"*Lost in Ghost Town* is a gripping, haunting portrait of addiction that's impossible to put down. Carder Stout lays bare his soul as he recounts the privilege he was born into, and the pain that led him into the bowels of hell once crack and heroin had him in its vice grip. The triumph of the book is Carder's ever-present humanity. It's an addictive, heart-rending read. This is an astonishing story."

—**Jessica Queller**, executive producer and writer of *Supergirl*,
bestselling author of *Pretty Is What Changes*

"This incredible memoir is a powerful and heartbreaking look into addiction and everything that comes with it. Dr. Carder Stout crafts a harrowing yet beautiful story and deserves all of the praise it's received."

—**Jennifer Todd**, producer of the Academy Awards,
executive producer of *City on a Hill* (Showtime)

"*Lost in Ghost Town* is a terrifying, hilarious, and ultimately moving cautionary tale. Like a modern-day Icarus, Carder Stout was born privileged, had to escape from a labyrinth, and flew too close to the sun. However, unlike Icarus, the labyrinth Stout escaped from was one of his own creation, and he miraculously survived to share his tale with the rest of us. He covers the distance from the top to the bottom unsparingly in this gripping, upsetting, beautifully written memoir."

—**Jonathan Marc Sherman**, award-winning playwright
(*Things We Want*)

"This book is a must-read for anyone doubting the possibility of personal redemption. Full of psychological insight and expertly told with an entertainer's instinct for a riveting crazier-than-fiction story."

—**Alessandro Nivola**, Tony Award–nominated actor
(*Laurel Canyon, The Many Saints of Newark*)

Lost in Ghost Town

A MEMOIR OF ADDICTION, REDEMPTION AND HOPE IN UNLIKELY PLACES

Carder Stout, PhD

Health Communications, Inc.
Boca Raton, Florida
www.hcibooks.com

AUTHOR'S NOTE

I wrote this book from memory and attempted to be as factual and accurate as possible. Due to my substance use during this period, there may be situations that are distorted. Certain names and places have been altered to protect the identities of those involved.

**Library of Congress Cataloging-in-Publication Data
is available through the Library of Congress**

© 2019 Carder Stout

ISBN-13: 978-07573-2354-6 (Paperback)
ISBN-10: 07573-2354-5 (Paperback)
ISBN-13: 978-07573-2355-3 (ePub)
ISBN-10: 07573-2355-3 (ePub)

Publisher: Health Communications, Inc.
          1700 NW 2nd Avenue
          Boca Raton, FL 33432-1653

Cover artwork by Richard Dupont
Photography by Trina Yin
Background mural by Mario Arteaga
Interior design and formatting by Lawna Patterson Oldfield

CONTENTS

For My Brother Craig
Who has always been my hero

FOREWORD

"**H**ow's Carder doing?"

I got asked that question about Carder Stout a lot from various mutual friends, circa 2003.

I'd usually say something like, "I think he's doing okay," but who could say for sure? I mean, he was living thousands of miles away, and I wasn't with him 24/7, so I could only make a semi-educated guess.

There was a vintage ceramic liquor decanter that used to sit proudly on the bookshelf in Carder's old apartment at 29 King Street in New York City. It said "The Jolly Twosome" on its base, on top of which were a couple of pickled drunks with their arms around one another and their eyes closed, sauced smiles on their faces. One of them was dressed to the nines in a formal white dinner jacket, while his unshaven pal was clad in patched blue jeans. Their common denominator was the elixir that altered their states.

For years, mostly in the mid-to-late 1990s in Manhattan, I was Carder's partner-in-crime. We were The Jolly Twosome.

We both came from privilege, but I was of the Jersey Jewish variety, with my big nose and big ears and aversion to shaving on a daily basis, whereas Carder came from prep schools and family drinking songs passed down from his Swedish ancestors. He looked like the antonym of a Jewish guy. What we bonded on from the start was our dark sense of humor, and the fact that we recognized kindred spirits who were then enjoying figuring out where the edge between life and death was, and toying with it. We were both in our twenties. That we lived through them still astonishes me.

So many of our old New York City haunts have closed: Rose's Turn, Wax, Spy, Moomba, Fez, Mondo Cane, and so on. My surprise that Carder outlived these bars is enormous, as is my gratitude.

I've probably laughed as much with Carder as I have with anybody on this planet. Some of that can be attributed to the fact that he's whip-smart, with a wickedly great sense of humor. Some must also be attributed to the fact that we kept longer hours than the sane people in our crowd.

I finally got clean and sober after I peered over the edge and decided it was time to make some changes in my life, back in May of 2001. (As of this writing, I've got eighteen years, three months, two weeks, and four days. Not that I'm keeping track or anything. One day at a time.)

In July of 2002, late on a Tuesday night which stretched into the wee hours of a Wednesday morning, a small band of friends—six of us—went from The Slipper Room, one of our go-to haunts on the Lower East Side, over to Milady's, a now-shuttered bar in SoHo. I was the only one of our group who was clean and sober. When our group had dwindled down to just three people, Carder—who had moved out to Los Angeles but was back on the East Coast for a visit—revealed to a mutual dear friend and me that he had been smoking crack and heroin for over six months back in Los Angeles. Tears were shed, and we begged him to change his upcoming travel plans, telling him in no uncertain terms that he should not go back to California. He looked unquestionably terrible. He'd lost his luster. The good looks and charm that could bypass any velvet rope in town were gone, replaced with a desperate, skeletal, scary frame, housing somebody who seemed not to have much longer to live.

We told him to stay in New York, not to go back to a city where there'd be thousands of miles between us. We told him if he got on his scheduled flight and went back to Los Angeles, he'd probably end up dead. We had no idea how right we were.

There's a version of this that could easily have begun, "I wish you had been able to meet my late friend Carder Stout..." Thank goodness, that's not the version I find myself writing.

When we told Carder that night that he was likely to die sooner rather than later, he wiped the tears from his face, solemnly nodded, and sincerely agreed with us. He said he'd stay in town. He was lying. He went back to Los Angeles.

He lived to tell the tale of what happened next. Shockingly and happily, he beat the odds.

It says a lot about Carder that when he asked me if I wanted him to change my name in this stunning memoir, and I told him he didn't have to, he did anyway. (I've been pretty much an open book about my own alcoholism and drug addiction.) When he sent me the draft of his book to read, I was now "Shane." That's perfect, I thought. Not only did he give me a name that's a hybrid of an Alan Ladd classic and a character from *Mean Girls,* but that simple move sums up Carder: one of the dearest friends I've ever known, taking better care of a pal than he took of himself, taking better care of me than I asked him to.

Lost in Ghost Town is a terrifying, hilarious, and ultimately moving cautionary tale. Like a modern-day Icarus, Carder was born privileged, had to escape from a labyrinth, and flew too close to the sun. However, unlike Icarus, the labyrinth Stout escaped from was one of his own creation, and he miraculously survived to share his tale with the rest of us. He covers the distance from the top to the bottom unsparingly in this gripping, upsetting, beautifully written memoir.

Carder has pulled off the trick of being so ruthlessly specific that his tale becomes universal. You might end up relating to it because of your own addictions, whether those addictions are to alcohol and drugs, or food, shopping, sex, toxic relationships, pornography, gambling—and the list goes on. Sadly, I can't think of anybody I'm close with who hasn't either struggled with addiction or loved somebody who's battled it.

Get ready to be drawn in to this harrowing account of pain, addiction, survival, and hope. My copy will sit proudly on my bookshelf, in a section alongside David Carr's *The Night of the Gun*, Mary Karr's *Lit,* and Jerry Stahl's *Permanent Midnight.*

How's Carder doing?

I know how to answer that question nowadays, even though I still don't see him 24/7, and he still lives across the country.

My friend Carder's doing better. My friend Carder's doing a lot better.

Jonathan Marc Sherman, playwright, *Things We Want*
New York
August 2019

PROLOGUE

So this is how it ends.

The door to the alleyway opened, and I could hear soft footsteps coming down the stairs. No wonder gangsters wore sneakers—better for sneaking up on anyone who crossed them. If I made a sound, I would die. I'd be murdered on the cold basement floor. I had seen the bloodstains on the sidewalks of Ghost Town and watched the wailing mothers and grandmothers try to scrub them away. This was real. I thought of my mother and how sad she would be. What would the papers say? *Former film producer found dead in gang-style execution.* And what they would say at my funeral? All those old friends. Perhaps they had seen it coming.

"He couldn't get out of his own way."

"It was the drugs. The drugs finally got him."

"Such a waste. He was a good guy in his prime."

"He used to make me laugh. How could he fall so far?"

"He had everything in the world going for him."

No silver spoon or diploma or charisma could protect me from a bullet fired at close range. Would it hurt? Would it be over before

I even heard the shot? I braced myself for a muzzle flash and held my breath. The footsteps came closer.

"Hollywood, you down here? It's Trech. Treacherous Wallace. I just want to talk to you. You don't need to hide no more. It's all good. Just want to hear your side of the story. Come out."

But I knew he was lying. If I showed myself, it would be over. I had disrespected him and, in doing so, put my life in his hands. And his hands were bloody. He had not risen to the top of the Shoreline Crips for being kind. He was ruthless and unforgiving, and I had pissed him off. I stayed in the fetal position, awaiting my fate. I heard him cock his automatic pistol.

Was it worth it?

She was off the streets, reunited with her little girl. Perhaps it was the noblest thing I had ever done. I guess it was worth dying for. No one would ever know besides us. Maybe it was better that way. I had spent a lifetime taking credit I didn't deserve, so it seemed fitting that my final act would remain unnoticed.

He was close now; I could smell the cigarettes on his hands.

"Hollywood? You back there?"

I was convinced he could see me.

"I got a surprise for you. Don't worry. It's not gonna hurt."

I waited for the bang.

By the code of the streets, I had earned it.

Chapter One

2003

I t had been a long time since I'd felt good in the morning. I cursed at the birds from under my covers—why did they hate me so much? Today would be a day like all the rest. I would spend most of it looking for money. I hated holding out my hand for loose change, but I did it anyway. I'd be ashamed if someone I knew saw me panhandling on the street corner.

At this point, my best options were to beg, borrow, or steal. Recently, I had done a lot of all three. I attended AA meetings pretending to be sober and hit up old friends for a $20 bill. This worked until they realized I was spending it to get high. I would have gotten some angry phone calls if I had a cell phone that worked. I'd gone completely off the radar and lost touch with everyone I used to know. This was fine with me—I had no interest in explaining myself. I lived a block from the beach in Venice, California, but rarely put my feet in the sand. My domain was further inland, where the rubber met the road. This part of Venice had appropriately been labeled *Ghost Town*. This was what the addicts called it, anyway—so many ghosts were walking the streets.

I scanned my room for anything I could sell. Heaps of dirty clothes on the floor were not worth anything. I had already sold my Armani jackets and Agnes B sweaters at a local vintage shop and had pawned my grandparents' heirloom silver a few months prior.

A signed lithograph by the renowned artist Adolf Gottleib hung on the wall across from my bed, and every day, it looked more enticing. I wondered how much I could get for it. It was of a small, brown puddle floating in a sea of red, and I imagined myself diving in, never to be seen again. My mother had loaned it to me years ago, before I moved to California. It had always been one of my favorite things and now was triggering a Pavlovian response. It looked out of place on the cracked wall—a reminder of the way things used to be in my life, when my family gathered around a kitchen table in our New England farmhouse. We would laugh and tell stories and eat French toast. But things were different now. I no longer felt a sense of connection to anything, especially my family. I was alone, really alone, but I didn't care. I was done apologizing for myself and asking for forgiveness. I was back in the tunnel of addiction, and there was no light at the end of it.

I got out of bed and pulled on a pair of baggy pants. I looked inside my mini fridge on the off chance that there was a beer waiting for me. Instead, just half a lemon, growing mold. I thought about eating it anyway. I'd had a slice of pizza the previous day at noon, and nothing edible had passed my lips since then. I was on the one-meal-per-day diet, and not by choice.

My stomach growled as I gulped down a mouthful of city water from the bathroom faucet, wincing at the chlorine taste. Picking cigarette butts off the street and smoking their remains was a common practice, but I had high standards for the water I drank. I was a man of contradictions—I considered myself an honest person, but had become a master thief. I loved people, but spent most of my time alone. My mother was an heiress, but I didn't have two nickels to rub together.

I looked in the dirty bathroom mirror. I had climbed Himalayan peaks in Nepal, swum with sharks on the Great Barrier Reef, and watched the Stones play a free concert for the newly liberated citizens of Prague, but these milestones were fading memories. I barely recognized myself anymore. I looked nothing like the boy I knew—the fair-haired kid with the golden smile. That boy was gone, and I missed him.

I walked outside onto Pacific Avenue, dodging a few bikes as I cut through an alley toward Main Street. It was a perfect spring day in California, and most of the folks on the street seemed to be enjoying it. In the past seven decades, Venice had been a cross-section of race, ethnicity, and class. There were the starving artists who lived cheaply in craftsmen houses next to African-American families that had moved into rent-controlled bungalows in the 1930s. Next to them, there were the surf rats and beatniks who kept the culture of the 1960s alive and drove their VW vans up the coast when the waves were big. Sprinkled among these eccentrics was a generation of Holocaust survivors and immigrant families that had moved in at the end of World War II.

In the air was the feeling that the neighborhood was about to explode with a surge of gentrification, and you could already see a few BMWs parked outside construction sites on Electric Avenue. But the most dominant presence of all was a gang called the Shoreline Crips, and they struck fear into the hearts of most everyone who lived there.

The Crips had moved into the Oakwood neighborhood of Venice with little resistance from anyone, including the police. They controlled the cocaine trade on the west side of Los Angeles and their numbers were staggering. If you pulled up to the community center on Seventh and California, your car would be bum-rushed by at least a dozen teenage boys and girls selling crack. The mob appeared confident, unruly, and intimidating. Most of the young dealers wore blue sweatshirts as a sign that they were active gang members and each tried to outdo the other to make a sale. There were often shoving matches at the car window, and fistfights ensued.

A few blocks over, on Brooks, there was a dealer on every corner and the flurry of activity that came with them. A constant stream of vehicles slowed to greet them, and you could watch a perpetual transaction of money exchanged for product. Law enforcement was seldom seen in these parts. When it did roll through, it seemed oblivious to what was happening. The officers would drive on by with little regard for the blatant infractions committed right in front of them. I wondered if the gang members paid them to look the other way. It seemed so.

There was usually police tape up on Broadway, and at night, you could hear the pop, pop, pop of gunfire. Sometimes, there were fresh bloodstains on the pavement, and old women scrubbed them vigorously, as if their removal would somehow cleanse the neighborhood. It would take far more than horsehair bristles and steel wool to disinfect the energy that flowed through the 'hood, and they knew it. But most of us were fine with the violence as long as the drugs flowed. We had landed here for a reason and had no intention of leaving.

When I had arrived in Venice six months earlier, I was unaware of all this. I was fresh out of rehab and intended to get my life on track. I had completed a twenty-eight-day stint at the world-famous Promises Treatment Center and been taught to love myself and embrace God. The teachings had fallen on deaf ears—my time there was more like a month-long nap. And boy, I had needed it.

I had been smoking cocaine and heroin for a year in my Hollywood bungalow. On the weekends, I would chase the dragon with several tabs of Ecstasy. In a year's time, I'd blown through my life savings—the $200,000 I had made from the sale of my penthouse in SoHo. My dark blue vintage Porsche was so neglected that it had become undriveable. I'd been so proud when I bought it, and in the end, it looked like a clown car with dents, scratches, and two donuts for back wheels. When my mother and sister finally arrived at my door, their intervention wasn't necessary. My bags were packed, and I was ready to get help, but I didn't really want any. I just needed a breather before the next run.

I thought that Venice would be a healthy place for me. I imagined the seaside air would be good for my temperament and I would be far away from the vampires that peddled their potions in the Hollywood night, but I was dead wrong. A few months after I moved there, I had my first encounter with a street dealer on Abbot Kinney. I was walking up the block when she called out to me.

"Hey, sweetie," she said. "What you looking for? What you need?"

"What you got?" I asked curiously, having no idea what she meant.

"I got rock. Real good rock," she said. "How much you want?"

In that moment, I was overtaken by a surge of electricity that radiated through my body, leaving me powerless. It had been several months since I had indulged, but in that moment, I craved it with every fiber of my being. I was working at a furniture store in Malibu and had a wad of cash in my pocket.

One more time. I'll just do it once more, and nobody will know. It'll be just like old times. I'll escape from the tedium that comes with sobriety.

"I'll take forty," I said eagerly. She took two big pieces of crack out of her mouth and handed them to me. My stomach was on fire, and I instantly had to take a shit. I ran to the nearest gas station, bought a glass pipe, and rocketed home.

I had been high every day since. My job, of course, was gone. My days were now an endless quest to acquire money so I could feed the demons inside. They had escaped from their cages and were ravenous.

I crossed Main Street and made a hard right onto Abbot Kinney. I walked past a neighborhood restaurant called Lily's and peered inside. I marveled at how happy everyone looked over their soup bowls and recalled the several times I had eaten there, years earlier. I plucked a long cigarette butt from the outside ashtray and lit it up with a match. The host came out and shooed me away. I was not welcome there anymore, so I marched onward, half on the sidewalk, half on the street, looking like a cross between Raggedy Andy and the Scarecrow from Oz.

I had made this trip many times before, and something always materialized. I never went home empty-handed. I asked a local shop owner if he could spare a few dollars but to no avail.

"Times are tough, man. I'm sorry," he said politely. "I may have to go out of business myself."

I thanked him anyway and rolled up the avenue like a human tumbleweed. I passed a few more boutiques and restaurants until I arrived at California Street. This is where I often took a left into the combat zone. This was the epicenter of drug activity in the 'hood and all of the characters who came with it. There were the junkies looking to score, the scammers looking to swindle, the hustlers looking to gain, and the dealers looking to get you hooked. They had become my tribe.

As I crossed Fifth Street, I was greeted by a familiar face. It was a hustler named Jamal who always had a plan in the works. He was tall and thin, with dark brown skin and a cluster of freckles on his nose. His teeth were bright yellow and his afro was matted down with several ounces of homeless grit, but he looked fine to me. I had done business with him on many occasions.

One time, Jamal and I had grabbed a few cases of tequila from a supermarket on Lincoln and pretended we were employees as we carried them out the loading dock door. Over the next few days, we traded the booze for money and drugs. Another time, we robbed a storage unit on Rose Avenue and traded some stereo speakers for crack. There was always the opportunity to barter in Ghost Town, and the dealers welcomed any type of currency as long as it was desirable. Jamal held out his hand and slapped it into mine.

"My man Hollywood," he said affectionately. He and many other folks in the neighborhood thought I looked like Viggo Mortensen. The film version of *The Lord of the Rings* had come out the year before, and Viggo had become a household name. While I was in rehab, my friends back east sent me a bobblehead of the character he played in the movie. This likeness to a movie star gave me tremendous street cred in the 'hood. Some people actually thought I *was* him, and I would play along. I had received several rocks of free product for this reason. Eventually, I told everyone that he was my cousin. Hence the name "Hollywood."

"I been looking for you. You needs to get a phone! I got business for us. Right now. I hooked that shit *up*," Jamal said, bouncing on his toes with urgency. "You still got your car?"

"Yeah, it's parked over on Vernon. Why?"

"I know a dude who needs one. A big dude. He can hook us up," he explained.

"Yeah, but that's the last thing I have. I can't lend it out to anyone. I need it."

"What you need it fo'? It's been sittin' over there parked for like two weeks now. You ain't been drivin' it."

"Yeah, but I can't just let someone I don't know take my car."

"I told you, I *know* the dude!" He was getting flustered. "Let's go meet him right now. He's waiting for us over at his grandma's house. Listen, Hollywood, he's a big dude and has mad respect in the 'hood."

"Sorry, man, but I can't."

"What!" he shouted. "This is some *bullshit*. You know you want to get high. He's got the dope. We got what he wants, too. Your car."

"Nah, man. Let's find something else."

I had bought the car with the last money I had. It was a gray Ford Taurus sedan with a pleather interior, and it got me from A to B when I was in a bind. I couldn't give it up.

"Hollywood, please!" he begged. "I got to get high."

I could see his eyes becoming more and more bloodshot. He put his hand on my shoulder and gripped it tightly.

"Please, man. I need a hit bad."

Something about his desperation touched me. I caved.

"Okay, man. It's cool. No need to get riled up. Yeah, fuck it. Let's go meet the dude."

We tromped through the back alleys of Venice to reach my car. I had found a spot that allowed me to park for a week without amassing any tickets and was sad to give it up. Perhaps it would be worth it if this panned out. You never knew with Jamal. Half of his schemes were so harebrained that I routinely refused to go along. He always had one foot in some sort of trouble. He had done a year for check fraud and was constantly asking me if I could open a bank account for him. The answer was no.

"Now this is what I'm talking about," Jamal said as he turned on the radio and fiddled with the air conditioning. "We need to get us some bitches and roll around the 'hood with the windows down." He smiled at me, and I laughed. The possibility of the two of us picking up any women was slim to none. Before we had traveled three blocks, Jamal put up his hand.

"We here," he said excitedly.

"Wait, what? We're here?"

"Yeah, his house is right there," he said pointing. "Park this bitch."

We had gotten in my car to drive less than a quarter mile.

"Why didn't we walk? It would have taken us like five minutes."

"Nah," he replied. "The car. He needs to see the car."

"Right." I sighed. I had almost forgotten why we had come in the first place. I was dizzy and spaced due to the lack of nutrients in my body. I had to eat soon, or I might pass out.

There was a neighborhood church south of Venice Boulevard that served bologna sandwiches to vagrants on weekdays at 11:30 AM.

I had become a regular and would walk there so no one would suspect I had a car. I feared they might turn me away if they saw me drive off with their brown bag in hand. Being homeless was a condition of entry, and I still had a roof over my head—barely. My father had agreed to pay six-months' rent and utilities, but that was coming to an end. I had two more weeks before $900 was due, and I had no idea where to get the money. I never thought that far in advance. It was moment to moment in the 'hood. I had to survive for the next few hours, and that was it.

We walked up to the front porch of a small stucco house and rang the doorbell. My foot tapped nervously on the ground, and I wondered if I was being lured into a trap. Much to my surprise, the door opened to reveal an elderly black woman with a wide smile.

"Hello, boys," she said. "My, you is handsome. Come inside. Come inside." She unlocked the iron gate and whisked us into her living room. "My name is Beatrice. I'm Franklyn's grandma. You lookin' for Franklyn?" she asked.

"Yeah, for Flyn," Jamal said. "He here?"

"Nah, he ain't here right now, but he's comin' back soon. Why don't you boys sit with me fo' a bit and wait on him?" she said.

"Of course," I said politely. I had nowhere else to go and rather liked her house. A floral pattern wove through her white linoleum floor and gave the place a country feeling. A TV set with rabbit-ear antennas sat on a stand under the front window, and it reminded me of the one in my grandparents' house. An old-fashioned radio stood on a table next to a bookshelf with colored figurines and sports trophies. The interior looked like it hadn't been updated since the 1950s.

Beatrice saw me looking around and said, "I been here a while. Still looks the same as when I moved in. I like it that way."

"I do, too," I said, and our eyes met. I could feel the sadness in her, and it seemed she could feel it in me. Her face was round and soft, and her dark skin had no appearance of wrinkles, but I knew she'd seen a lot. She reminded me of Lillie B., the adoring nanny who brought me up as a child. They were both women from another era.

"Well, you boys ain't lookin' like you been eatin' too well. You hungry?" She looked over at me with a knowing gaze.

"No, that's okay—"

"I'll bring out some chicken and ice tea," she interrupted. And as she got up, she stumbled forward a bit. "Damned arthritis," she grumbled.

I stood up, held her arm steady, and walked with her down a narrow hallway to the kitchen.

"I'm all right, baby," she said. "Now sit down and tell me about yourself." She moved over to an old Sears icebox and pulled on the rusted lever to open it. I sat down at a glass-topped table and followed her directive. There was no getting around it.

"My name's Carder. I'm from DC originally, and New York. I came out here to make movies, but it didn't really work out. I'm trying to figure out what to do next." It was strange to hear myself summarize my life in a few short sentences.

"Just be yourself, baby," she said. "Where is your family at?"

"Mostly on the East Coast."

"Do you miss them?" she asked.

"I do. Very much."

"Family is everything," she said. "Franklyn's daddy left us, and then his brother was taken from us. Don't seem fair sometimes. I miss those boys every day. Franklyn's the only one I got left, so don't go messin' with him. He just got home from jail. Will you help him? Will you help my grandson?"

I was deeply moved. In that moment, I would have done anything she asked.

"Yes. Yes, of course I will," I said.

"Thank you, baby. I knew you would. Now let's get you some of that chicken."

She brought out a platter overflowing with a mound of barbequed chicken. She handed it to me and removed a glass pitcher of ice tea from the fridge and placed it on the table.

We gathered the feast and carted it back into the living room. Bob Barker chuckled from the TV, and his silver baritone voice had lulled Jamal to sleep. His head was tilted back and his mouth hung open, catching flies. Beatrice smiled and put her finger up to her mouth.

"Let him sleep. He must need it," she said, and led me into a small dining room just down the hall. We sat across from each other and remained quiet for a moment. It took everything I had not to grab a piece of meat and devour it like a stray dog. I was that hungry, but I knew that restraint would go a long way. She folded her hands, bowed her head, and began to pray.

"Heavenly Father, I thank you for bringing this child into my life. Please bless him and protect him and keep him safe. And I ask you, O Loving God, to help my grandson Franklyn straighten out his ways so that he may find truth and happiness outside of jail. Give me the strength, O Lord, to keep on fighting in your name so that these boys and girls stop dying out on the streets. The hurt is too much, Lord. The pain is too much. Amen."

I had never heard a prayer quite like this before. In that moment, my petty little problems seemed ridiculous. She radiated the truth and vibrated with a frequency of the divine. Although I had not met him, I was envious that Flyn was her descendant instead of me. She raised her head and smiled. I noticed one gold tooth that had been hidden by her upper lip. It beamed at me.

"Now dig on in," she said.

I attacked the chicken, disregarding the manners I had learned from my own grandmother. Beatrice laughed and watched me eat. It was obvious that I had not been taking care of myself. I hadn't showered in several days, and my clothes were tattered and stained. I could tell that she didn't care and was glad to have me there. It had been a long time since I had eaten a home-cooked meal in the company of such a maternal figure, and I needed all the mothering I could get.

My mother had come from repressed parents who were afraid to hug and rarely uttered the words *I love you*. They passed this tendency on to her, I guess. I didn't blame her, but had looked for validation from other women ever since I was a small boy. I once asked my preschool teacher if she would take me home for the weekend. All of my many girlfriends had assumed the role of caretaker, and I loved nothing more than to get lost in the bubble of security they created.

But my addiction had taken that away. I was not capable of being in a relationship these days. My mistress had become rock cocaine. It demanded my full attention and took care of me during those long nights of walking the Venice canals. There was no room in my life for anyone else.

The telephone rang from the kitchen, and Beatrice got up to answer it. I could hear her muffled voice a few rooms away as I continued to stuff my face with breasts, thighs, and drumsticks. When she returned, she had a peculiar look on her face.

"Franklyn said he's over at his apartment, and he won't be coming back 'til tomorrow. Said he would be here at four. Said for you to come by then. And he told me that he didn't know you."

I froze mid-chew. I felt like such an opportunist. Here I was in the grandmother's house of someone I had never met, eating like a king.

"Don't matter to me," she added. "You's my friend now."

"You see, I was supposed to meet him here for—"

"It don't matter, baby. You can come over whenever you want. I enjoy the company. But promise me you will take care of him when you see him. That boy can get in a world of trouble just walking down the sidewalk."

"I will." I nodded. I was her friend now.

I walked back into the TV room and gave Jamal a shake. He was out cold. I tried tickling his ear with my finger. "Jamal," I sang as if to a sleeping child.

"You is terrible," Beatrice giggled. "Pop him a good one on the nose."

Pop! I batted him square on the nose, and his eyes flew open in rage.

"You motherfucker!" he said, launching off the couch. "Don't you ever—"

Beatrice's cackle stopped him cold. She began to laugh so hard that she keeled over and braced herself on her ample thighs.

"Oh, shit, I thought you were robbing me!" Jamal said, shaking his head to wake himself up.

"No, but we *should* rob you for all that snoring in my living room," Beatrice said with a pat on his arm.

Jamal and I hugged Beatrice and walked out into the hazy afternoon. She stood in her doorway and waved at us as we climbed into my car.

"Remember what you promised me," she said.

"You have my word," I replied, and we zoomed off into the 'hood with the windows down. I felt better than I had in months. My belly was full, and my heart had been touched by the kindness of an old woman. Beatrice had spotted my soul buried under layers of soot. I was lost and barely knew myself, but for a brief moment in her home, I remembered something vital that the smoke and solitude had taken away from me. I remembered that maybe I was good, no matter how terrible I felt inside. At the center, there might be something good.

"What promise?" Jamal asked, rubbing the sleep from his eyes.

"Just something between me and Miss Beatrice," I replied. No way I would talk about our agreement with a sleazy character like Jamal. Any information he could get his hands on was used for purposes of blackmail and extortion. I knew better than to tell him my secrets, no matter how hard he pried.

Jamal had arrived in the 'hood a few years back in a bright new pair of Air Jordans, driving his own Ford F-150, and with a wad of cash in his pocket. All that was now gone. He'd smoked it away. I had told him that I'd once lived in Hollywood and produced movies for a living, but that was all I revealed. We were not curious about each other's stories. Our relationship was based on necessity and fueled by the desire to extract anything we could from the marrow of the streets. We were good partners and fed from each other's will to survive.

The only cocaine available in the 'hood was crack, and both of us were addicted to it. It was really no different than powder cocaine, other than a simple process of cooking with a sprinkle of baking soda and water. The cocaine in both was the same and targeted identical pleasure centers in the brain, but crack had a bad rap. It had exploded in the inner cities during the 1980s and was considered a drug for the down, dirty, and destitute—but that wasn't how it came into my life.

The first time I smoked crack was two years before at my friend's house in Beachwood Canyon. Dave was VP of marketing for a major film company and had arrived from New York a few years earlier. The two of us were drinking beer and watching *Caddyshack* when Dave suggested we get some crack. I thought he was joking— I had never even considered the idea. But he was deadly serious and, a few hours later, had procured a large rock from a local dealer. I was curious and sure that smoking the drug once would have no impact on my life.

The two of us stayed up for twenty-four hours smoking crack from a long, glass tube. Within a few months, I was smoking it every day. I liked the high better than snorting powder because the delivery method was more powerful and immediate.

There was no waiting with crack.

The crystalized nuggets were smoked in a glass pipe that could be purchased at any gas station or liquor store for 99¢. These pipes were displayed on the counter like small bud vases, but everyone knew what they were for. I always found it funny when I saw a businessman buying one, pretending it was for some other purpose—a Valentine's Day gift for a tiny girlfriend.

Frequent smokers called their pipe a "horn" or "stem." I only used mine at night, as I was too paranoid to smoke while the sun was up. I felt like everyone was looking at me, and I would never enjoy the high. Often, I ended up huddled in my bathroom, peering under the door at imagined shadows. But when the sun went down, the landscape changed, and my horn became a fixture in my pocket. Presently, my horn was empty. I would need to fill it soon or suffer from withdrawal. I pulled the car over to the curb.

"I got some things to do right now. I'll catch you on the street," I said.

"Cool, cool," Jamal replied as he got out. "See you, Hollywood."

I was glad to see him go. In order to get a rock, I had to hustle my way into a $20 bill before sundown. It was easier to work alone, unless it involved a bigger, more complex con.

The walking streets of Venice were filled with treasure that could be monetized rapidly. I surveyed the landscape. Something beautiful—an oversized moving truck—was double-parked up the street. Movers often left a truck unlocked as they went inside to load up. This was an optimal time to grab something out of the back and run. I had once stolen a turntable from a truck on Broadway and pawned it the same day for $50. Not bad for a moment's work.

Even better (and legal) was the possibility of finding something that had been tossed out during the move. People threw away all kinds of valuable shit when they were headed someplace different, like shedding a skin. I walked past the truck and headed down the alleyway behind the half-empty home, and there, right in front of me, was a stack of about thirty CDs. Fucking gold mine. I fell to my knees and thanked God for the invention of the iPod. If the CDs were in decent condition, I could get at least two bucks a piece for them at the used record store on Windward Circle. I scooped them into my forearms and hightailed it toward the boardwalk. It was not unusual to see an unkempt white male trolling through the 'hood with an armful of stuff, so no one batted an eye as I passed.

I walked into the store and plopped the CDs down on the counter. I hadn't bothered to look at them. Behind the counter, a weathered old guy wearing a Harley Davidson vest glared at me over his John Lennon specs.

"What you want to do with these?" he asked. He seemed annoyed, and short-tempered. "And what kind of shit is this anyway?" He picked up a CD case with a photo of Lawrence Welk on the cover. He opened it—it was empty. He raised his head and grimaced.

"We don't ever buy Lawrence Welk. This ain't West Hollywood, you know. And even if we did, there's no CD in here. We definitely don't buy Lawrence Welk CD *cases*." He threw it in the trash. "What else you got in here?"

The next CD was the Olivia Newton-John classic *Xanadu*. "You know what you can do with this one, right?"

"Not a Newton-John fan, I guess."

"Nope."

He kept digging in the pile and pulled out eight of the remaining thirty.

"I'll actually take a look at these," he said. "The rest is total garbage."

He sifted through the small pile, taking out each disc and inspecting it in the light.

"Three bucks a piece for these and two for these. Yeah?"

"Yes, totally." I could hardly believe it. He handed over a $20 bill with a $1 chaser. I stuffed them deep in my pocket and set off down Main Street. The 'hood was safer during the day, and I had a few minutes left before the darkness came. It was time to score some dope.

I could feel the nervous excitement in my stomach as I took a hard right onto Brooks. Even though I'd done this a hundred times, there was always an element of fear. First, you had to find someone who you knew and had done business with. Then there was the art of the trade. The money you held out could easily be snatched away by someone who had no intention of parting with the goods. A deal was a dance. I would stroll up and inquire with a broad question like, "You got what I'm looking for?"

Usually the response was, "Yeah, I got it. How much you looking for?"

I would respond, "Twenty." Then I'd wait for the dealer to take out a folded piece of waxed paper and open it up.

The dealers used waxed paper because it glided easily up their sphincters if they felt the heat of law enforcement nearby. They called it "putting it up." There was often a pungent odor of excrement on their fingers as they handed over the goods. This didn't bother me at all. I couldn't care less about a shit smell when I was about to get high.

After visually confirming that the dealer had crack in his possession, I would take out my money and hold it in my left hand. The final exchange was simultaneous. I'd take the rock with my right hand, and the dealer would thrust the bill into his pocket. At the same time, we'd keep an eye on the passing cars to make certain there were no police around. If the cops witnessed the transaction, the dealer would simply put it up. The one place the cops would not search was the inner cavity of an asshole. I'd never been arrested and was determined to keep it that way.

As I walked up Brooks, I saw a food truck parked across from the Bethel Church on Fifth. I used my extra dollar to buy a bottle of Evian water that I poured on my face.

I noticed that all four corners on Sixth and Brooks were empty, which was peculiar and troubling. Sometimes, the crack chefs that were cooking around town were late. This had a ripple effect on the streets. There were even times when the 'hood was dry for a few days, and the junkies patrolled the sidewalks like zombies infected by the plague.

I walked all the way up to Seventh and strode toward the park on Broadway. Men were seated on stone benches playing dominoes under the shade of an oak. This was a region that whites did not enter, no matter what. It was an all-black venue, and anyone else who tried to walk through would get pummeled. I had seen it happen a few times—it was not a pretty sight. This was an unwritten law in Ghost Town.

I veered right again and walked down Broadway, hoping to find a rogue peddler in the shadows. In the distance, I could see a heavyset man leaning up against a brick wall. As I approached, he smiled and nodded his head at me. This was usually the signal that greenlit the process. I didn't recognize him, but he looked the part; he was wearing a blue sweatshirt with the hood up. There were always new recruits on every block, so this didn't bother me, but I proceeded with caution.

"Hey, what's up?" I asked politely.

"Nothing," he replied. "Just out here on the streets doin' my thing."

"Cool, cool," I said. "I ain't seen you around here before."

"Nah. I'm new here. Been here a few weeks, though. All good. What you lookin' for?"

There was something about him that seemed off. I couldn't put my finger on it, but the hairs on the back of my neck rose up. There was a myth floating around Ghost Town that if you asked an undercover officer if he was a cop, he would have to tell you. In this moment, I believed the myth.

"You're not a cop, are you?" I asked.

He laughed.

"Fuck no, Cracker. I done more time than Al Capone."

I laughed with him. That was good enough for me.

"You got some?" I asked.

"Yeah, I got it," he said.

"Could I get a twenty?"

"Surely so," he said as he reached into his pocket. He held up a large rock of crack between his thumb and forefinger and looked at it in the fading sunlight.

"I'm feelin' generous."

He handed it without emotion and sent me ambling down the sidewalk. Victory. I felt like a kid with a fresh snow cone heading toward the big-top circus. I cupped my fingers around the rock and quickened my gait toward home. I imagined what the smoke would taste like as it entered my lungs, and the thought propelled my feet faster and faster.

In my peripheral vision, I could see a woman about twenty yards away, running at full speed in my direction. I turned to see if someone was behind me, but the street was clear. She was white and middle-aged, which was not a common sight on Broadway. Her blonde hair was cropped short, and she was wearing blue jeans and a windbreaker. She was moving like a thunderbolt. As she got closer, I could see that she was flashing something in her hand. It was a badge.

Seconds before impact, I thrust the crack into my mouth and swallowed hard. She dove across the asphalt and hit the center of my chest with her shoulder. Her body landed on top of mine, and she tomahawked my throat with her closed fist. I looked her straight in the eyes as my head connected with the curb.

And then the world went completely black.

Chapter Two

1975, SEVEN YEARS OLD

Of all the big brothers in the world, Craig was the best. He was like a superhero. Sometimes, he wore a cape, like on Halloween, when he pinned a red one on his shirt. I wished I had a cape on *my* shirt: a long blue one that went to the floor so I could fly around and save people. Craig always saved things. One time, he put a bandage on a frog that I squashed with my bicycle tire. And one time, he pulled me out of the street when a silver motorcycle was going like a zillion miles an hour. He took care of me. He told the bigger kids at school not to push me, "Or else." I did anything Craig asked me to—one time he dared me to drink from the toilet bowl and I said, "No way," but I did it anyway. He could eat six and a half hot dogs at lunch. I'm not kidding—I took a picture with my Polaroid.

That morning, I howled and raced down the stairs of our townhouse. I leapt onto the wooden banister and slid down to the third-floor landing. Craig dove and grabbed my ankle, pulling me to the floor. I knew his knuckles were coming, so I closed my eyes. It didn't hurt, but I pretended it did.

"Ow! That *hurr-rrt!* Truce." I held up my left pinky.

"Truce," he replied, linking his pinky with mine.

A truce never lasted long, but this time, Craig looked serious.

I remembered why today was different. Today we were running away.

We weren't running away from anything bad. We had bikes and could ride them around the block by ourselves. Our parents let us watch an hour of TV every night after dinner. My dad was always at work, and my mom was busy with her friends, so we mostly did what we wanted.

My dad had hair like Clark Kent. It was always neat and brushed to the side with goop in it. He didn't wear glasses, though. And he wasn't a *real* superhero—I checked under his shirt, and there was no "S" on his chest or anything. My dad was my hockey coach, but he only showed up for two practices and three games. Ed took me to practice and school most times. He was a cab driver who worked for us. I didn't mind. It was kind of cool being the only kid to pull up to school in a cab.

When I asked my dad a question, he would usually ask me a question right back. It was really annoying.

"What does your tattoo mean?" I asked, and he said, "What do you think it means?" and I said, "I don't know, tell me," and he said, "If I tell you that, you will be as smart as me." Boy, I wished I was.

Sometimes, my dad got mad at me. Like if there was a lightbulb out in my lamp, he would get mad. He would say, "How hard is it to replace a lightbulb?" And when he spanked me, it felt like he was swatting me with a ping pong paddle. It was hard to sit down after that 'cuz my butt was red. Once, he chased me up the stairs after I threw a Frisbee in the living room and broke Grandma's china on the mantelpiece. He got me on the stairs and pulled down my pants, and *thwack*. He spanked me until I couldn't cry anymore. I was scared of him after that. The only one who would protect me from him was our nanny, Lillie B.

Lillie was my second-best friend after Craig. Her big arms felt good when I leaned back in them. Her lap was my favorite place to sit. My mom's lap was too bony, and she always said I was too heavy, but Lillie never said that. Lillie said we were her children. At the grocery store, people would think she was crazy when she called us her kids because her skin was black. One time, a man brought over the store police, but they let us go because we didn't break the law or anything. We told him she was our second mom, and we thought that was right.

My real mom's hair was blonde and wavy, and her face looked like a painting—not like something you would make in art class, but something in a museum, like the Moaning Lisa. I saw the Moaning Lisa when I went to Paris. Other grown-ups stared at my mom and then smiled. Grown-up men, mostly. Why couldn't they smile at their own moms? Geez. My mother smelled like perfume and gasoline. She dunked her fingers in smelly chemicals when she developed the pictures she was always taking. I liked the smell and would sniff her hands when I could. Most of the time, she pulled them away and told me to stop. She pulled away from me a lot, so I would get hugs from Lillie B. Then I would sneak into my mom's room and try on her long leather boots, wear her velvet hats, and put on her jewelry. I made sure that no one saw me. One time, I walked around all day with one of her purple scarves wrapped around my head. No one seemed to care.

But none of this would matter anymore. We were running away, and this time it was for real.

We pushed through the swinging door and stood around the butcher-block table.

"Good mornin', my boys. You better stop hollerin' when you on the stairs, cuz if you wake up your baby sister, I'll pop you upside your heads," Lillie said. "Now, who wants French toast?"

We both raised our hands. She brought over a stack of thick, eggy slices already covered in butter and syrup. Yum.

I filled my mouth with syrup and bread and scooped a slab of butter onto the end of my knife like a catapult. I waited 'til Lillie was at the stove and slung the butter across the room. It hit her in the ear and began to drip down her left cheek. She looked over, super mad.

"Why you tryin' to break bad with me, Coda? You see I'm busy. I'll take this spoon and pop you wit' it."

This was just what I was looking for.

"Oh, yeah?" I said. "I dare you."

Before I could run away, I felt a pain on the top of my leg. Her wooden spoon came down so hard that a purple bump was already showing.

"*Ow!*" I cried as I jumped out of my chair. I fell to the floor and pretended I was dying.

"Get yo ass up off the flo'," she commanded. Craig laughed so hard milk came out of his nose. Lillie B. started to laugh, too. She could never stay mad at me.

After breakfast, Craig pulled himself onto the counter and took a bunch of cans from the top cupboard. He handed down two cans of tuna, a few soups, some condensed milk, refried beans, and four cans of corn. I stacked the cans on the counter like stairs. I was Watson, and he was Sherlock Holmes. I liked being second in charge. If you were first, you had to make too many decisions.

"What in the hell do you think you's doin'?" Lillie said, hands on hips.

"We're getting provisions," Craig said.

"Provisions!? Provisions fo' what? I ain't see no war going on 'round here."

"We're running away," I said.

"Yeah, we're running away," Craig said.

"You boys is crazy," Lillie said. "Who you runnin' from?"

"No one," Craig replied. "We're just running away."

"You know, like running away. Like fugitives," I said.

"We're going on the lam," Craig added.

I had no idea what that meant, but it sounded good.

"Yeah, on the lam."

"The only lamb I know 'bout 'round here is in the freeza!" Lillie said. "Remember, you ain't s'posed to cross the street. So, run away all you want, but stay on the block."

Craig and I nodded and ran up the stairs. Mom said we couldn't cross the street without a grown-up, so running away was like running around the block—and there was a lot of cool stuff to see in our neighborhood. But Craig was in charge, and sometimes, he broke the rules, like when he took a candy bar from the 7-Eleven without paying.

We dumped the cans onto the floor with a loud thump. Good thing my mom always slept late. We had time to make our getaway.

"Take the pillow cases off our pillows," Craig said, "and put the cans inside."

From the closet, Craig took the handles of two brooms that he had stolen from the kitchen and sawed off in my dad's basement workshop. He tied the end of a pillowcase around the broom handle.

"This is the way hobos carry around their stuff. If we are really gonna run away, then we have to be like real hobos," he said.

"Of course!" I had seen a hobo on *The Andy Griffith Show* with a pole and satchel over his shoulder. "Can you make mine for me?"

"Sure." He made another one, and it was perfect.

"Hold on one sec," Craig said. "I have to get a few more things."

I waited with my broom handle on my shoulder like I was in the army. My stomach felt weird. I wondered what running away really meant. I mean, if he was getting food and making hobo sticks, then maybe he wanted to run away for real.

I put the stuff down and got a little bit sad. I wasn't ready to say goodbye to Lillie and my mom and dad. Not forever. And besides, on Monday, my class was taking a spelling test of words that start with the letter D. I didn't want to miss that. So, when Craig came back, I asked him.

"Are we really running away? Or is this like pretend?"

"We are really running away," he answered. "For real."

"But why?" I asked. "I like things the way they are."

"You know *why*. We talked about it. It's because Mom and Dad don't want us anymore." He was scaring me. He looked mad.

"They don't?"

"No, they don't. So, we're going to go away and live on our own. It will be much better. Don't worry, I'll take care of you," he said.

I began to cry. I never really believed that my parents didn't want us. They spent a lot of time away, but I knew they had important things to do. My chest felt like it was burning, and I gulped three times. Maybe I *was* too much trouble for them. I was always messing around and not cleaning up after myself. I guess I understood why they wouldn't want me.

"Yeah, okay," I said, sniffling. "As long as we stick together."

Craig opened his sweatshirt and pulled out two green bottles of beer. We'd never done anything as bad as stealing my dad's beer.

"That's Dad's beer," I said.

"Not anymore," said Craig. "Now it's ours."

"He's going to notice it's gone, and we'll get in trouble."

"Stop being such a baby," Craig said. "First of all, *we'll* be gone, so we *can't* get in trouble. Second of all, he never checks his beer. I took one once."

"You *did*?" I couldn't believe it.

"Yeah," he said, as he stuffed the bottles into his hobo sack, "and it was delicious. Tasted like a million bucks."

I could not wait to taste one. My dad had let me pour his beer into a tall, frosty glass, but I didn't want to taste it. It was a grown-up thing, like briefcases.

I was getting excited as we jumped down the stairs.

"Hold on a second," Craig whispered on the second-floor landing. "We need to get one last thing."

"What?" I whispered back.

"You need to sneak into Mom's room and steal her pack of cigarettes."

"What!? No way!"

"I got the beer. Now you have to get the cigs," he said.

This made sense, but still...

"She's in there," I said, pointing down the hallway toward my mother's door. "She's in there sleeping."

We could both hear my mom's loud snores bouncing off the ceiling. Her nose was always stuffed up, so she snored like an animal —a hyena or pig or something.

"So, sneak in there and grab them before she wakes up."

"What do we need them for?" I asked.

"We're going to smoke them, dummy," he said, laughing.

I crawled across the green rug toward my mom's bedroom, but no matter how quiet I tried to be, the floorboards still creaked at me. Maybe it was the ghosts of Georgetown. Our house was a hundred years old. There could be a lot of ghosts.

I looked back at Craig, whose eyes were wide. He waved his hands at me. *Go,* he said with his lips.

I crouched outside the door and turned the doorknob slowly. I knew my mom slept with one eye open. I stopped at the end of her yellow canopy bed and reached into the air. I almost had the cigarettes when I heard a rustle.

"Carder?" she whispered.

How did she know it was me? I grabbed the pack and froze, not even making a sound.

"Carder? What are you doing on the floor?" she said in her gravel voice.

Maybe if I didn't answer, I could still escape.

"Card? Do you need something? I'm very tired and need to go back to sleep."

"Uh, Mom. I was looking for my shoes. Found them. Go back to sleep." I prayed she would.

"Okay." She put her head back down. "What are you and your brother up to this morning?"

"Nothing," I said. "We're just running away."

So stupid! Why did I just tell her our secret plan? I was like a spy who told the bad guy everything. Sometimes, I couldn't help blurting things out. I was kind of a blabbermouth.

"Running away? Okay. Have fun." She was half asleep.

"Okay, Mom. We will. Love you," I said.

I couldn't believe it. I was home free. I slithered across the floor toward the open door.

"Just remember not to cross the street," she said.

"We won't," I said. "No way. You don't have to worry."

I clamped my hand over my own mouth to stop the words from coming out and hurried out of the bedroom. I ran past Craig on the landing, with the cigarettes held high in the air.

We had everything we needed and were on our way. When we reached the corner, my brother crossed the street.

"Promises were made to be broken," he said.

"I know, but Mom said that—"

"Don't worry about it," Craig said. "Just follow my plan, and everything is gonna work out. When you run away, there are no more rules. It's just us and the open road."

We had our hobo sticks over our right shoulders and pretended we were two Union soldiers deserting the ranks. Craig began to sing, "Hi ho, hi ho...it's off to war we go...with hand grenades and razor blades...hi ho, hi ho."

"What are you two boys doing all by yourself without your parents? Maybe I should call the police!" It was Mrs. Atherton, walking her dumb dogs.

Craig was cool as a cucumber.

"Oh, no. That won't be necessary," he said, "We are off to the store to pick up my mother's groceries. Go ahead and call her. *I dare you.*"

"My heavens!" she said.

"And stop being such a busybody!" Craig added.

I wanted to be rude, even though my dad said it was wrong to be rude to grown-ups. But she was always angry at us for no reason. I opened my mouth, and it just came out.

"Yeah, why don't you mind your own business for once?" I yelled.

"Don't you *dare* speak to me that way. I am going to call your mother!"

"Go ahead, Shorty," I said like a gangster from an old black and white movie. "Why don't you pick on someone your own size?"

I'd always wanted to say that to someone. It sure felt good.

We both put our thumbs on our noses and wiggled our fingers at her as we ran away.

"We can say anything we want to!" Craig said.

"No more rules."

Traffic sounds filled the air when we got to M Street. This was a busy intersection; there was no way would I ever cross it by myself. A yellow cab sloshed through a puddle and picked up a man wearing a cowboy hat. A construction worker was using a jackhammer. Lots of people were stopped at the crosswalks.

People kept turning around and shaking their heads at us. Sometimes, I figured it was my hair. We hadn't been to the barber in a long time. We didn't ever comb or wash it. I thought bedhead was better than some slick kind of hairdo. Tommy Mallen had a crew cut, and he looked dumb. My mom said that we had hair like her great grandfather. It was thick and blonde and hard to brush. She told us that he came over on a boat in the 1800s from Sweden and didn't even speak English. She said I had his eyes, and Craig had his nose. I liked having his eyes and wondered about all the things he saw. I daydreamed about the boat he came on, with tall smokestacks and splintery wooden planks. I wondered if it hit any icebergs on the way. Probably not because it didn't sink like the Titanic.

When we crossed M Street and until we reached the canals, I stayed right behind my big brother. We stopped and watched a boat-man stick a long pole onto the bottom and push his helmet-shaped boat under a bridge. The canals were a secret. Sometimes, we walked by them with our dad because they were near his boat club on the river, but he was gone now. He was riding on a big airplane to England. The only good thing about that was he would bring me back shiny new beer cans from the pubs. He stuck them in his suitcase, and nobody bothered him in the airport. He was good at hiding things. Like when he forgot my mom's birthday and said he had made a hiding place for his presents but couldn't remember where he put them.

We passed a bum in a cardboard box, and it made me shiver. I walked fast and tried not to look him in the eye. He smelled like alcohol, like my mom's breath when she tucked me in. I wondered if all grown-ups smelled like that.

Underneath the bridge, there were a bunch of tin houses and wooden shacks next to the river. They looked like old forts from the Wild West. Craig and I pretended we were bandits and outlaws like the men who lived here. Sometimes, we said hello to them when we walked by. They could tell that we were outlaws, too, so they let us pass without a toll. We knew not to cross them or try to steal their gold. People had been turned into varmint food for less.

We found a good spot next to a crackly old parking lot and sat down. We could even build a campfire if we wanted. My brother untied his hobo pouch and took out some beer.

"It's time for a drink," he said. Craig popped off the metal cap and took a guzzle.

"Better than the milk from a bowl of Cap'n Crunch."

I knew how much he loved cereal milk—he would guard it with his life—so the beer must be even better. But when I took a sip, I didn't think so. The beer kinda tasted like rusty nails.

"*Mmm*, that is awesome," I fibbed.

When we finished the first bottle, my head started spinning. The clouds and trees mixed together, and I felt woozy and happy, like it was my birthday. Now I could tell why my mom carried a drink on her way to bed and snuck booze into her OJ first thing in the morning. I totally got why my dad had a silver flask on hunting trips and tipped it into his mouth when we waited for the ducks. Everything made sense. When I grew up, I wanted to drink as much as them, or maybe even more.

"I feel great," I said. I put my arm around Craig. "You are my best friend," I said. "Very best! Bestest of all time. You are."

"Thanks, my brother," he said. "You are my best brother friend, and also Tristram is my other best friend. But you would win in a contest, because we live in the same house and sleep in the same room."

I nodded at him.

"You know what goes perfectly with a beer?" he said.

"What?"

"A cig."

Right! My mom always had a cig when she sipped her wine. She smoked two packs a day, and there were ashtrays all over the house. They were always full, and the brown ends and ashes would spill all the time and leave messy piles on the floor.

My mom would say, "Darling, I put my ciggies down somewhere. Be a sweetie and find them for me." This was my special job. I found her cigs in so many places around the house that she called me the best tobacco detective in Georgetown. Once, I found them behind the toilet bowl, crumpled up next to the wall. My mom smoked on the toilet. She could probably win a prize for smoking.

My brother pulled out two cigarettes and handed one to me.

"When I light the end, you want to puff on the smoke and make sure it stays lit. Then, after a few puffs, you want to breathe the smoke deep into your lungs," he said.

"Deep into my lungs? What does that mean?"

"You know when Dr. Strong tells us to take a deep breath and hold it in for a few seconds before blowing it out?"

"Yeah." Sometimes, Dr. Strong would put his hand on my balls and ask me to cough. It made me feel weird.

"So suck the smoke in like you're taking a deep breath and hold it in before blowing it out," Craig said.

I wanted to do it right and show Craig that I could be a good smoker, like Mom. I didn't want to let him down. He lit the end of my cigarette, and I breathed in with all my might. It felt like someone had thrown a bomb in my mouth. I gagged and coughed and sneezed at the same time.

Craig cracked up. "Your face is turning purple!"

The whole world was spinning around me. Everything was out of control. My worried voices, like the ones that told me Mom and Dad didn't love me, were gone, and my brain started to pound. Everything that ever scared me flew from my body when I sneezed out the smoke.

I took another puff and then another, coughing every time. I closed my eyes and saw bright-colored planets in my head, and I flew through the universe at light speed. I could feel the cold air of space against my cheeks. I watched as a star burst in front of me, and it looked like a million fireflies swarming inside a volcano. I felt my body fall through space until it hit the ground with a thud. I was back.

"What happened to me?" I asked Craig.

"You just got high," he said. "That's why people drink and smoke. To get high."

"Yeah, I was really high. I want to get high again."

"Me too," Craig said, and he took a puff of his cigarette. "It works even better if you spin around in a circle after you take a puff."

I watched Craig spin around and around, laughing and falling to the ground. His eyes were closed, and he had a huge grin on his face. Until today, I thought that playing hockey, eating coffee ice cream, and finding old beer cans were the best things in the world, but not anymore. I had a new favorite thing. It was called getting high.

I sucked a huge amount of smoke into my lungs and spun around with my arms out like I was a red-tailed hawk. I fell to the ground and watched as two sunsets fell behind my eyelids. This was a magic place where nothing bad happened, my mother and father were home all the time and let me sit on their laps for hours, my whole family snuggled together in one big feather bed under a soft blanket big enough to cover our toes, my dad squeezed me tight and told me he loved me, and my mom would never be on the phone with her friends when I had something important to say. I wanted to stay here forever, but the magic place vanished when I opened my eyes.

Craig looked over.

"Why are you crying?" he said. "Are you okay?"

My face was soaked with tears and snot.

"Yeah," I sniffled, "I just wish Mom and Dad were around more. I mean I wish that they cared more about me."

"Yeah," he said, "I know. But I love you, bro. So don't worry about it."

That felt good, but the sad voices were back. I wondered how I could feel so happy and sad all at the same time.

"Let's drink another beer," Craig said. "It will make you feel better."

The beer made me feel better, a little bit, but I still felt really bad. Even when I won first prize in the spelling bee and got picked first for kickball, I still didn't feel like anyone wanted me. All I really wanted was to sit on somebody's lap. But everyone was too busy—even Lillie B., sometimes. I was afraid that I would wake up one day, and everyone would be gone. They would leave me alone cuz I was a bad kid. I wished I wasn't bad, but I knew I was. Sometimes, I stomped up the stairs so loud that my mom said it sounded like an earthquake. Sometimes, I felt sad and I didn't know why. Sometimes, I cried in my room when no one was listening.

We looked up at the clouds. I remembered Tom and Huck on the old river in *Huckleberry Finn*.

"We should build a raft out of driftwood and float away," I said.

"Okay, but I'm too dizzy right now," Craig said back.

"Yeah, I mean later. We could float down the river, catch fish, and have adventures. And no one would ever tell us what to do."

"Let's make a pact and never tell anyone what we're gonna do," Craig said.

"Do you think they'd miss us?" I asked. "I mean if we built a raft and floated down the river?"

I held my breath as I waited for his answer.

"I think they would," he said. "Yeah, I think so. You know Mom and Dad aren't so bad. They just don't understand us, that's all."

I nodded my head. But I wasn't sure.

"It's just that they're always too busy for us," I said. "And when Mom does anything like pick us up from school, she acts like it's such a big deal."

"And she's like an hour late," Craig said.

"And she's drunk," I said. "But maybe that's okay because that's when she lets us stand up in the back seat."

"Yeah, we can do whatever we want. Tristram has way more rules, and he hates it. He says we're lucky."

My brother was good at making me feel better, usually, but I didn't feel lucky. I felt sad. I didn't know where my dad was most of the time. There were always bags in the hallway, and I didn't know if he was coming or going. When he was there, he got mad a lot, and when he yelled, it felt like the whole house shook. He was like the big bad wolf or something.

But there was a happy part of him, too—like at our farm, when we went skinny-dipping in the lake, no matter how cold it was. When we were naked, I could see the freckles on his shoulders and birthmark on his hip, and he didn't seem so scary. Sometimes, I sat on his lap when he was driving. That's the only time I sat there. Other times it was off limits.

"I wish Dad was home," I said. "Maybe if he knew me better he'd like me more."

"Remember that thing I said about Mom and Dad not wanting us?" Craig said.

"Yeah."

"That wasn't true. I was just trying to get you to run away with me."

"I know," I said, but I wasn't sure.

"They do love us."

"I know." I hoped it was true.

The sky was really dark, and a streak of lightning hit the river next to us. Thunder banged like a cannon battle above our heads. Then the rain started. Maybe it would take the sad from my body. Maybe all the bad stuff would wash away. Maybe I was the only kid in the world who felt this way. Sure seemed so.

Craig sat up and put his arm around me.

"What do you want to do now?" he asked.

"I want to go home," I said.

"Me too," he said.

We waved goodbye to our camp and stood up. Craig gave me his jean jacket and walked one step in front as the raindrops stung our eyes.

He held my hand tight 'til we reached our front door.

Chapter Three

2003

Everything hurt. My wrists felt like they were wrapped in barbed wire. *So this is why people hate handcuffs.* It was a first for me, and I felt completely helpless. Even with my arms bound, I could feel the swelling on the back of my head. My heart pounded through the bruise on my skull, and it hurt to breathe. When I looked up, I had no idea where I was or who the people in front of me were. Then I recognized the policewoman who had tackled me standing a few feet away. Her expression was one of disgust. She waved at a man in a black sedan.

"Roll tape," she said.

She turned toward me and began to speak. "What is your name?" I stared and realized the severity of my predicament. She raised her voice. "*What is your name?*"

"Christopher Jeppson." There was no confirming otherwise—I hadn't carried a wallet on me for several months.

"Well, Christopher. You're in a lot of trouble right now. Do you fully understand what's happening here?"

"Well, actually, I have no idea," I said, with a croak in my voice.

"My name is Detective O'Mara, and I'm an undercover agent with the LAPD's narcotics squad. And *you* are in possession of a large amount of crack cocaine."

"I have absolutely no idea what you're talking about," I replied.

"Don't play dumb with me, shithead. We all saw you make the buy from this alleyway. We have photographs of it." I looked over at two middle-aged men flanking an old Chrysler LeBaron. One of them had a camera with a telephoto lens around his neck. He smiled at me and nodded.

"Yeah, we can print you up a glossy eight-by-ten if you want, so you can submit it to your agent." He chuckled.

"I still have no idea what you mean." I was scared to the bone and could feel myself shivering but somehow continued with my unequivocal rejection of the truth. Thank you, adrenaline. "That guy was asking if I had a dollar to spare, and I gave him one. Being a good Samaritan, you know. Sometimes, if I have extra—"

"Shut the fuck up," Detective O'Mara spat. "We saw the exchange. It's proof enough to bust your ass. Now you better come clean, or we're going to stop being so damn nice."

"Listen, I live a few blocks away, and I went over to the food truck to get some water, and on my way back, gave a homeless guy some dough. That's it, I swear."

"Do you know that lying to an officer is also a crime?" She turned to her two partners. "Should we arrest him now and let him spend some time in jail? What do you think?"

"Let's give him another shot," one said.

"We saw you put the crack in your mouth and swallow it right before I got to you. You know we can get a warrant to pump your stomach, right? Whatever's inside you is admissible as evidence. We can take you to a doctor's office right now. Or you can start talking," she said.

"I'm sorry, but I already told you. You guys have made a mistake—"

"We're trying to help you. Don't you see that? This neighborhood is no place for a white guy like you. You could get killed out here. We've seen it happen before," said the third officer.

"Thank you, sir," I said, "but I'm fine. I live in this neighborhood, and I'm not afraid of what goes on here. I mind my own business and keep to myself."

"Does your mother know you're a drug addict? I bet she's really proud of you. Coming into the 'hood. Smoking crack. Lying to the police. I bet she thinks you're a real prize." O'Mara's voice was thick with disdain.

"My mother's dead," I lied. "But I know she was proud of me. You have it all wrong."

"Yeah, right," she said. "One last chance to tell the truth before we book you."

"Sorry, but I'm innocent. I think this might be harassment. You have nothing on me."

I waited, holding my breath.

"He's right," the one with the camera said quietly. "We don't have enough to hold him. Stop rolling tape."

"God damn motherfucker piss-ant cocksucker," O'Mara shouted, inches from my face. She then turned toward her partners and shook her head. "I am so sorry, you guys. This is totally my fault. I should have wrestled that crack from his mouth. I got there too late. Shit. I was so close."

"So, can I go now?" I asked.

"Just a minute, scumbag."

The third cop nodded to her. "We have eyes on him. We'll get him soon. Very soon."

"Did you hear that, Chris?" O'Mara crouched beside me. "We know where you live. We know who your friends are. We may just show up at your crack house door one day with a warrant. You can expect us soon. Count on it."

"Anytime. I'll make us some tea and crumpets. We can have a nice chat."

"I don't drink tea, you stupid fuck," she said.

"You kiss your children with that mouth?" I couldn't help turning the screw a bit—they couldn't touch me.

"We'll be seeing you, shithead. You and your pipe will be locked up soon. You have my word," she fumed.

"Pinky swear?" I said.

She stood me up and turned me toward a chain-link fence that ran through the alley. I could hear the click of my cuffs and rubbed at my throbbing wrists and fingers. I backed slowly onto the street and began to jog away. I had to thank my defiant streak for defending me long enough to evade incrimination. They were trying to tape an admission of guilt so they could arrest me. I had learned back at St. Paul's that when confronted by an authority figure, the only way out was to deny, deny, deny. It may have been the most valuable information I gained from three years of boarding school.

Back at my apartment, I headed straight for the bathroom. It wasn't long before the acid in my stomach would break apart the cocaine. I cupped my hands and drank several long gulps of water from the tap. Leaning forward with my head above the sink, I forced myself to throw up with a simple contraction of my stomach muscles. It was easy for me. I had learned to purge my system at age twelve, and for the decade that followed, I had suffered from bulimia. It had taken me to dark places, but for the most part, I was cured of *that* addiction. I could feel the yellow nugget of crack rise into my throat and drop into the porcelain. I washed it off and dried it on my shirt. Good as new. And now, the ritual began.

Most crack smokers had their own way of doing things. I was no different. I was meticulous about how I handled my equipment. The pipe only worked if it was lined with a screen made from the clippings of a steel wool pad. The best pads were called Chore Boy and were available at most grocery stores around town. They were easy to steal and lasted for a long time. I'm pretty sure that this brand of cleaning implement was used primarily to smoke dope. I had never seen one beneath a kitchen sink, but they were always present on the grimy coffee tables of the addicted. A two-inch section of the brass-colored strands, once packed together, was ready for charring. Because there was no stove in my small efficiency, I would hold it with an old pair of tweezers over the flame of a Bic lighter. After the gold turned black, the screen had to cool off for a few moments. If it were not properly cured, the draw from the pipe would be strained, and the crack would be wasted. I would then wedge the screen through the end of the glass pipe while thrusting a coat hanger through the other side. The hanger provided the perfect amount of torque to assist the metal tendrils in their adhesion to the glass walls. The optimal resting place for the screen was about an inch from the top because it provided ample space for the crack to be loaded. This process could not be rushed, as the result would guarantee an inferior high, so even the most crazed and strung-out maniacs had to be patient.

In the past, I had smoked with friends, acquaintances, low-lifes, dealers, and prostitutes—everyone and anyone I could. When I first began to smoke, I was the life of the party, sharing my self-proclaimed wisdom with anyone who would listen. I had weeklong fiestas at my Hollywood bungalow starring several cases of bourbon and no sleep. I loved to commune with others. I told jokes and laughed and danced through the night, with little thought to the downward trajectory of my life.

But as my appetite for the drug grew, I became more and more reclusive. It happened slowly and subtly. Like the setting sun falling into the ocean, there was no way to stop my descent. I began to distrust everyone around me. I looked over my shoulder to make sure I wasn't being followed.

And then the voices came. They were terrifying. I was so frightened that I sometimes ran out the front door of my place and down the middle of the street. Several times, I climbed onto my roof to try and catch a glimpse of the perpetrators. I believed they were coming to get me. It was like a sinister cocktail party was happening inside my head, and the guests pointed their fingers and chased me down the hallways under my skin. But when the drugs wore off, they disappeared, leaving me baffled and alone. I was in Hell.

At first, I thought that the voices were coming from real people, but as time wore on, it became clear that they were not. As soon as the smoke filled my lungs, they would arrive, and they would not leave me alone until I came down. But I smoked anyway—as much as I could get my hands on. My paranoia increased with each day, and eventually, I refused to open my door for anyone until my family arrived and brought me to rehab.

The voices were different now—or maybe I just understood them in a different way. They no longer tormented me. I thought about them constantly in the few months I was sober and realized that they were not there to hurt me.

I concluded that the cocaine opened a channel in my mind, connecting me to another realm. The properties of the drug had unlocked a doorway that led to the resting place of souls. These spirits spoke to me when the portal was open, much like in the shamanic experiences that inform the beliefs of many indigenous peoples. I thought of it as a gift. The voices I heard were not random but rather those of my ancestors. I discovered this when I actually began to listen and heard my paternal grandmother, Maxine, with her low grumblings and distinct hyperbolic gasps.

My grandmother had always professed her clairvoyance. When she was a small girl, her mother had brought her down south to visit with a friend living in a beautiful antebellum mansion. As they were sitting together in the living room, little Maxine asked her mother's friend if the trapdoor still existed behind the fireplace. Maxine then took them into an adjacent parlor and reached into the fireplace to release a hidden lever. A door sprung open in the back of the fireplace and revealed a passageway that connected to several tunnels underneath the house. The owner of the house was astonished—she had no knowledge of the passageway.

"This is where the slaves were brought to hide them from bad people," Maxine told them. She explained that she had seen a vision of a black woman climbing down the ladder. Her mother was humiliated and rarely spoke of it again.

When my father was at boarding school, he fell on the ice and sliced his Achilles tendon. Before he reached the infirmary, Maxine had called several times and asked how her son's leg was doing. The school hadn't contacted her—she'd seen the accident in her mind. My father was proud of his mother's gift and told us her powers might be passed down. I believed the cocaine caused my powers to surface.

The pipe was now ready for a load. I pinched the crack between my thumb and forefinger until a big chunk detached, and I dropped it into the cylinder. I brought the pipe to my lips and lit the glass underneath the crack. It bubbled and made a cracking sound as it vaporized. I took a long hit of the smoke and held my breath for about fifteen seconds before exhaling a thick stream into the room.

When I visited with my ancestors, I didn't like to stay at home because the room felt too crowded. I would head onto the backstreets and canals of Venice with the full weight of my bloodline in tow. Lillie B. was there, as well. I felt protected by her, but even so, I knew the 'hood would not be safe after dark. My route was through a much more gentrified and family-oriented part of town. I wore my Red Sox cap with the brim pulled down over my eyes, my pipe and dope tucked neatly in my front pocket. Every few hours, I found a quiet spot to smoke on the open road.

Maxine was already cackling away as I hurried down Pacific toward Venice Boulevard.

"I'm angry with you, my boy. You want a family and children. You will never have them if you keep this up."

"Yeah, but if I stop, I won't be able to talk with you. You're one of the only people I can count on," I replied.

"You gots lots of people, my child. You just ain't looking in the right places. An' why you wearing that dirty ole hat again?" said Lillie.

"Who? Who do I have in my life that I can count on?"

"Your new friend Flyn. He's a good man," a voice said.

"I haven't met him yet. Besides, he's a business prospect. Nothing more."

"He's gonna be your brother. Just like Craig," the voice said.

"Craig's too busy with his own family. Besides, I've let him down too many times." A young couple walked past me on the street and turned around to get a good look. I suppose they wondered why I was talking to myself. But I wasn't, really. I had a whole crowd behind me.

"Be careful, people are watching you," another voice said.

"You need a shave and a haircut. Two bits in my time," said an old man.

I had a newfound respect for those diagnosed with schizophrenia and wondered about the discourse between their ears. Mine was a cacophony of sounds, declarations, and idiosyncratic phrases, each with their own particular accent and cadence. Some were Brits and others Scots, intermingled with a few Swedes and New Jersey blue bloods. There was a refined twang to some voices, while others seemed unschooled and even Paleolithic with their grunts. I thought about what it would look like if they were all visibly surrounding me as I meandered down the street. It would certainly be colorful, with all of the parasols, bloomers, top hats, capes, and fur.

A few dogs barked as I passed, and I wondered if they saw the ghosts that surrounded me, as I had heard that the sensory perception of a canine was more evolved than that of its owner. A couple waved to me from their back stoop and invited me up for a toke from their joint, but I politely declined. My dance card was already full.

I doubled back on Strongs Drive and peered into the open windows and doors of its affluent residents. Then it was up to the canals. This was my favorite part of Venice. Industrialist and real estate baron Abbot Kinney had built them in 1905 to copy the canals of Venice, Italy. There were six main canals, each about a quarter mile long, that were connected by a series of nine bridges. At night, with the streetlights sparkling off the water, they were a sight to behold. They were relatively deserted after dark, and offered safe harbor for an upscale downtrodden figure like myself. I was white, with no visible scars, wearing clothes that were not stained with my own urine, and was therefore allowed to walk the canals with little or no incident.

Sometimes, I would sit for hours with my feet dangling down a dirt embankment, quietly replying to the voices. The beautiful homes that lined the canals were packed in tightly, and their lights went off about 10:00 PM, so I tried to mitigate my outbursts by pretending I was a child in a library. The canals were my midnight playground, and I didn't want to spoil the opportunity to move freely about them.

I walked up the Grande Canal and gazed skyward at an amazing array of yellow stars overhead. My people were quieting—a clear indication that I needed a hit. I never smoked on the canals because there were too many eyes around, so I cut out of the waterways and headed down Dell Avenue toward Main Street.

A small craftsman bungalow halfway up Seville Court had a row of bushes brushing up against a white picket fence. This seemed like a prime spot to twist into; both the fence and bushes would provide cover from anyone passing by. I dropped to my knees and crawled through the hedge.

"Shit!" I shrieked when a sharp branch scratched my left cheek. A moment later, the outside light came on, and a middle-aged woman popped through the front door.

"Hello?" she said. "Is there someone there?"

I kept dead silent. I was caught halfway between a crouch and a bear crawl, with one hand on the ground and one hand caught behind my back. I didn't dare move a muscle. Suddenly, my nose itched like it had just been bitten by a mosquito. I blew a silent stream of air toward my nostril in hopes of some relief, but this maneuver failed miserably. Almost unbidden, my hand flew to my nose, and I face-planted in the dirt. I heard the screen door slam and prayed that it would drown out my predicament. If not, I was certain to have a broom thwacked over my head.

I waited for several seconds. The coast was clear. I sat up, pulled my stem from my pocket, and loaded it with a large rock of crack. I heated the pipe gently with a low flame so that the cocaine would melt onto the screen. This eliminated the possibility of my precious cargo dropping into the darkness. I lit the end and pulled my breath in hard. I could feel the dense fumes suffusing the passageway to my lungs, and almost immediately, my friends were back.

"Get yo ass out them damn bushes. You ain't a possum, is you?" Lillie chided.

"Yeah, yeah, yeah," I said. "Just keep it down for a minute. Sometimes you guys are so damn loud."

"Don't be rude. We are only here to help," a Swedish man said.

"You better not turn on us," another voice said.

"Sometimes I wish you would just leave me alone," I begged.

"As long as you smoke, we'll be here," said a man with a thick Cockney accent.

"We are *always* here. When you medicate, our voices can reach you," a Scottish woman added.

"We have been with you since you were born. Well, most of us, anyway." This voice sounded like that of a young child.

This was an interesting notion to consider. Were these spirits forever assigned to follow me about? It was reassuring and annoying at the same time. Of course, it felt supportive to have my ancestors surrounding me, but it also felt invasive. When I was high, even my thoughts were fair game. In fact, just bringing an idea into my mind would provoke a number of fervent opinions. I didn't always agree with them but had a strong sense that they would steer me in the right direction. If they told me not to go down a certain street, I didn't. If they told me to avoid a certain person, I did. They were like an overbearing posse of uptight parents trying to mold their defiant child into something he was not. I had fun tormenting them once in a while. I would intentionally imagine something preposterous, like stealing an ATM machine, just to instigate a flurry of concern. It made me laugh.

I strolled down Brooks Avenue toward the water. There was always a colorful cast of characters on the boardwalk at night. The long, paved road running adjacent to the beach was filled with addicts of all kinds. There were drunks stumbling about, who barked angrily at passersby. There were stoners tucked in the alleyways, dancing to the Grateful Dead from their car radios. There were the meth heads darting around, anxiously looking over their shoulders at imagined conspiracies, and there were the fixers nodding gently inside their heroin dreams. Every type of drug that existed was available on the boardwalk. This attracted both the gutter rats and the working-class stiffs who came to make their purchases—and the police looking for a bust. I had no interest in being hassled by cops for a second time that night and proceeded on my way.

When I reached Rose Avenue, I headed onto the beach toward an empty lifeguard tower: a perch that I could inhabit for hours without interruption. I had spent many nights listening to the waves and pulling on my pipe. Tonight would be no different. I sat and chatted and smoked the night away. And when the first hint of dawn showed its ugly face, I headed toward home.

As the drugs slowly wore off, I lay naked on my bare mattress and thought about the women I had loved. Girlfriends who sobbed in my arms as I whispered goodbye or slammed the door in my face after I cheated: Kate, with her sun-kissed face, Doc Marten boots, and wicked sense of humor. She could never make up her mind about anything until she decided she'd had enough. And Amy, with her heart of gold, blonde cowlick, and Anna Wintour style. She would never trust me again. I imagined their faces—their remarkable faces—and I fell asleep wondering if I would die alone.

When I finally woke up, I could tell by the light that it was late afternoon. I leapt out of bed and pulled on a pair of khaki shorts and a wrinkled polo shirt. I wanted to look respectable for my four o'clock meeting with Flyn. I doused my face with water and attempted to brush the gristle from my teeth with an outstretched finger. I couldn't even remember when my toothbrush had disappeared. I sighed when I looked up and stared at my face in the mirror.

My eyes were bloodshot red, and my lips were cracked and swollen. There were dark black patches underneath my eyes. My hair resembled a bird's nest. I was Pig Pen from Peanuts all grown up, and there was no way to remedy this. My hot water had been turned off the month before, so a shower was out of the question. This also made shaving next to impossible, as my patchy beard could not be tamed by cold water and a used razor blade. I was a mess—no two ways about it. But I had a bargaining chip. I would never have guessed that a gray Ford Taurus would be my most valuable possession, but it was.

Before I left my apartment, I took my horn from my jeans pocket. I positioned it vertically in an old Ray Ban case, wrapped it in a cloth, and placed it carefully in my top drawer. As a kid, I used to stow away my prized stuffed animal, Liony, and I would refuse to go anywhere until I knew he was comfortable. Old habits never die, I guess. *Sleep well, my good girl.*

The car started right up. It felt good to be behind the wheel, and I had an urge to cruise through the neighborhood for a bit. I took a right on Fifth and a left on San Juan, tapping my car door through the open window. As I took a right on Seventh, I saw a cluster of blue hoodies and slowed down to watch a few of the younger Crips square off in a fist fight. A crowd of boys and girls surrounded them, chanting and jeering. A teenage dealer named Bee who I had bought from on numerous occasions came over.

"What's up, Hollywood?" he said. "You need somethin'?"

"Nah, I ain't got no money right now," I said. "I'm going to see Flyn. Takin' care of some bizness. You know Flyn?"

"Flyn!? Yeah, everybody in the 'hood know Flyn. He a big dawg. Nobody fuck with Flyn. He connected. All the way to the top."

"Yeah, we got somethin' goin' on. Bizness. You know." I was trying to speak 'hood and failing miserably. I realized that I was bragging to a thirteen-year-old street dealer about my potential association with someone I still had not met. But I had no one else to converse with, brag to, or try to impress. Bee liked the fact that I drove around in a car that mimicked the Crown Victorias driven by the undercover units. The Taurus was a smaller version of the Crown Vic but could be easily mistaken for one from a distance. Sometimes the dealers scattered when they saw me pull up, especially at night. Bee told me that I looked like a cop and probably believed that I was, until he watched me smoke his crack. He trusted me after that and sometimes sat shotgun and rolled around with me when the action was slow at the community center.

"Cool. Cool," he said, putting up his fist for a pound. I touched his knuckles with mine and pulled a U-turn back toward Vernon Avenue. In a matter of moments, I was parked outside Flyn's front door. I smoothed out the wrinkles in my alligator shirt and walked up to the front stoop. Before knocking, I closed my eyes and thought of Lillie B. She always put a smile on my face.

Beatrice peered down at me through the iron bars of her gated front door. Her smile cut through my apprehension about meeting a "big dawg."

"Come in, baby. We's been 'spectin' you." As I entered the brightly lit kitchen, I laid eyes on Flyn for the first time. And he *was* a big dawg: six foot three and two hundred and sixty pounds' worth. He was stocky and thick like the trunk of an old redwood, and his hands were larger than my forearms. I considered what it would feel like to be on his bad side. I never wanted to find out. Underneath his tank top, the light brown skin on his shoulders wore the distinct lines of jailhouse tattoos, and he had a large diamond earring in his right ear. His eyes were emerald green and looked kind, inviting, and sincere. He got up from his chair and greeted me with a gentle slap on the shoulder.

"So you're Hollywood? I've heard good things."

"Carder, yeah... or Hollywood is fine. Whatever you want to call me is fine," I said sheepishly.

"Word on the street is that you're a stand-up dude. Get all my intel from the street."

"And from your old Grandma, too," Beatrice added with a laugh.

"Word! Of course. That's where I get everything. From my BeeMa. She knows everything." Flyn put his arm around her and squeezed. He was so much bigger that I could imagine one over-enthusiastic hug being the end of her, but he was as gentle as a parent with a newborn.

"You ain't lyin'," Beatrice chuckled. "Can I get you boys somethin' to eat?"

"No, BeeMa. We're leaving now. Got a few things to take care of. See you tomorrow morning for pancakes and sausage."

"Sounds good, baby. Don't get into trouble. Now, Codder, you remember your promise." She patted my arm gently.

"Yes, I remember. Don't worry," I said, following Flyn out into the backyard. I had no idea if I could keep it.

We rounded the side of the house, and as I walked behind Flyn, I marveled at his sheer size. He barely fit between the house and the chain-link fence that bordered their property. Nervous energy contracted in my stomach, like I had just picked up my date to the prom. We walked up to my car, and he began to assess it.

"So this is the ride? All right, all right. I can work with this. Does it have AC?" Flyn asked.

"Uh, yeah, AC and a CD player and leather seats. Runs great," I said.

"Okay. I like it. Inconspicuous. Tight. Clean. Could be perfect. Might be the one."

"For what?" I asked.

He turned his head and looked at me without responding. It wasn't quite a glare—it was almost a blank look—but it spoke volumes. I was not to ask such questions—not yet, at least.

"Okay, let's take this bitch for a spin," he said.

We jumped inside the car, and I slowly pulled away from the curb. Flyn's ease put me at ease right away. He fiddled with the radio, and 50 Cent began to rap through the speakers. Flyn bobbed his head and smiled.

"Now that's some good shit," he said. We both sang along. "I never knew a white dude who could rap," he laughed.

"Ha, me neither," I said. "I can't sing worth a shit, but that don't stop me."

"I hear that." He turned up the radio and pumped his hands to the beat of the lyrics. I could tell by the way he spoke that he was educated. He didn't sound like most of the people in the 'hood. He exuded a level of sophistication that was usually lost in the gutters and alleyways of Ghost Town. He had no street accent and enunciated his words as if he had been schooled by a Catholic nun. For a moment, I imagined that I was rolling with some old friend from college.

"So, you don't sound like you're from around here," I said brazenly.

"Ha. Not all us black folk is ignorant," he joked. "My grandma always made sure I studied and did well in school. I read a lot of books. I also like movies. You know, you look just like that dude from *Lord of the Rings*. Word. You could be him. I mean really."

"That's why they call me Hollywood."

"So, what you want to get from life, Hollywood? What are you about?" he asked.

I paused for a moment. There were about a million ways I could answer this question. I wasn't sure if Flyn wanted to hear my sad story or even my scattered philosophy about life, so I kept it brief.

"I'm just trying to get by. Get high. Be sly and comply."

I immediately felt like a fool. The rap music had gotten to me, I guess.

"I ain't interested in all that, man. I mean, what is it you want?"

Relieved to have another shot, I constructed my second response with sincerity. "I don't know, really. I suppose I'm just trying to find my way. Trying to find a way to be happy."

"Now that's real," he said. "Where's your family at?"

"Well, my dad lives in England, my mom is in Massachusetts, and I have two sisters and a brother scattered about. I haven't spoken to any of them in months." I shrugged. "They're kinda done with me."

"Family is everything," he said. "You should call them up sometime. Tell them you thinkin' about them. Ease the pain. You only got one life. You need to forgive and move on. It's the only way to be."

I found myself nodding, almost tearing up. He was part preacher, part therapist, and part giant. I had never met anyone like him. His interpretation of my circumstances was dead on. He seemed to understand the depths of my regret without even knowing my situation. I was glad to have met him. Just his advice would be compensation enough for my new role as chauffeur.

"You want to take a ride with me? Take care of some business? Shouldn't take long and be good for both of us."

"Sure. What the fuck. I'm in."

"My man, Hollywood," he said with a grin, putting his knuckles out for a pound. "I think this is gonna work out just fine. I'll take care of you if you take care of me. Cool?"

"I'm down. Just as long as we're not gonna do anything illegal," I joked.

"Baah," he replied. "You mean *legal*. We ain't gonna do anything *legal*. Take a right on Lincoln and head up toward the marina."

"Where we going?" I asked.

"The 'hood in Inglewood. Onto the block of some stone-faced killas. So watch out. White boy like you is fair game."

I glanced at him. His serious expression made my heart start to pound, but then a smile began to crack.

"Baah! Don't worry. You with Flyn. And nobody fucks with me. Not now. Not *ever*."

This was a different side of Flyn: a thug alongside the spiritual guru. I could understand why he commanded respect on the street. He could out-talk, out-think, and out-muscle his adversaries, to be certain. I felt safe in his presence and intuitively believed that no harm would come to me when we were together. We headed through the marshland of the marina and sped up the hill toward the danger zone.

It had all been so easy. Strangely so, in fact. I already trusted him. *Why*, I wondered, *did he seem to trust me?*

"So, can I ask you a question?" I began.

"Yeah, shoot."

"So, I'm totally psyched to be taking care of business with you, but I was wondering how you know that I'm cool. I mean, I could be *anyone*. A cop or detective or whatever. I mean, I'm not. Of course not—but what if I was? How can you tell I'm okay and you can trust me?" There it was—my acceptance speech for *Best Shady Newcomer*, granting me the highly touted opportunity to collude with a gangster.

"All right, all right," Flyn responded. "Good question, though. First off, we haven't done anything wrong yet. So, if you was a cop, you'd have nothing on me. Secondly, just the fact that you bring this up lets me know you're not a cop. A cop would never get into shit like that. Never. But I knew right away that you was cool. I can tell by looking in a person's eyes. I've been around cops all my life. On the inside, around the 'hood, trying to bust me, get info, all that shit. You ain't nothing like them. And, your thumbs have black spots, and there's burns on your fingers. You got hands like a dope fiend."

I stared at my thumbs on the wheel and looked at the thick black calluses covering the tops of them. This was a direct result of handling burnt screens and pushing the glass pipe for hits of resin. My finger had several pipe burns, as well. Flyn was absolutely right. No police officer would exhibit the scars of crack addiction—or have the wherewithal to fake them. He was a smart motherfucker.

"I guess you got me," I said, embarrassed. "I mean, is that cool with you? That I smoke. I only do it at night, and—"

"I got my horn right here." He held up a shiny new crack pipe. "And we're gonna test out this mofo later tonight." He laughed heartily. "You funny, Hollywood. What you think, I was gonna judge you for smoking dope? I been smoking this shit for twenty years."

I was totally surprised by Flyn's admission. He did not bear the marks of crack addiction in any way. His clothes were pressed, and his face was clean. He was muscular and hulking, with a few extra pounds to shed. His eyes were clear, with no visible bags under them. He was jovial and calm and full of wisdom. I imagined that he used differently than me, in a way that was somehow less severe. Perhaps he was a weekend smoker who dabbled with the substance from time to time. I was happy that we shared a habit in common. It somehow made our new alliance more solid. There was a kinship that smokers shared.

Smokers could sniff each other out for the most part, but in some cases, it was hard to detect. I tried to hide my addiction, keeping my hands in my pockets to conceal the evidence. A few years prior, when my mother was visiting LA, I smoked in the janitor's closet of a restaurant as she sat alone at the table. She had no idea. But Flyn had pegged me right away, and I was the one left in the dark.

"Take a right on Arlington," he said. I had never been in Inglewood before but could immediately tell that it was dangerous. A large contingent of young black men populated the corners in their signature navy blue. This was Crips territory, and as we ventured deeper, I realized that I was the only white person around. The sun was down now, but I could still make out the faces of everyone we passed. None of them looked friendly. In fact, they stared at me with burning eyes of hatred as I drove by. I was obviously not welcome here. I took a deep breath as I followed Flyn's direction through the neighborhood.

"Okay, pull up over here," he said. "Give me like ten minutes. Don't get out of the car. Be cool." He jumped out of the passenger's side and disappeared into a building halfway up the street. Ten minutes seemed like an eternity, and I could feel my heart pounding at its maximum speed. I realized with a jolt that the street smarts I was so proud of only extended to the streets I knew well. Here, I felt like a target. I needed a cigarette to calm my nerves. I leaned down and reached under the seat, to no avail. I opened the glove box and rummaged through an assortment of documents, and plop—a beautiful, pristine, unsmoked Camel Light fell directly onto the seat. With a gasp of joy, I grabbed the cigarette and popped it into my mouth. I exhaled a lung full of bitter, glorious smoke as I rolled down the window. I felt better—much better. *Everything's going to be fine*, I thought to myself.

Flicking ashes onto the asphalt, I peered into the side mirror. Four men were approaching the back of my car with noticeable— terrifying—momentum. They looked wild, unkempt, and truculent. I could see that one of them was brandishing a pistol. In full panic mode, I grabbed the keys from the ignition and thrust them deep into my pants pocket. They surrounded me.

"Man, what you doin' here?" said one of the pack. He was wearing a blue sweatsuit with no shirt. His hair was braided in corn rows, and he looked like he hadn't eaten in a week. "You *know* it ain't safe for a cracker like you to be down here."

"I'm just waiting for Flyn. He's my friend, and he went inside. I'm cool. I don't want any trouble," I said. I willed my voice not to shake.

"Flyn?" he turned to his friends. "Flyn who?" They all shook their heads.

"Uh, you know, Flyn. He's a big guy. Tall. Black. I don't know his last name," I said frantically.

"And he don't know yours, neither. You need to get out the car."

"Uh, no, it's okay. Flyn will be back in a moment and—"

My words were cut off by the butt of a gun slammed to my left cheek. I blacked out for a second and was unable to resist as he reached in and yanked me through the window. I was dragged across the street, receiving a few kicks to my ribs and derisive words from his friends.

"Ain't shit right now, is you?"

"You 'bout to die, motherfucker."

"Say goodbye to Mommy and Daddy, 'cause you goin' to heaven."

I whimpered as they pulled me down the sidewalk and into an alleyway. They were having a hoot. Each slap came with an insult or burst of laughter. They stood me up against a brick wall and took turns kneeing me in the stomach.

"Give me the keys, motherfucker."

"Yeah, give us the keys."

"That car belongs to us now."

I withstood the strong temptation to hand them over for one reason—I knew that if they got the keys, they would end my life, so I stalled. I needed a minute to think. I had never allowed anyone to rob or carjack me before, and as a matter of principle, I decided to fight back. Psychological warfare was my only option.

"I left them in the car. Under the mat." I thought this response would confuse them, and I canvassed the landscape for an escape route. One of the four men trailed off and headed back to my car.

"You better not be lying to us. If you is, you getting a bullet to the brain." He held the gun up next to my temple and stroked the barrel up and down my face. A few times, he pretended that he was pulling the trigger. I prayed for a miracle. And just as I thought I was a goner, the man came back with Flyn by his side.

"Jayden!" Flyn yelled from down the alley. "Ty, he's with me."

"Who's that?" Jayden said. "Oh shit, Flyn? That you?"

"Yeah, it's me," Flyn said. "He's cool. He wit' me." Immediately, Jayden backed off, and I slumped down the wall. I could tell that he was afraid. All of his cronies wore concern on their faces as well. Flyn was like a superhero.

"Flyn, my man, had no idea. I didn't know he wit' you. My bad," he said, embracing Flyn in a big hug.

"All right, all right, cool. But this here's Hollywood," he said, pulling me up and putting his arm around me. I could barely stand. "He's allowed on the block. In fact, treat him with respect and love. He's my brother. Tell everyone on the block, no one fucks with Hollywood." They all nodded—they had gotten the message, and they quickly regrouped and hustled out of sight. Flyn looked at me and shook his head.

"You all right, my brother? I tol' you there was some stone-faced killas out here."

"Yeah, I'm okay," I lied. I had never been more scared in my life. "I'm cool."

We walked back to my car and fled the scene of the crime. I wanted to leave this neighborhood forever, but something told me that I would be back soon. Flyn handed me a loaded crack pipe as we turned left on Jefferson. We smoked and talked and laughed all the way back to Venice. And my ancestors joined us along the way.

Chapter Four

1977, NINE YEARS OLD

Jimmy Arnoff wasn't like the other kids at the playground. He had a ponytail, for one thing. I thought ponytails were for girls, but he didn't act like a girl. The girls in my fourth-grade class were pushy and grabby and loud. They were always complaining about this or that or skipping rope or something. Jimmy never complained, and I don't think he had a jump rope, either. Jimmy was cool. He was like one of the bad guys on TV who was always getting into trouble, but he always got out of it, too. Craig and I loved his stories, like the time he stole his dad's car and drove around the neighborhood, or the time he frenched a girl in his tree house. He always wore the same blue jeans, and they smelled bad. Sometimes it was so bad that I gagged, but I just covered my nose and looked the other way. He was older than any of the other kids we played with and always talked about his secret missions. He made my mom nervous. When we talked about him, Mom made a face like she'd swallowed her cigarette.

Jimmy told us that he'd been in juvie for shoplifting and had pulled a knife on one of the guards. I didn't know if it was true or not. I kinda believed him, I guess. He had one droopy eye, like he got stung by a bee on his face. We always wanted to see what he would do next. He and Craig were real friends, but he invited me over to his house, too. We smoked cigarettes, drank rum from his dad's liquor cabinet, and watched R-rated movies. Jimmy freeze-framed on the naked scenes and traced the boobs with his finger. We lied to our mom and said we were at the arcade.

Jimmy told us to meet him at the park at eleven on Saturday morning and to make sure we could hang out all day. His dad was away and had left him alone in the house. "You're gonna come over as boys and leave as men," he promised.

Jimmy had one of the coolest backyards we had ever seen. Ten feet above the ground was a big tree house that his dad built. His dad was an engineer. Inside the tree house, there was one window covered by a thick blue curtain, and it was really dark inside. A red lightbulb hung from the ceiling and made everything the color of fire. On one side of the room was a leather couch sitting next to a La-Z-Boy chair, but I liked to sit on the floor. The orange shag carpet ate most of the things we brought inside. It had eaten my pocket knife, two packs of matches, and the queen of diamonds.

On Saturday, we met Jimmy at the park and walked up O Street toward his house. We had sticks in our hands and banged them on parked cars as we walked along. The sun was bright and made us squint at Jimmy, who smiled like the Cheshire cat.

"What are we doing today?" Craig asked.

"You'll see, my good friend. You'll see," Jimmy replied.

"Can you give us a hint?" I asked, hurrying to catch up.

"And you, my little Dude—you are about to have the time of your life, so don't worry."

I *was* worried. I did not want to put on a ski mask and rob a liquor store or something. Jimmy was older and tougher, but I didn't feel safe when I was around him. I wanted to hang with the big kids. Sometimes, I wanted to be alone and far away from the troublemaking, but today, I was going to be brave.

Jimmy had something small and silver sticking out of his pocket. It looked like a metal straw with a dime attached to the end or something, like he had been building a model car and pulled out part of the engine.

"Hey, what is *that*?" I asked.

"Something that's gonna get you high," he said.

"Oh, right," I said, having no idea what he was talking about.

"Why do you *always* have to ask so many *questions*?" Craig said.

"Don't tell me not to ask questions. It's why I'm so smart." I got all A's on my fourth grade report card and was proud of my brain.

"You may be smart," Craig said, "but you don't know shit."

Jimmy and Craig laughed. I wanted to roar at them, but my voice was too high and my hands were so small. I wanted to put up my middle finger and walk home, but I didn't. I tried to pretend it didn't bother me.

They were right—I didn't know about a lot of stuff. I had no idea how to untie a square knot and had overflowed the bathtub three times. Sometimes, I confused my left and my right, and other times, I spilled food onto my shirt during dinner. Last summer, I dove into the pool at our farm in Massachusetts and hit the bottom with my front teeth. The left one cracked in half. My mom said it made me look low class, and my dad wanted to take me to get it fixed, but I kept it anyway. It was my thing, and I felt like it belonged. I was now the kid with the chipped tooth.

Georgetown was really cool. People hung around on the corners and had nothing to do. They weren't like beggars or bums or anything—maybe they just had nowhere to go. They were strumming guitars, handing out flowers, or saying hello with peace signs and smiley faces and stuff. Craig and I loved to walk around M Street because we never knew what we might see. There was an old record store next to an ice cream parlor. A few movie theaters played movies you never heard of with almost-naked girls on the posters. There were fabric shops and shops to fix your typewriter and jewelry stores and flower stands. Our favorite arcade was around the corner.

Then there were the head shops. We knew they were called head shops because my mom told us never to go near them, but when Craig and I were alone, we stopped and stared at the colored glass pipes in the big square windows. We pretended we were workers on strike at a glassblowing factory, but we never went inside—we knew that we had to be grownups. But today was different.

As we marched up the stairs, Jimmy held out his arm like he was carrying a sword. The owner looked up from a comic book.

"Jimmy, my man!" he said, and he came from behind the counter to give him a hug. "How's it hanging?"

"A little to the left," Jimmy said, and grabbed at his balls.

"And who are these righteous dudes that you have with you?" He winked and then eyeballed us. "Hey, are you guys old enough to be in my shop?" I smelled the clove cigarette in the ashtray and stared at the brownish-yellow lumps he had for teeth. Sometimes my mom smoked cloves, too. I stood behind Craig for cover.

"Well," said Jimmy, "this dude is my man Craig. Craig, meet Six-Pack Jack." He pushed Craig toward the shop owner. Craig shook his hand and stepped back.

"And this little dude here with the chipped tooth, well, we're not sure where we found him," Jimmy said, laughing. "No, seriously, this is my dude Carder. He looks little, but he can party."

"How old are you, little man?" asked Six-Pack.

"I'm nine and a half," I said. "Ten next year."

Six-Pack began to crack up. I thought he was going to cough up a lung.

"Ten next year! Well, I'll be damned. I didn't start getting high until I was twelve, like Jimmy here. Nine years old—this might be like a world record. Somebody get Guinness on the phone!" He started to wheeze.

"No, I've never smoked before. Not yet," I squeaked.

"Not until today," Jimmy said. "Today is the day we take your virginity."

"Time for you to get some Chinese eyes," Six-Pack added.

"No big deal," I said, but I could feel my stomach gurgling. I had no idea what would happen. I wanted to run away and never come back, but Craig would never forgive me. Maybe I could sneak out later. For now, I just played along, like everything was okay.

"Yeah, I know all about it. I'm cool with it," I said. Everyone laughed at me, again.

"First time I smoked, all the people I was with looked like either giants or midgets. I got totally freaked out and thought I was shrinking," Six-Pack said. "Also thought my heart had stopped beating in my chest."

That did not sound fun to me. I was just under five feet tall and didn't want to shrink—not even an inch. Also, I liked that my heart was beating and didn't want it to stop up in a tree house where the ambulance couldn't get to me. But maybe it would be different for me. Maybe the weed would make me feel better. I could even pretend that I wasn't myself. I could be someone else, like James Bond or the Six Million Dollar Man, and never have to apologize for anything. No one would make fun of me and everyone would love me. If I became Steve Austin, my dad would definitely stick around and do stuff with me. If I were a secret agent, my mom would stay home from her cocktail parties. Pot might be the perfect thing I was looking for. I tried to tell myself that as I looked around.

Jimmy, Craig, and Six-Pack were in the corner of the shop poking the metal thing that Jimmy brought from his tree house, so I walked around the store. I had wondered what it would be like to go behind the velvet curtains, and now I was here. It was everything I imagined. There were glass cases filled with every kind of trinket you could think of. There were silver rings with skulls, serpent belt buckles, and leather wallets with blue stones on them. There were wooden crosses, rose petals made out of gold, and mugs that looked like shrunken heads. There was a huge wall of lava lamps, sort of like my beer can collection, that made shadows like barracudas swimming across the cement floor. I wondered if the lava lamp makers got high together before they made them.

One corner of the shop was full of bongs. One was so big that I could only reach the top if I stood on my tippy toes. Others were round with dots on them, like a group of mushrooms growing from a log. A few of them were small like they were made for little kids.

Even though I had never smoked before, I wanted a bong for myself. I opened the top of a case and reached for a purple one with writing on the side that said "Purple Haze." It was warm and felt like a bottle that had been out in the sun. I wondered if Jimi Hendrix had ever smoked it. I put it up to my mouth and pretended to play it like a flute. It was about a foot long and fit perfectly in my hand. I had no idea how to use it. I wanted to put it on the shelf in my bedroom next to the beer cans I found in the woods. I would take care of it like my Indian tomahawk, my eagle feather, and my shark's tooth. I didn't let anybody but Craig touch those things.

I walked back to the front of the store and took my chances.

"Six-Pack Jack," I said, "I want to buy Purple Haze."

No one said anything. Jimmy put his hand over his heart like he was saying the Pledge of Allegiance. Craig grinned at me like I had just scored the winning goal in a hockey game, and Six-Pack gave me a double thumbs-up. I felt like I was a full member of the club.

"Nice choice," said Six-Pack. "You can never go wrong with this one. It has good pull, ideal size one-hit chamber, stashable body, and bears the mark of the greatest guitarist of all time. I have one in my car right now for my mobile sessions."

"Great first bong," Jimmy said. "We can test it out in a few."

"Well done, bro," Craig said, with a proud older brother face.

"That will be ten bucks," Six-Pack said. "Usually twelve, but I'm giving you the friends-and-family discount. I am honored to be popping your cherry."

I reached in my pocket and pulled out a crumpled $10 bill. I had been saving up to buy a new baseball glove, but my old one was good enough for now. Six-Pack took the money and put the bong in a crumpled paper bag.

"If anyone ever asks you where you got this, don't mention my name," he said. "The bulls are already after me, and the last thing I need is another headache with the law."

"Of course," I said, "I'll say I found it in the bushes."

"Good idea," Craig said. "Don't worry about my brother—one thing about him is that he never squeals."

I could have told on my brother lots of times, but I never did. Once he sliced my leg open with a big hunting knife, and I told my mom I fell on a brick in the garden. I kept his secrets like they were mine. He kept mine, too, and there was no one who could make us tell, not even if we were captured by the enemy and tortured.

Jimmy walked over to the glass case and looked down. He kept looking down as he spoke.

"Uh, hey, Six, man, uh, do you think you could maybe, uh, set us up with a dime?"

Jimmy's voice creaked, and he gulped twice. He sounded like me when I got scared. Six-Pack smiled and went over to lock the door. He flipped a sign over to read "Closed" and lowered the curtains.

"Yeah," he said, "I believe I could oblige your request."

He held up his finger and went into a back room.

"I can't believe you just asked him for some weed," Craig whispered.

"I know," Jimmy said, eyes wide, "I never bought any from him before. I didn't think he was a dealer. You never know."

Six-Pack came back with a small backpack and put it on top of the counter. He took out three plastic baggies and put them side by side.

"Now, first of all," he said, "I don't normally do this. I don't sell dope to minors, but being that this is a special occasion—and due to the fact that we are all friends here—I am willing to make an exception."

All three of us said "Thanks" at the same time. We nudged each other to say *Jinx*.

The shop smelled like a skunk when Six-Pack opened the baggies and took out some pot from each. Each piece was green and looked like something that might fall off a tree in the jungle. Six-Pack held one up in front of his face and looked at it like he was a scientist who had just discovered a rare species of baby turtles.

"Now this," he said, "is decent weed. Nothing to write home about, but gives you a good, mellow high. You can still function on it. I call it 'Your Majesty'."

He put it on top of the bag and picked up the second one.

"Now this," he smiled, "is some skip-and-go-naked kind of weed. Smoke a bowl or two, and all you want to do is take off your clothes and find a woman. It makes you horny as shit and full of good energy. I call this 'Free Love'."

We listened to his speech like he was the mayor or the president or Jane Fonda or somebody. My mom liked to watch Jane Fonda on TV. She said that Jane was a rebel. Six-Pack was a rebel, too, in my book. And who even knew there were different types of pot? 'Til now, I thought that there was only one type of pot, and it grew on a stalk like corn.

Six-Pack picked up the third one and held it in his hand like it was a baby grasshopper with a broken leg. There were small red hairs running down the side like raspberry racing stripes, and I wondered how they would taste on my tongue.

"Now this," he said, "this comes from a guy I know in Humboldt County. This will make you see things that may or may not be there and laugh 'til your head falls off. Only smoke this if you have several hours to kill. I call it 'The Holy Grail.' It will cross your eyes and dot your knees. It will turn you into a believer."

"That one," said Jimmy. "We'll take that one."

Craig and I looked at each other. I had never expected to be part of a drug deal. I felt dirty—not like when you roll around in the mud with your brother, but something else. Mud always came off if you had enough suds. This was a different kind of dirty. It was more like a gooky feeling that somehow got under my skin. I was afraid it would stay there forever. I wanted to wash it off and run far away, but I didn't say anything. They would think I was a baby.

On the way to the house, Jimmy ran through the cars like a figure skater, and Craig ran after him. I could barely keep up with them and almost got flattened by a Chevy Lumina.

"Wait up!" I could see them turning left at a crosswalk a block and a half away. "Wait up! Hey, guys, wait for me!" I yelled. I thought they would treat me better because of my new bong. I ran with all my might. I was scared of being ditched. I was scared of a lot of things. Sometimes, I slept on my parents' floor when I had nightmares. I was scared of red bullet ants, hats that were too pointy, my dad's temper, and flying on airplanes. I was scared of getting a bad grade, being picked last, Mom leaving forever, and not getting invited to someone's birthday party, but the thing that scared me most was getting left behind.

When I got to Jimmy's house, I could hear my heart in my ears. I bent over and fell down to my knees to catch my breath. I could see that the trapdoor on the tree house was shut, and I could hear them laughing inside. My brother had never ditched me before, not even one time, but Jimmy made him different. I was the bull's-eye for Jimmy's jokes. Sometimes, I treated my sisters that way. I teased them and laughed when they tried to fight back. I loved them, but I still wanted to see them cry. I guess part of me was sick, and I wanted to spread my germs.

I pounded on the trapdoor to get in.

"Hey, you guys. It's Carder. Come on, let me in," I whined.

"Carder who?" Jimmy's voice laughed from above. "No, there is no Carder here. Sorry, you've got the wrong place."

"No, it's me, Carder! I'm here! Come on, this isn't funny." I hit the wood as hard as I could with my fist.

"Sorry, we're not buying any subscriptions to the Encyclopedia Britannica today," Jimmy said. "Please try next door. They're rich."

"I'm not selling anything!" I yelled. "Now let me the fuck in!" I began to cry. "Let me in. Let me in. Let me in." I pounded and pounded. I could hear my brother inside.

"Hey man, I think my brother's crying. Let him in, okay? He has that new bong."

"Right, right. That new purple bong," Jimmy said.

I heard the latch open, and my brother pulled me up.

"Sorry, bro. We were just kidding around." His face looked guilty.

"I know," I whimpered, with tears still coming down. "I know."

"Little man!" Jimmy acted like nothing was wrong. "Great to have you in the tree house. Don't worry, you're our little dude. We were just foolin' with you."

"Yeah, okay," I said. I felt like someone punched me in the side. I thought we were all part of the club. I was wrong again.

"Let's try your new baby out," Jimmy said, "if that's okay with you, little dude."

"It's okay, right bro?" Craig asked.

"Of course," I said. "I dunno how to use it, so you go first."

There were two other bongs in the corner, up against the knotty pine two-by-fours that crisscrossed the walls. Jimmy grabbed one of them and tipped it so the water inside drained into the top of mine. The whole room stunk bad, like a wet dog or underwear with skid marks or something.

"Ah, the sweet smell of bong water," Jimmy said.

"Smells more like rotten fish mixed with toe cheese," I said.

"Well, at the end, the new guy always has to drink the bong water. That's tradition among stoners," Jimmy said.

No way in hell was I going to do that. My mouth got dry, and my armpits felt wet.

Jimmy started howling. "I'm just kidding, man. That would be disgusting. I would never make you do that."

"That would be gnarly," Craig added.

I could see Jimmy take the pot out of the plastic bag and pinch it between his fingers. He dropped a small pile into the silver bowl at the bottom of the bong.

"She's ready," Jimmy said. "Who wants to fire her up first?"

Craig and I stayed quiet. Neither of us wanted to look stupid. There was no turning back now—I was about to get high. And from what Six-Pack Jack said, I was about to get *really* high. Maybe it was for the best. Maybe I would turn into a superhero. Maybe it would kill the monster inside me. Maybe it would make me feel happy. It had been a long time since I'd felt really happy.

"I guess I'll do the honors, then," Jimmy said, lighting a flame on the silver bowl.

Jimmy began to suck, and I could hear the bubbling of water, like someone was boiling eggs, and I could see the thick, white smoke inside the purple tube. Jimmy took his thumb off a small hole and pulled the smoke into his mouth like he was a vacuum cleaner. His face turned red, and his body began to twitch like a fish. Jimmy looked like he was swelling up, and just before he would burst like Violet in *Willy Wonka*, he blew the smoke and raised his right arm. "Yeah!" Jimmy yelped. "Now that's what I call an ear ringer."

Then he passed the bong to Craig. I watched my brother put stuff in the bowl just like Jimmy. Before he started, he looked at me and said, "Here goes nothing." I didn't know why he said that to me. We weren't going for nothing, because that didn't make any sense; we were doing something. Maybe it was what people said before smoking on a bong, like singing the national anthem before a baseball game.

Craig blew out a huge cloud of fog and sat down on the orange carpet. I was the only one left. It was my turn to grow from a boy to a man. Maybe I would have muscles after. I sprinkled some pot into the bowl and covered the hole with my thumb. I turned toward Craig and said, "Here goes something." This sounded better and was much more honest.

"Here something goes." I waited a moment and then said, "Something goes here."

At the same time, Craig and Jimmy yelled, "Stop talking and smoke!" So I did. And right away, I felt different.

Right when the smoke was in my throat, I felt like I was an eagle feather. I floated out of my body and up to the ceiling. I saw myself lying on the carpet with my mouth open like I was asleep, but I wasn't. I watched myself start talking in a language that was like French or Swahili or something. Or maybe it was Egyptian hieroglyphics that were coming out of my mouth. This was at least thirty-seven times more powerful than drinking beer and smoking a cigarette. Craig and Jimmy pointed and laughed at me. I tried to talk, but my brain was moving so fast that the words couldn't catch up.

I said, "You know," and I heard myself say, "Mum mum."

I tried to slow everything down in my brain, but I was traveling at light speed.

Jimmy's eyes began to droop until the skin of his eyebrows completely covered them. He looked like an alien.

Is he an alien?

And then the Bee Gees came. "You Should Be Dancin'" was inside my head, and when I closed my eyes, I was dancing on a lighted dance floor under a glitter ball.

But I hate disco.

In my head, I watched Barry Gibb turn into Yosemite Sam, who danced with the Tasmanian Devil and Road Runner. They chased each other around in a circle so fast that they turned into a ring of fire spinning all around the world. I opened my eyes and began to laugh from my belly. I laughed and laughed and laughed. I watched Jimmy and Craig through the red smoke, and they were on the floor laughing like me. Everything was funny, like we were at the best circus with the silliest clowns tripping all over the place.

When I opened my eyes, Jimmy looked so strange to me, as if someone had inflated his head like Bob's Big Boy. I pointed at Purple Haze and reached out my hand. How could he even see with that skin covering his eyes? For the first time in a long time, I didn't feel bad. I decided that I was never going back. Not to my house, not to school, not to anywhere I had ever gone before. I wondered if I could stay high forever, but I bet that Lillie B. would be able to tell. I would get an ass whooping.

But I wanted to smoke anyway. I smoked bong after bong after bong—nine, one for every birthday.

After five hits, everything got blurry, so I closed my eyes and went on a magic carpet ride. I flew out of the clubhouse and over the gray sidewalks of Georgetown. I could see the rooftops and backyards that filled each block. I soared above the busy streets and saw all the little people walking around on the ground. They looked like ants marching everywhere, and I wasn't part of their colony anymore—I had been granted the special powers of a caped crusader. Suddenly I fell into the whirlpool of a black hole, and I started to remember.

I was three and sitting on the potty. Lillie B. folded a piece of toilet paper and said, "This is how you do it, baby, so the B.M. don't get on yo hands." And I was standing in a line of four-year-old skiers on the slopes in Austria. My mom and dad waved goodbye and disappeared over the hill. I had tears on my little face and peed in my snowsuit. And then I woke up in the fields when I was five. I was all alone in the hay and screamed for my mommy. My babysitter forgot that I was taking a nap inside the hay cart. Then I was six and getting pushed on the playground by a big bully who kicked his rain boot on my shin. I was seven and I punched the suitcases outside my dad's bedroom until my knuckles hurt. I was eight and my brother put his arm around me and told me everything was going to be okay.

I opened my eyes and Craig was next to me holding my hand. I had been crying out for him.

"Everything is gonna be okay," he said, again—this time out loud and in front of me. He put his arm around me, and I could see his blonde hair curling around the bottom of his ear.

"Don't worry," he said, "it's just the pot making you feel weird."
He was right, I guess. Not even the pot could take away the sad
place in me.

"Hey, remember that time when we took Mom's tear gas gun
out of her drawer and shot it out the window?"

"Yeah."

"You remember that the wind blew back all that gas into our
faces, and it hurt super bad? Remember how much we cried, and
we didn't ever think it would stop?" he said.

"Uh huh."

"Well, if you could get through that, you can get through anything, okay?"

I nodded and then asked, "Do you think we're going to be high
forever? I mean, is this forever, and we will never be normal ever
again? Because I don't think I wanna be this way all the time."

"No, bro, it will just be a couple of hours, and then we'll be back
to normal," Craig said.

"You promise?" I said.

"Yeah, Stout's honor," he said, laughing.

The pot showed me where the bad memories lived, and they
dove at me like bats from the sky. I tried to hit them away, but there
were too many, and for the first time ever, I felt like I could die. I
saw my father yelling at me and spanking my bare bottom. I saw
myself crawling down wooden stairs and falling on my face. I felt
a diaper pin poke my leg. I watched them like a movie in my head.
It was a grown-up movie, and I wanted it to stop.

I opened my eyes, and Craig's face was over mine. He was singing, "*Our house* . . . is a very, very, very fine house, with two cats in the
yard, life used to be so *hard*, now everything is easy *'cause of you.*"

I wanted to find someone who could make everything easy. I wanted someone to take away all the bad feelings inside me. I didn't know anyone who could do that. I started to sing along and slowly began feeling like myself again.

But I was hungrier than I'd ever been. We had smoked all day and forgotten to eat our salami sandwiches before we left home. Getting a burger and fries from Roy Rogers was definitely the best idea we ever had—maybe the best idea of all time. We put down the bong, tied up our laces, and raced out the trapdoor.

Roy Rogers was full of people munching on roast beef and slurping chocolate shakes. This was one of my favorite places. Craig and I ate here once a week, at least. We ordered three cheeseburgers, a melted ham and Swiss, a roast beef, three large fries, two chocolate shakes, and one vanilla. I wanted vanilla. We would probably need to go back for seconds.

I was pretty sure that my cry-baby stuff was over in the tree house. I was part of the club now, and that's all I wanted. I picked up a ketchup dispenser and squeezed it too hard by accident, and it sprayed all over Craig's shirt. It was hysterical.

"You are so dead meat." He grabbed the dispenser and blasted me in the face with a long squirt of ketchup. I reached into the next booth for the barbeque sauce and squeezed it at Jimmy. I aimed too high and hit a fat man on the back of his fat head.

"Hey, guy, that's so not cool," he yelled, but we didn't care and squirted a bloody battle all over the place. The fry man jumped over the counter and chased us out the front door. We looked like we had been hacked by zombies in some bloody massacre, so we pretended we were.

"I can't believe he bit me!" I screamed, falling down on the sidewalk.

"Help me, I'm dying!" Craig yelled from his knees. An old woman wearing a white wig like she was in Parliament or something grabbed at her chest.

"Oh, my God," she screamed. "Somebody call a doctor! These boys are hurt!"

We played hurt 'til the crowd got so big that we could get in trouble. It was time to make a clean getaway.

Craig got up first, and I ran through the crowd after him. We waved goodbye to Jimmy and jogged all the way home, looking as though we had been run over by a Mack truck. When we rounded the corner on our block, I was glad that the adventure was over. I had smoked a ton of pot and had not gone outer limits crazy.

That would come later.

Chapter Five

2003

I awoke to a slight tapping sound coming from my apartment window. I rolled over in bed and glanced at the clock on my nightstand. It read 4:15 AM. There could only be one person who would stop by at this hour. Her name was Tisha. I saw her young face pressed against the glass and got up to let her inside. It was a cold winter night, and I could see that she was shivering. Ghost Town could be unkind to those without homes in the wee hours. She was one of those rare ones who had survived on the streets for several years without being locked up or killed. She was barely five feet tall but protected herself like a panther from the hunters that stalked her through the night. She made it a habit to visit me when the wind was blowing hard and her teeth were chattering.

I had often seen her walking up and down Brooks, and one day I decided to strike up a conversation. She asked me if I wanted to have sex. Until that moment, I had not realized she was a prostitute. Sex was no longer an elixir to me—I hadn't had it for quite some time. The cocaine took away my drive, so I turned her down politely, and asked if she would like to talk instead. Over the next few weeks, we walked through the 'hood, sat on stoops, leaned on chain-link fences, and revealed the stories that had put us there. I liked the company and asked her to come by my place one night if she had dope. She began showing up a few times a week. If I wasn't home, she would draw a heart on my window with an arrow pointing down to a small nugget of crack on my windowsill. She wasn't a smoker but often had product for her preferred clients. In a strange and dysfunctional way, I thought of her as my girlfriend, and she called me her man.

Tisha was beautiful in a weathered sort of way. She was only nineteen, but the streets had put about ten years on her. Her skin was light brown and smooth, with a few rows of pronounced lines on her forehead. Next to her left ear was a discolored scar about the size of a quarter. She had the eyes of a large cat—her pupils were the color of old-fashioned root beer. Her face was oval with high cheekbones and full lips. She resembled a beautiful doll that someone had left to gather dust and cobwebs on the attic floor. She smelled of sweat and decay, but I didn't mind. I didn't mind at all. She made me feel wanted at a time when no one wanted me. She made me feel attractive when I was at my worst. She listened when no one else did. I would gladly have given her anything I could muster. Unfortunately, it wasn't much, but she seemed happy. She climbed through the window and landed firmly on my bed.

"It's cold out there. How's my man doin' tonight? Did you miss me?"

"Of course," I said. "How you doin'?"

"You know, it ain't easy for a workin' girl out on these streets. Just glad I'm here now."

"Me too, me too," I said, lighting a candle next to the bed. The power company had cut off my electricity, so this was my only source of light. I got up and lit a few more that I'd strategically placed around the room.

"You sure you don't want some sugar tonight?" she said, taking off her jacket and shirt. The smell was worse when fully exposed to the air. I exhaled from my nostrils and held my breath. It would take a few minutes for my nose to adapt. Her round, full breasts spilled out of a leopard print bra, and she pushed them together seductively.

"We could put you right in there." She pointed to her cleavage. "So soft. So good. Mmm. I can taste you, baby." It was tempting, but I simply did not have the urge. Besides the stench, she was glorious, but she was my friend.

"One of these days, you're gonna get me," I said. "But not tonight. Not tonight. Let's just chill, okay?"

"Okay, baby. That cool."

"Tell me about your day."

"My day," she said. "My day? Well, what you want to know? Some dude stiffed me for twenty bucks. Another dude smacked my ass so hard that I'm bleedin'. I called my daughter, but no one picked up. I haven't eaten anything. What else?"

"That sounds pretty bad. I'm sorry," I said.

"No, sweetie. Today was a good day. I'm still here, ain't I? I got nothin' to complain about. I know God loves me and will protect me. That's it," she said. Although the scars of her profession were obvious, she exuded a kindness that one would expect from someone whose circumstances were vastly better. She was never angry—there was no bitterness in her heart.

"I didn't know you had a daughter. Why didn't you tell me?"

"I don't tell many people about her. She belongs to me and no one else. She's my whole world," she said, with a light in her eyes. "She lives in Detroit with my momma. Jayla. Her name Jayla. Couldn't keep her here. This ain't no way for a child to grow up."

"You must really miss her."

"I think about her every moment of every day. She my sunshine. Soon as I save up enough to give her a good life, I'm goin' back. Prolly next year," she said hopefully.

"Can you get some money from her daddy? To help, I mean?" I asked.

"Don't know who that is," she replied. "Got pregnant on these streets. Went home to Detroit to have her. Left when she was one. Ain't nothing goin' on in Detroit. Can't make no bread there. So I came back. Came back to find you. My man." She smiled at me.

I could feel myself about to cry. I couldn't imagine what it was like to be separated from a child.

"You know, if I had a million dollars, I would give it all to you. Every penny of it. I would. But I don't right now. Maybe someday."

"I know. Thank you," she said. We lay down next to each other on the bed, and I pulled her in tight with my left arm. I was angry at myself for being destitute. I wanted to take care of her. If I added up all the hits of crack, it would have easily surpassed a hundred grand. That would have bought Jayla a lot of nice things. Fucking crack.

"You know, I got some things going on with Flyn now. Big things. Maybe I can get you some money," I said.

"Flyn? He the big dawg. Be careful," she warned.

"Nah, it's not like that. He's my dude. We look out for each other," I said, exaggerating the truth. "I meet with him every day, and we do our thing."

"Every day?"

"Yeah, since last week. I roll with him and take care of things," I said.

"He was away for a stretch. Inside for slingin'. Everyone got mad respect for Flyn. Crips let him do what he wants."

This was all new information to me, but I pretended that it was old hat. I had heard rumors about Flyn but hadn't had the courage to ask him about his past. It was all making sense now. I knew that Flyn moved freely about the 'hood making deliveries and selling crack. The 'hood was the territory of the Shoreline Crips, and you needed permission to spit on the sidewalk there. Dozens of people had been shot because they impinged on the boundary line, and this created decades of bloody turmoil that still existed. If you tried to sell dope in Ghost Town without the go-ahead from the Crips, your days were numbered. If you were caught within the borders of the 'hood with product, you would first get beaten up and warned. The second time, a person known to you would walk up in broad daylight, take out a pistol, and fire several shots into your head and chest. These were the unwritten laws of the territory. Flyn, apparently, was above them, and I was safe from the potential carnage because I was his driver. Mom would be so proud.

"What if I could get you a whole bunch of money?" I had no idea how to do this, but it sounded noble.

"Don't bother, baby. I give everything to Trech," she said. "He makes sure I'm taken care of."

A pimp? I had never heard of him before. The idea that someone owned her burned a hole in my skin. I felt a little jealous.

"Why can't you be on your own?" I asked.

"That's not how the streets work, baby. Wouldn't last a week without protection. Just the way it is. He gives me some money when I need it." This seemed like an unfair arrangement to me. She did all the work and kept none of the take. "So, what's in it for you? Why you play with that glass horn?" she asked, pointing at my top drawer.

A great question, and one that I was not fully prepared to answer. I guess I didn't know the full extent of the reason. I smoked because I was lost. That was obvious. I had lost my way a long time ago, and every time I hit the pipe, my memory faded for a bit. I blew away my failures with gray smoke.

I smoked because I was sad. I had always had grandiose visions of my life. I thought I'd be famous, with a name that landed on the tips of tongues and carried weight. I imagined that I'd be surrounded by influential people making vital decisions about this and that. I had dreamed of being married at twenty-five and a father at thirty, but those benchmarks had come and gone like rest stops on the Mass Pike.

Maybe I smoked because I never felt loved by anyone, or maybe I never let anyone love me because deep inside, I knew my heart was defective. There was a stone in my heart that blocked my ability to love. It was wedged in tight. If I ever tried to move it, its size would only grow. Yes, I smoked because there was a stone blocking my heart, but this was a secret that I was terrified to reveal.

"I smoke because it makes me feel good," I said.

"Really? You lie. I see how you get when you smoke that thing. You get all strange," she said.

"Nah, it just makes me think a whole lot. About stuff. You know. About my life."

"Who you talkin' to, anyway? Who's there?" she asked.

"Just my thoughts. Just talking out loud."

"You lie," she said again. "I see you. It's like a crowd a people all around you, all talking to you at once. Tell me who they are."

"Nobody, baby. Nobody," I said. I realized it must have been alarming to see me in conversation with invisible people. I mean, Tisha was understanding, but she was also rational and deductive. I tried to frame it in a context she could understand.

"It's God, baby. I talk to God and his angels when I smoke," I said.

"You crazy. God ain't got nothing to do with this. Smokin' crack ain't no *Godly* act. He don't approve of shit like that." She was right. He did not. But my God was all-loving, a God of forgiveness and compassion. Unfortunately, I had turned my back on Him. God was nowhere to be found in my little efficiency a block from the beach. He was probably out surfing.

"I got that thing for you if you want it. Even though it makes you act like a fool—I still got it for you." She took a large nugget of crack out of her bra and handed it to me. "Thank you for taking me in on a cold night," she said.

I thought about my options. I could stay inside and pretend that the spirits were not bearing down on me or take my pipe and hit the road. I decided to stay, mostly because I didn't feel right leaving Tisha after she'd shared about her baby daughter. So, I unwrapped my stem from its Ray Ban sarcophagus, loaded it with the trimming from my cocaine nub, and sucked on it like a teenage porn star. Tisha watched me carefully and stroked my hair as I pulled from the pipe.

"I love you, baby," I heard her say, as my head filled with voices. "Don't hurt me, baby. I got you, baby. Take care of me. Love me."

The intimate nature of her admission and the intensity of her request were a bit overwhelming, so I pulled away from her and slipped into a tattered armchair at the foot of my bed. I needed some space to get my bearings. The room began to spin, and my vision blurred. My ears rang like they had just heard close-range cannon fire, and for a moment I didn't know where I was.

I flopped from the chair and lay flat on the floor, staring up at the ceiling. My chest tightened up—I felt like my heart was under attack. The apartment walls crumbled around me, and my feet went completely numb. I gasped for air but could find none. My limbs convulsed and twisted uncontrollably. I was having a seizure.

This is how it all ends. Goodbye to the people I passed in the night. Goodbye to the children I never had. Goodbye to the wife I never met. Goodbye to the happiness that never found me. Goodbye to the love I once knew. Goodbye, Mother. I will miss your gravel-throated laugh. Goodbye.

And I was gone—gone to the other side.

Lillie approached me on a long, open path in a birch forest. The birch had always been my favorite tree—I had read that it was the earth's largest living thing. In a birch forest, all of the roots find one another and wrap together to form a single DNA structure. Thousands of trees become one living entity, bound together in one life, sharing the same soul. As I walked down the path, I could feel millions of thoughts wrapping themselves around my own. I noticed everything and understood it all. Knowledge covered me like heavy snow, and I could see the past and future fuse together in one single stream of consciousness.

"We ain't ready for you yet," Lillie said.

"Where are we?" I asked.

"You know where this is." Lillie smiled. "Love yourself, Coda. Or no one else will."

"I miss you, Lillie. Mother Lillie. Take me with you! I don't want to go back. There's nothing for me down there," I cried. She wrapped her arms around me, and for a brief moment, I was lost in the sweet.

"Everything is waiting for you. Stop hurting yourself, and the answers will come," she said.

"I want to die," I said, "so I can be with you. I'm not afraid to die. It's okay."

"Not yet, Coda. Not for a while. A moment here is a thousand years there. You will see." She laughed. A thousand yellow butterflies swirled around her and lifted her off the ground. I knew how to fly in my dreams, and I tried with all of my might to launch from the bricks at my feet. My soles felt anchored to the earth, and I held out my arms as Lillie flew higher and higher into a purple sky. Beautiful music played from above, as if the clouds were wired with surround sound, and I could hear Lillie sing the lullaby that she sang to me as a baby:

> *Mama right here, my baby bird,*
> *Mama right here, don't say a word.*
> *I'm here today,*
> *But I'm goin' away.*
> *Back in the morning when the sun is stirred.*

I looked up and marveled at the way she soared through the air. She swooped down toward me, and her body silently collided with mine. Her essence dispersed into my limbs, and I could feel her trying to move the stone from my heart. My chest felt like it was on fire.

BAM. BAM. BAM.

"Hollywood! Hollywood! Baby! Wake up! Wake up!"

I opened my eyes to see Tisha straddling my waist with her hands clamped together. With all her might, she pounded repeatedly on my chest with a double fist. She had become a human defibrillator and was in the process of saving my life. I gasped. Cold air filled my lungs. I felt like I had been run over by a steam shovel and then buried in a field of quicksand. My whole body hurt, and I carefully motioned for her to get off of me. It felt like she weighed a thousand tons. I leaned up on my elbows and caught my breath.

"Damn, where did you get this dope anyway? Strongest shit I ever smoked," I gasped.

"Baby, you okay?" she cried, with tears coursing down her cheeks, her leg still flopped across my lap. "I thought you was *dying*. I thought you was *gone*."

"I was." I nodded. "I did. I saw the other side. I was dead. How long was I out for?"

"A few minutes," she said. "What you mean you was *dead*?"

"Just that. I died. Wasn't my time to go, so I came back. No big deal." I shrugged and shook my head.

"*Shit*, baby. I don't want you to die."

"Where's that crack? I need to hit it again. Ride of my life," I said.

"You crazy," she said with a sigh. She handed me the coke and got back on the bed. "You white boys are crazy."

I pinched another dollop onto the screen and lit the glass pipe. I wanted something to happen immediately, so I held the smoke in my lungs as long as I possibly could. If now was not my time, maybe I could be as reckless as I wanted without any consequences. Did Lillie just give me the green light to abuse myself even more? So what if I overdosed again? She would be there waiting for me and literally take me for a walk in the park. I had nothing to fear anymore.

I suppose I didn't really want to die. Not quite yet. I had made one botched suicide attempt a few years before. I ingested an entire bottle of Advil PM with a fifth of bourbon and a heroin chaser. I ended up sleeping for thirty hours and waking up naked on my living room floor. Not a pretty sight. There were several pools of yellow vomit next to my head, and my stomach felt like it had exploded. I spent the next few days stumbling round my bungalow, confused and tired, but after a few lines of coke, I felt normal again and the party continued.

I had never told anyone about that night. Not the textbook therapists, the underdeveloped counselors, the narrow-minded doctors, the shallow life coaches, or the best friends who tried and tried to help me. No, that was a memory just for me.

There were so many secrets that I held inside, but this was the crown jewel at the top. There was the stealing, the eating disorders, the cheating on girlfriends, the lies, the betrayals, the evil wishes, and the time I wore girls' underpants to school in second grade. Yes, there were a lot of secrets that no one would ever know or even suspect. I kept them locked away like a room full of disabled children, disowned by their upwardly mobile parents. It was the secrets, the fetishes, and the filthy little habits that kept me imprisoned in a world of shame, and I could blame no one but myself. Well, I blamed Mom and Dad regularly as well, only they were too narcissistic to realize it, so I was stuck in a shadowy mandala of gloom, and the sand kept shifting under my feet. It was getting increasingly difficult to stand.

The room became crowded with voices from the past, and when the ringing subsided, I felt like I was at a carnival. At least two dozen of my ancestors began talking to me at once.

"Slow down, everybody. Slow down. I can't understand anyone. One at a time. Please. It's the only way," I pleaded.

"Not again," a childlike voice said.

"Just look at yourself," said another.

"Help the girl. She needs you."

"Fuck all this destruction. Time to be a man now, Carder."

"We love you," said my grandmother Maxine.

And through all of the words and accents and voices, I could feel Tisha's eyes watching me. She began to cry and covered her head with a pillow. Maybe this was how I was supposed to redeem myself from the years of selfishness. Maybe I was supposed to take care of this precious girl who shared my room. She never had a trust fund or an education, or even a chance. I had been given everything and had thrown it all away. I got up from the floor and sat next to Tisha on the bed. For the next few hours, I held her tight.

Flyn was expecting me at his house the next afternoon. It felt great to have somewhere to go and something to do. I had wandered aimlessly for so long, and to have something definitive on the calendar—even a date with a drug dealer—made me feel responsible. I had something to get up for. This used to be the norm. I moseyed through four years of college actually doing most of my work and showing up to my morning classes. In New York, I held down various jobs and arrived at my appointments with a fresh face and clean clothes. My superiors appreciated the work I did for them, and I rose through the ranks in the casting office. My friends waited for me at bars and clubs with happy greetings and bottles of Rolling Rock. I always put on a smile for them, although for the most part, I felt detached and inferior.

Flyn was happy to see me. He opened his arms and gave me a big, burly hug. It reminded me of the embrace my brother gave me after he had been traveling the world by sailboat. I could feel that it was genuine. Luckily, he hadn't minded when the spirits reared their mischievous voices as we drove back from Inglewood. Flyn hadn't batted an eye. He grinned as he hopped into my car.

"We doing something special today, Hollywood." When I pressed him for more information, he said, "Just wait and see, my new Caucasian friend. Just you wait and see. Roll down Vernon and take a left on Electric."

We scooted through the sparsely inhabited streets and slowly merged into a line of seven Harley Davidsons. The riders were all wearing Hell's Angels jackets, so I drove timidly among them until Flyn spoke again.

"Left here on San Juan," he instructed.

I wondered why we were taking such an obscure path directly back into the heart of the 'hood.

"Where are we going?" I asked.

"Go down a few blocks and park at the end. That's my spot. Right at the end."

I continued down San Juan until we approached Seventh Street. There was an open space at the end of the street next to the curb. It was partitioned off with three orange construction cones, and Flyn got out to move them onto the sidewalk. I guess this space *was* reserved for him. I tucked my Taurus neatly into pole position and turned off the engine. Flyn climbed back into the front seat and got comfortable.

"What are we doing?" I asked.

"Today, we're gonna watch. Got to be in touch with the heartbeat of these streets to know what's really goin' on. We sit and watch and learn," he said.

"So this is like going to school in the 'hood?" I joked.

"Shit, you about to get a PhD in crime, motherfucker." Flyn started to laugh. It was the kind of belly laugh that made my whole car shake. But he was serious.

"See there?" He pointed to a man walking down Seventh. "You see that dude walking around like nothing is goin' on? Wearin' that raggedy old suit and those brand-new tennis shoes? That dude is undercover Five-O. Narcotics squad. Spot that motherfucker a mile away."

I watched as the man reached into his pocket and pulled out a fresh pack of cigarettes. He stood for a moment packing down the ends in his open palm. As he looked over his shoulder and lit a match, I could tell that he had no intention of smoking. He then stopped, turned round, glanced into the park, and began walking across the street toward our car. He walked quickly without looking up, but it was clear that Flyn was not going to let him get away.

"Afternoon, Officer," Flyn said as the man passed by my open window. He looked at us, startled, with the burning eyes of a guilty teenager, and began to pick up the pace. Flyn slapped his knee and laughed again.

"He ain't foolin' nobody. Look at that fool scurry down the road like a scared little rabbit. They'll never learn. Stupid motherfuckers. Cops are the worst scum on earth," he said.

"How did you know he was a cop?" I asked. I desperately wanted to know because, to me, he looked like an average, conservative middle-aged man walking through Venice.

"Motherfucker, please. He might as well have a badge tattooed on his forehead. You see his shoes. Brand-new Adidas. Standard undercover issue. And then there was his suit. Men's Warehouse. Fresh off the rack, but tussled up to make it look like it wasn't new. His haircut, shaved on the side with the top slicked back. That's the haircut that every prison guard has in every jail on the Westside, like they all got the same country-ass barber or some shit. Then you look down at his left pant leg, and when he walked, it didn't break naturally. That's because he has a Glock 9 holstered on his calf.

"You see the way he was just standing there scoping the park, hoping to see somethin' go down? Normal people don't just stand around lookin' over their shoulder. And then that stupid cigarette pack, but no lighting a smoke. He's obviously new at this game. He's got a lot to learn. Now we know that undercover has a few men in the streets. That's what you find when you watch the 'hood," Flyn said.

I was amazed at the precision with which Flyn dissected every aspect of law enforcement's attempt to fool him.

"Man, I'm impressed. How did you know all that?" I asked.

"Grew up in these streets. Venice is my backyard. Saw it all. People getting shot right here on this corner." He pointed to a spot a few feet from where we were parked. "People getting mugged, robbed, beaten. I did some of that, too. All of it. Started rolling with the SLC when I was eleven. Nothing else to do. Had to do it to keep my grandma safe. Started slingin' dope when I was twelve. Got busted a few times and spent some months in Juvenile Hall. Kept on slingin' so my grandma could keep her house and I could have some change in my pocket. Ran with crews in Compton. South Central, too—that's where the shit went down."

"Sounds dangerous, man."

"Yeah, it was. Still is. I got popped when I was a teenager. Went away for a few. When I got out, I kept quiet. Kept smart. Rose through the ranks. *Everybody* gettin' popped. *Everybody* gettin' killed. Not me. I watched the 'hood. I learned the game. Saw *everything*. Couldn't take me down. By the time I was twenty-five, I was the big man. I ran the whole shit. The 'hood was mine. Everybody else was gone. Had a hundred little soldiers armed in these streets, making mad dough. Defending the territory. Making moves. It got crazy for a while, but we came out on top. Did it right."

"Shit, I'm hanging out with royalty," I joked.

"No, not anymore. I don't run with the Crips anymore. I got popped a second time with some weight. Did some hard time for that. Promised my grandma I would distance myself from my brothers when I got out. I keep my promises."

"They let you do that? Just leave like that? The SLC?" I asked.

"Not usually, no. But with me it's different. I made millions for them and didn't roll on anybody when I got busted. I'm protected now. No one can touch me. I can do what I want as long as I don't mess with the rules."

"What rules?"

"Can't really tell you that, my inquisitive homie. That's part of it. Got to take some things to the grave."

"Crazy shit, man," I said.

"You have no idea how crazy. I've done shit that haunts me every day," he said. "But I did it to stay alive for my family. So my grandma could have a good life."

I nodded. "You never have to worry about me judging you, okay? That's not who I am. I only met you a few days ago, but you're already like a brother. I can feel it," I said in earnest.

"Your *brother*?" he said. "You mean 'cause I'm *black*? I'm a *brother*? Really, did you just say that?" He turned his menacing gaze on me.

Sweat beads broke out on my forehead instantly. "No, I didn't mean that, I, um, meant like a real brother—"

"Because I'm a *black man*? I'm a *brother*? I thought you were deeper than that, man."

"No! I meant 'brother,' like—"

"Brother this, brother that, what the fuck are you trying to say? Are you a *racist*?"

"No, not at all! I just meant that you are like family to me." I looked over, and Flyn had a huge smile on his face. He covered his lips with his fingers, trying not to laugh. He waved his index finger at me and shook his head.

"Aah," he said with a chuckle. "I got you. I got you good."

I exhaled out loud. "You're fucking with me? I almost pissed my pants! Don't worry, payback is a bitch. I never forget," I joked.

"I feel you. My brother," he said, as we pounded our bare knuckles together.

There was now a lightness in the car that provided an opening for my next question. "So, what happened to your parents?"

"I barely knew my pops. He left when I was a kid. Last thing he gave me was a $100 bill. He said, 'That dude on the bill. His name is Franklin. You're named after him. Your name means money.' So I've been trying to make some ever since. And my momma, well, she's gone, too. My grandma raised me and taught me to be good. I owe her everything in the world. She made me read books every week. I'd come home from thievin' and sellin' dope, and she would put *Tom Sawyer* in my hand. Make me read for an hour. First time I killed somebody, I was reading *Treasure Island*. Still got blood on the pages. First time I got locked up, I brought *Catcher in the Rye*. Holden Caulfield is my dude.

"Grandma B knew what was goin' on but still squeezed me with all her might. Had to survive in those streets. Didn't mean I was bad. I love everybody now. No more hate in my heart. I meditate every morning and clear my mind of negativity." He took a meditation pose in jest. "Still got to make a living, though. I ain't the Dalai Lama." His face broke into his signature grin.

"That's for damn sure." I felt more comfortable around Flyn than anyone I had met in a long while. We were from totally different backgrounds but seemed to be cut from the same cloth. There was a spiritual warrior lurking underneath the violence of his misdeeds. It was the same warrior that lived in me, and spending the afternoon with Flyn was a reminder that mine was still there.

We watched as a young mother and father walked hand in hand with their two young boys. The man picked up his boy and positioned him high on his shoulders. The woman twirled her boy around in circles. Heaven.

"What about your pops?" Flyn asked.

"He lives in England," I said. "Doesn't get me at all. Tried to help me by paying my bills for a while, but he's done with that. He's been abandoning me my whole life. He finds a lady and runs off somewhere and leaves his kids behind. I used to think he was bulletproof. Now I feel sorry for him."

"Least you had him. Any pop is better than none," Flyn said.

"I guess you're right. It's just that we never saw eye to eye. He's a small man with a big opinion of himself, and he lies all the time."

"Sometimes, lies are better than the truth," Flyn said. "And your mom?"

"Well, I got mad love for her. Always have, but she lives inside a bottle of vodka. She's confused and angry and counting her days. I almost don't recognize her anymore," I said.

"Do you tell her you love her?" Flyn asked.

"Not in a long time. She doesn't want to talk to me right now. No one in my family does. Not since I started smoking."

"Maybe you should stop, then."

"Yeah, right. Only thing that keeps me going. I hear things. See things."

"You smoke enough of anything, you're bound to hear things."

"No, it's not like that. I hear my family talking to me. My family from hundreds of years back. They all have something to say," I explained.

"Some kind of spirit world, huh?" He laughed long and hard. "My man, *Holy* Hollywood!" I couldn't help but laugh, too. I didn't take it personally. I knew I sounded like I should spend a few nights in the psych ward.

"Listen, right back atcha," he said, catching his breath. "I'm not gonna judge. Only got love for you, Hollywood."

We were like two kids on the first day of school who met at the bank of cubbies and instantly became inseparable. The 'hood was our playground, and it was now recess. I didn't want the day to end, ever. In *my* book, we were both orphans who grew up without real parents. Mine were so wrapped up in their own bullshit that they had no time for me, or anyone else. When they did show up they tried to convince me that my blood was pure and, therefore, I deserved a seat in the church of the elite. They felt that money and breeding were the ingredients to a happy (if ignorant) life and, for a while, so did I. But look at us now.

My father had been run out of the United States after *60 Minutes* aired a segment about his willful conning of 100,000 veterans. He had promised to build a memorial wall in Caen, France, to commemorate the fiftieth anniversary of D-Day but instead took their $4,000,000 in donations and booked a room at Claridge's.

And my mother, well, she had been the Grand Dame of Georgetown society, throwing lavish parties in her palatial mansion. After my father left her, she had a string of drug-addled boyfriends who robbed her of her dignity before they left. After allowing several homeless men to live in her house, she was excommunicated by her friends and retreated to her farmhouse in Massachusetts. She continued to drown her sorrows there with another opportunistic man who mixed her drinks with care. I felt sorry for her, too.

And, of course, I felt sorry for myself. I was no prize. Born with several silver spoons up my ass and sent to the finest schools, but here I was in Ghost Town, side by side with someone far more interesting. This was my new stomping ground, and I wanted to mark my territory by peeing all over it. This was where I felt understood and alive. I had no truck with blue-blooded sycophants anymore. They were replaced by a breed of philosophers with darker skin and much more to say. Yes, I was finally home.

"Look at this dude," Flyn said, pointing to a middle-aged white guy heading toward a group of teenage dealers. "He is gonna try to swindle them. Just watch."

To my amazement, it became apparent that the man was doing just that. We watched as he held up a few junky pieces of jewelry and a gold-looking pocket watch. He began to argue with a heavy-set girl who slapped him across the face and pushed him down the block.

"Take yo fake shit and give it to yo ho wife," she said, as a steady stream of her followers collected behind her for support. They started to jeer and yell at the man as he ducked into an alleyway down the block. Tough crowd.

"How did you know he was gonna do that?" I asked.

"You see the way he was walking with that shifty shuffle? I could tell he was a hustler. Can spot a hustler a hundred yards down the block. They don't come at you straight. They come at you all sideways, with some kinda story to tell. Gotta shut 'em down right away," he said. "She did good."

Next came a twenty-something couple who looked overly groomed and nervous. They timidly walked in the street and veered toward the crowd with small, unassuming steps.

"Now they're lookin' to buy some weight. Maybe even an ounce or two. White and privileged. Best customers in the world," he said.

I could see the well-dressed woman counting out at least ten $100 bills and placing them in the dealer's hand. We were watching a street-level retail transaction at its best. There was no President's Day sale happening on Seventh and San Juan. Not today.

"Man, that's crazy. Are you ever wrong?" I said.

"Not about the commerce of dope. No sir, I am not," he said seriously. "Can't afford to be wrong. Wrong means dead."

"You seen a lot of death?" I asked.

"Been around it my whole life. Contributed to it. Believed in it. Suffered through it. Felt it on my fingers. Tasted it in my mouth. Watched the life drain out of a dozen eyes. Killed a few. Had a few killed. Last words my best friend ever said to me was, 'Don't let 'em get away.' So I didn't. Tracked down every motherfucker who was in that car and took 'em down. One by one. Didn't love it. Just did it. You know, like in the Nike commercial," he said.

"Not sure I could kill somebody," I said.

"You would, Hollywood. If it was you or him. You would."

Maybe he was right. I had never been in a bona fide life-or-death situation before. More than a decade earlier, I was trekking in the Himalayas with my two best friends from boarding school. One of them got horribly ill with acute mountain sickness, and the other took him down to a lower altitude in order to acclimate. I decided to trudge on, alone, up to an eighteen-thousand-foot pass, because the next day was my twenty-first birthday. That night, I found shelter in a stone hut with no windows. It was twenty below zero with the wind chill, and I found myself huddling under a yak blanket with a Danish man named Jan who I had never met before. I honestly believed that I was freezing to death and could not stop my teeth from chattering at a rate much faster than my heart. I prayed to God to keep my fingers and toes from turning black, and by the next morning, I was perfectly fine. That was as near death as I had been.

Later, on the same excursion, we were hiking a steep trail with thousands of stone steps leading up the mountainside. A weary traveler hundreds of feet above us dislodged several large rocks and sent them hailing down upon us. I looked up to see a sizeable rock falling toward my face and, at the last moment, jerked my head to the left. If the stone had connected, I would have been a goner.

But I did not know danger like Flyn. He lived in a perilous world where bullets flew by like wind-blown raindrops in a summer storm, leaving puddles of blood for the children to jump in. The first time I ever had a gun put to my head had been a few days before, but for some reason, I knew I would survive. At least for now.

I could see Flyn's posture straighten up as a black Cadillac Escalade turned from California onto Seventh and stopped in front of the recreation center. The entire community of adolescent foot soldiers surrounded the car in a whirl of excitement. There was something ominous about the vehicle, and I watched as the tinted windows came down to reveal what was inside.

Flyn sat motionless and peered through the windshield with a combination of intense absorption and nonchalant complacency. I had not seen him behave this way before, and it worried me. I could see a man behind the wheel exchanging words with the crowd. Every one of the kids was vying for his attention, and they all stood back a few paces out of respect. I could hear rap music blazing from the speakers with the bass turned up.

"Who's that?" I asked, thinking that I may already know the answer.

"That, my homie, is Trech. He's the big man on the block. He's a ladies' man. He's a killer. He's a snake. And he's my cousin."

"Yeah, I heard about him," I said.

"From who?" Flyn asked.

"Girl I know," I said. "Why they call him Trech?"

"His name is Treacherous Wallace, that's why."

"Kind of like Furious in *Boyz n the Hood*?" I was pleased with myself for making the reference.

"Seriously, dude? With all that education, that's the best you can do? A fucking John Singleton movie? I'm not impressed. Movie was bullshit anyway."

"Okay, give me a better reference then," I challenged.

Flyn thought for a moment, and I could almost see the gears turning in his pupils. He began to nod his head and do a little car dance.

"The Circle of Treachery from Dante's Inferno. All about love and betrayal." He grinned.

"Dante's Inferno? Where did you pull that out of? Well done, brother. And by brother, this time I do mean black man," I said. Flyn began to laugh and gave me another fist pound.

"My man, Hollywood," he said.

Treacherous spotted us and came screeching over in his SUV. He pulled up beside my car, headed the wrong way down a one-way street. Nobody seemed to mind very much.

"Yo, Flyn. That you?" he said, bending down to look past me.

"Yo, Trech. What up, Cuzz?" Flyn said, leaning into my seat.

"What you doin' in that cracker's ride?" Trech said. He was frowning.

"This Hollywood. He cool. We chillin'. You know. Watchin' the 'hood," Flyn responded.

"Watchin' the 'hood. That's how we do it. That's how we know. Learned that shit from you, Cuzz," Trech said. "Hollywood, pleasure to make yo acquaintance. Heard 'bout you from Tish. Good lookin' out, shorty."

"Good to meet you, Trech. Thanks." I tried to act cool, but I was petrified. I could sense he was sizing me up and knew that he could press a button on me any time he wanted. His command of the streets was palpable, and I was now a guest in his backyard. My temperature rose several degrees during the conversation.

"Any friend of Flyn's is a friend of mine," he said, but I could tell he didn't really mean it. He stared at me with razor blades in his eyes before pulling away and thundering down San Juan. Something told me that this would not be my only encounter with Treacherous Wallace. I had a gut feeling that he would impact my life permanently, and my intuition was never wrong.

Chapter Six

1983, FOURTEEN YEARS OLD

When I finally arrived at St. Paul's, I couldn't wait to get out of the car. The two-hour ride from Logan airport had been painful, my parents were barely on speaking terms. I wasn't supposed to know yet, but the paperwork for their upcoming divorce had begun. They tried their best to put on happy faces, but it wasn't working. This was a big day for me, and it felt ruined already. I had heard about St. Paul's since I was in diapers. Grampy had gone there in 1917, and my Dad in '57. If you wanted to get into an Ivy League college, it was the place to go—that's what my Dad drilled into my head, anyway. But I didn't care about all that; I just wanted the yelling in my house to stop.

The fall in New Hampshire was amazing. The leaves were turning a raspy orange, like the sun had thrown up on them before calling it a night. I had seen colors like this at our farm in Massachusetts, but I was still blown away. Maybe nothing bad could happen here. No one would have to decide which parent they loved more. No one would cry when they woke up in the morning. No, not in a place like this. I felt optimistic as I walked down a dirt path toward my new dormitory. Parents and their perfect children walked past and waved hello. Everyone seemed excited, well-dressed, and polite. It was like a Learjet had landed in the woods and dropped off every good-looking kid on the East coast.

I was five-foot-one, and the peach fuzz under my arms was just beginning. I prayed for some five o'clock shadow as we passed a preppy blonde wearing a flowered summer dress. *Damn, way out of my league.* But I stared anyway and smiled. She smiled back at me. Man, that felt good. I almost forgot about my parents as I stumbled over my luggage. I shrugged my shoulders, and she laughed a little. For a minute, I felt like I had muscles under my turtleneck and lifts in my shoes.

After we dropped off my bags and said an obligatory hello to the dorm master, we were off. I didn't really like the guy. He seemed like a geek who was trying way to hard. He shook my dad's hand like a hundred times. My dad bragged about his long, important affiliation with the school as we neared the chapel.

"I spoke to the rector just the other day, and he thinks this may be the best year the school's ever had. I've raised a lot of money for this place, so don't let me down." He was a trustee and thought he was such a big deal. He made sure to tell me not to screw up for the umpteenth time. Like I didn't already know that.

It was hard to live up to my dad's expectations. He was a force to be reckoned with. We were not much alike. He rarely dressed without cufflinks and a monogram somewhere on his clothing. If someone gave me a pair of cufflinks, I would melt down the gold and make a ring. He walked around like he was better than everyone, like he knew all the answers. And if you weren't white, he would look down his nose at you. Man, I hated that. He would say, "Those type of people are different than us." And the crazy thing is that he didn't even know he was racist. We were alike in some ways, though, like our tempers. I used to smash things up pretty good when I was mad, but I'd gotten better about that ever since I'd started taking drugs. My dad was clueless about this, too. He was clueless about a lot of things. He never really paid attention to me, not really.

He was complicated, my dad. My whole life, he told me he was two inches taller than he was. I knew this because I measured him once with the same measuring tape I used on myself. He told me that stretching the truth was okay if you could get away with it. "Always appear like you have money, even if you don't," he would say. When someone asked what he did for a living, he would brag, "I am the head of a vast publishing empire." That wasn't true, either. Humility was not his thing. He grew up in a military family, and I guess he had a lot to prove. A family trust paid for his education, but while he was in school, he didn't have money. He acted like he did, though. Sending me to St. Paul's was his dream, and that was fine with me. I was happy to be getting away from him.

The chapel on St. Paul's campus looked like a gothic cathedral borrowed from some village in Tuscany—like something you would see on a postcard or something. When we walked in, I couldn't believe how quiet it was. I looked up at the stained-glass windows and got lost in the blues, greens, and purples. This definitely seemed like it was the house of God. What a sight. We walked into the main chamber, and my father stopped suddenly.

"This was my chapel seat in my fifth-form year," he said. I knew from my indoctrination that meant eleventh grade. "I remember walking from my dorm on mornings in January and having my hair freeze solid. Hard as a rock. It would start to thaw out during morning prayers and drip down onto my face. I went through a lot of handkerchiefs in this place."

What a strange thing to remember. It wasn't an amazing sermon or favorite hymn or beautiful girl who sat across from him, but a frickin' handkerchief. Totally lame. My mom, who had barely spoken since we got out of the car, let him have it.

"Now they all have lipstick on them," she hissed.

My dad glared at her and walked away from us. I clutched my mother's hand and gave her a smile. She needed to know I was on her side. I had just picked one, right then and there. Fuck my dad.

My mom was really beautiful, and I couldn't understand why he wanted to be with someone else. All the other moms wore tweed coats and had fat ankles, but not her. She could have been a model if she wanted. I guess success had gotten into his thick head. DC was a small town, and he had started a big-deal political magazine called *National Journal*. I hated politics and never read his stupid magazine. He was like a second-rate soap character—the ones who cheat on their wives with some steamy secretary at the office.

One of the stops that morning was to visit the student who had been assigned to look after me. St. Paul's had a tradition that every freshman (third-former) would be paired up with someone from the senior class (sixth-former), sort of like an older brother or something. At St. Paul's, a freshman was called a "newb," and seniors were called "old boys" or "old girls." My old boy was a guy named Bartholomew—*Buzz*—Cooper. His parents belonged to the same country club as mine, and I grew up watching him destroy other teams on the hockey rink. I didn't really know him, not well, but I prayed he'd take a shine to me.

I had watched Buzz parade around the country club pool with his tennis racket and white Lacoste shirt. I envied just about everything he did. He walked around like nothing bothered him. I imagined him putting his arm around my shoulder and saying, "You have potential, my young friend, and I am going to show you how to beat the system."

Buzz lived in a dorm called Armor that lay on the outskirts of campus. Craig had told me that it was a good location for old boys because of its closeness to the woods, which allowed them to sneak out in the night to visit girls. It was a loosely supervised dorm where elite students would talk about Salinger, smoke bong hits, and listen to the Grateful Dead. I was with my parents, so I had a free pass to enter—otherwise, I would have been stopped at the gate.

We knocked on a door in the first-floor hallway, and Buzz popped his head out.

"Carder!" he said with fake excitement. "I heard you were around and was hoping you would stop by."

He greeted my parents like a true blue-blooded gentleman. My dad ate it up.

"Mr. and Mrs. Stout, such a pleasure to see you. Amazing. Come in. Come in."

I noticed the smell of skunk as we entered his room and looked up at Buzz's eyes. Bloodshot red. I knew the stench of good weed when I smelled it. We must have just interrupted a morning bong session.

"Please sit down and make yourselves comfortable," he said.

My parents settled on a ratty old corduroy couch. They seemed ridiculously overdressed on the second-hand furniture, like they were at a costume party or something.

"So, Bart, old boy," Dad said, "I hear you have taken on the responsibility of mentoring Carder. We could not be any happier it's you. Fantastic stuff."

"Yes, I heard something about that," Buzz said. "Don't worry about a thing. I will take good care of him." He winked at my mom, who sat quietly with her hands folded on her lap.

"Just try to keep him out of trouble," my mother said seriously. "We had so many problems last year with Craig that I hope the school doesn't put a target on his back."

"Mom!" I screeched in embarrassment. "This has nothing to do with Craig."

My brother had been kicked out of St. Paul's the previous spring after a long string of infractions. He had been caught drinking in a girl's room at two o'clock in the morning. He was failing several of his classes, and he constantly wore jeans to class even though it was against dress code. His reputation was mud, and my mom was worried that I would have to roll around in it.

"No, don't worry about that," Buzz reassured her. "Carder is his own man and is going to pave the way for himself. With my help, he'll sail through the fall term."

I liked that he called me a man. I didn't feel like one—I mean there wasn't even one hair on my balls, and my voice hadn't changed much, but maybe all that would change.

"So, will I meet with you regularly?" I said.

"Yeah, something like that," Buzz replied. "Just have a good time. I remember third form. Yikes, not always easy. So long ago."

This comment sent a feeling of uneasiness all the way into my fingers, and I began to fidget with my belt buckle. *Shit, what am I in for?*

"Just don't be a cocky newb," Buzz warned. "That's my only real advice. The school doesn't like cocky newbs."

My parents looked confused but remained silent, looking back and forth between Buzz and me.

"I won't," I promised.

Craig had told me that being a cocky newb was possibly the worst thing you could do as a third-former. If any upper former decided that you were too confident or thought you were too cool or something—you were fucked. All it would take was one person's opinion to tip the scales. Others would then agree and remember small ways that you were acting cocky. This was a label you'd wear for life, like shoplifting. There was no explaining your way out of it. Once you were cocky, you were done for.

I didn't speak with Buzz for weeks. His parading me around campus and introducing me to the cool crowd had been a fairy tale. In fact, there were several times when he passed me on a crowded path and didn't even look my way. I felt shunned. All his kind words in front of my parents were bullshit. It was a reality of St. Paul's that I was a lowly third-former, and newbs were at the bottom of the ladder.

I had never been away for more than a few weeks, and I was homesick. I missed our house in Georgetown, and I longed for my real bed. I hadn't really made friends, and I felt completely alone. I tried to look cool, but it just wasn't working. Every morning, I put on my Levi's jean jacket and baggy corduroys, which I had been told by my brother was how you dressed if you wanted friends. I thought if my threads looked like the older kids', someone would notice me, but I was dead wrong. I spent most of the first month crying on the pay phone to my mom.

"I don't want to be here. I just don't fit in," I whined.

"Do you want me to come get you?" she replied.

My mom had always been good in a crisis. She would light a cigarette, take a swig of vodka, and give fantastic advice. She had a knack for this sort of thing. When the chips were down, she knew what to say to make me feel better.

"Yeah, I want to come home. I don't like it here. I miss Jasper."

Jasper was a stray black lab that I had gotten as a puppy. Most nights, she slept on my bed. She was as close to a girlfriend as I had ever had.

"Jasper is right here next to me," said my mom. "She can hear your voice, and she is wagging her tail. She misses you, too."

I cried even harder.

"Listen, Weed, Thanksgiving break is just a few weeks away. Do you think you can make it that long? Then you can come home for a whole week. What do you think?"

"Yeah, I guess so."

"Weed" was the name my mom had given me a few years earlier. She said that I'd grown like a weed one year—six inches, to be exact. The nickname stuck, and I didn't think it was funny until I actually smoked some.

There was plenty of weed on campus, but you had to know where to find it. Even though I could smell it in the upper hallways at night, I didn't know how to get any. I mean, what was I supposed to do, go up to some sixth former and ask him for pot? That would be stupid. I would later find that it was right under my nose, anyway—or more specifically, over my head. This is where a sixth-former named Sophocles (people called him Soggy) lived in a room called the Bowling Alley. It was one of the best rooms in the school because it had a blocked entryway. This allowed stoners a few needed seconds to stash the bong if a teacher walked in without knocking. This natural barrier was referred to as a "delay," and many rooms on campus tried to copy its layout. Students stacked bookshelves on top of dressers and hung purple tapestries over the edges. It's amazing what a few seconds could do. Like having pole position at the Indy 500, it gave the stoners a clear advantage.

"I love you, Mom," I said quietly and put down the phone. I could sense someone was standing behind me. It was Soggy, and he was staring.

"So, we have a cocky newb in our midst," he said. I tried to ignore him, but he hovered over me like a gnat.

"Last I heard, you were on the list to get ponded. Beware, my friend, beware."

I ducked past him and retreated to my room.

Ponded? Shit, really? This must be a mistake. He's just trying to mess with me. But my heart was pumping so hard I thought I might be sick.

Ponding was the worst thing that could happen to you as a third-former. I had heard terrible stories of innocent third-formers being ponded in the dead of winter. It was St. Paul's folklore, and everyone seemed to know about it. Several seniors would grab you from your dorm room or sneak up behind you on the path. They would carry you to the bridge that connected campus to the hockey rink and throw you into the icy waters. Sometimes naked, I heard. There were usually three or four that came for you, but sometimes a dozen students would stand and watch. Word of the ponding would spread, and students would duck out of lunch early to get a good seat on the bridge. Once you'd been ponded, you had a black eye forever. There was no recovering from this kind of disgrace. Your reputation would be ruined, and you would never, ever be invited to sit on the blue couch. The blue couch was reserved for cool kids only.

This was the worst possible news I had ever received, and it made me want to go home immediately. I wanted to run far away and find a hole to hide in, but instead, I sat frozen in my closet with the curtain pulled shut. I tried to breathe lightly so that no one would hear me if they came in. Thankfully, the outside hallway stayed quiet, and the windy afternoon turned into night. I felt like I was a hostage and awaited my fate. After an hour, I snuck into the downstairs bathroom, locked the stall door behind me, and threw up in the toilet. I always felt better when I emptied my stomach.

For the next few days, I tried to avoid people as much as I could. I looked over my shoulder and listened for footsteps. I peered into every room before I entered and made a mental note of possible escape routes and illuminated exit signs. I wouldn't make it easy for them. I was a fighter. I had endured busloads of my dad's elitist bullshit and successfully grabbed the steering wheel when my mother was headed for a tree. I would survive this, too. At least that's what I told myself.

One night, after dinner, Buzz approached me in the hallway of a dorm called the Upper that led to the dining room. He was walking with a beautiful brunette from Greenwich named Alexandra, who dressed like a hippie in high heels. Buzz stopped me and pretended like everything was fine. *Is he part of the conspiracy, too?* I shuddered.

"Alex," he said, "have you met my newb, Carder Stout?"

"No, but I know about you. You're Dough Boy's brother, right?"

"Dough Boy" was my brother's nickname during his two years at the school. Craig had always been chubby, but it didn't seem to bother him. Most people at St. Paul's looked like they were auditioning for a movie about the rise of the Aryan nation. They were tall, muscular, blond, and full of themselves. My brother was different. He was like a rogue wave that smashed everything in its path. He had left quite an imprint on St. Paul's before he was expelled.

"Are you like...Little Dough?" Alex asked, chuckling.

"Little Dough Boy! I like it!" Buzz said.

"I guess so," I stuttered. It would be a strange nickname for a scrawny kid like me.

"Well, it's nice to meet you, Little Dough," said Alex. "I've heard a few grumbles about the way you flip your hair. Some of the sixth-formers think the way you flip your bangs to the side is a cocky move."

"Yeah, it seems kind of cocky," Buzz added.

"Uh...okay," I replied.

"There's been talk of ponding you because of that hair flipping move," Alex warned, "so maybe you should just lose it."

"No problem. I can do that." I nodded eagerly.

"Listen," Buzz whispered, "no newb of mine is going to get ponded. I won't let that happen. I've already made that clear to the instigators. But don't act like a cocky newb."

"And having an older brother like Dough Boy is another layer of protection. He was the coolest. But it won't protect you forever," Alex said.

"Okay," I replied. "Thank you, guys, seriously. I thought it was going to happen, like, any moment." Relief flooded my veins.

"Believe me, it was," Alex said.

"You were close to going in head first," Buzz laughed, "but your skin is safe for now."

"So what's your brother doing?" Alex asked.

"He's sailing a boat from Tahiti to St. Maarten."

"And getting fucked up along the way," Buzz added.

"Sounds like Dough Boy," Alex said. "Give him a big hug for me when you see him. I love your brother."

As they began to walk away, I could tell that Buzz wanted to say something else. He had a weird look on his face. He told Alexandra that he would catch up to her later, and he put his arm around my shoulder.

"I'm going to call you in a few weeks when we're both in DC. I've got a surprise," he whispered.

"Sounds awesome," I said, hesitantly.

I certainly wasn't cool enough to hang out with Buzz Cooper during Thanksgiving break. Maybe he was just kidding around or planning to put me through some kind of test. Maybe this was all a joke, and he was just making me feel comfortable so the ponding would be more of a surprise. All the relief in my body quickly turned to suspicion.

I'm being set up. This is even worse than before. And for a hair flip? What does that even mean? My bangs are long, and I can't see with them in my eyes. I could get a haircut ... or maybe some sort of barrette. Could a barrette be cool? I'll only flip my hair when I'm alone. I'll be a secret hair-flipper. Either way, I am destined for the icy waters of the pond. Either way, I'm fucked.

But the ponding never came. As I boarded a plane for Washington three weeks later, I felt as if I had avoided some catastrophic event, like a hurricane survivor clinging to a palm tree. Boarding school had not lived up to the hype. I had envisioned a posse of new, colorful friends, as making friends had never been hard for me before. But I was wrong. I had spent most of my time alone and had become insecure and shy, like the kids I'd known in middle school who were bad at sports and had pimples.

When I finally arrived at our house in Georgetown, it was like I never left. Everything was just the same. My mother opened the front door, and our four black Labradors burst into the hallway and mauled me with their tongues. I lay on the floor and asked them for a hundred licks on my face.

"I went to the store and got you all your favorites," my mom said. "Bagels, yogurt. Stouffer's frozen pizzas, salami, and brie cheese. I'm so happy you're back."

"Me too, Mom. You have no idea."

"Well, I guess it's time for a noon balloon," she said grinning. She poured a large glass of white wine and lit a Marlboro. I reached for her pack of cigs.

"Can I bum one?" I asked.

"Well, why not?" she said. "Would you like a beer or a glass of wine?"

There had never been a drinking age in my house, and I had been smoking in front of my mother since I was thirteen. She had given me smoking permission at St. Paul's, allowing me to smoke in certain areas around campus with other kids who had permission. She couldn't fight it—she had smoked two packs per day for as long as I could remember. I had grown up in a cloud of gray and believed that smoking was my birthright. No one had ever told me differently or tried to stand in the way. By the end of eighth grade, I had a running smoke ring competition with my mother. She usually won. It was good to be home.

Sometimes, the phone rang ten or fifteen times in our house before anyone picked up. On about the tenth ring, several shouts of "Someone pick up the goddamn phone!" would echo at once. For some reason, answering the telephone was something that no one in my family wanted to do, like picking up the heaps of dog shit in the garden.

The next morning, after the twelfth ring, I ran to the phone in the library. It was Buzz Cooper.

"Oh, hey, Carder. How is it going, man?"

He was actually calling me. This was just incredible.

"Oh, hi, Buzz. How are you doing?" I stumbled over my words.

"Good, yeah, good. Hey, sorry to call so early, but I need to see you."

"Uh, sure." I was baffled. "Do you want to come over later? My mom and sisters are going ice skating at the club, so it will be just me at the house."

"Perfect," Buzz said. "Oh, and make sure you have at least $400."

"Okay, sure."

I honestly had no idea what Buzz wanted. Does he need to borrow money? Is he in some sort of trouble and needs to get out of town? Maybe he got a girl pregnant. Well, I would help him out with whatever he needed. I had cashed a birthday check from my grandparents and had $500 in my desk drawer. Maybe this kind of gesture would improve my social status at St. Paul's. If I handed him a wad of cash, I bet Buzz would return the favor and introduce me around. It was totally worth it.

A few hours later, the doorbell rang. We lived in a seven-thousand-square-foot mansion in the heart of Georgetown, and the "ding-dong" echoed off the fourteen-foot ceilings and polished wooden floors. My mom always bragged that the Kennedys had lived here, but I wasn't sure it was true. It was definitely one of nicest houses in the neighborhood, but to me, it was just home. I had a bedroom and my own TV just like every other kid. There were nine bedrooms in the house, to be exact. The servant wing was occupied by a Filipino family who looked after us and did most of the cooking and cleaning. The fridge was always stocked with special egg rolls, and the dining room windows were spotless.

Before Buzz even got inside, his mouth opened and his eyes locked on mine.

"Have you ever tried cocaine?" he asked.

"Uh, of course," I lied.

I had never done it, seen it, or known anyone who used it regularly.

"Really? Wow, you guys start early in Georgetown. How old are you?"

"Fourteen," I said. "Fifteen next month. My brother gave some to me before he left on his trip." Another lie.

"Cool," Buzz replied. "Is there a good place we can weigh it out? We're the only people here, right?"

"Yeah, no one else is home. Let's go up to the library."

We walked up the long staircase to the second floor and pushed open the paneled mahogany door to my dad's study. It had always been my favorite room in the house. The walls were lined with carved bookshelves filled with leather-bound books he had gotten at Harvard Law School. His grandfather's heavy wooden desks flanked the room. My brother and I tried to do homework at them but usually ended up lobbing tennis balls back and forth. Next to the desks was a pair of red down sofas that were perfect for watching movies on our VCR, which was one of the only VCRs on our block.

On the floor was an antique marble chess board that we rarely used. All the pieces had been lost, and the board had been in the same spot for years, collecting dust.

Buzz eyed it immediately.

"Ah, that's perfect," he said, "for doing lines."

I had seen people doing cocaine in a movie or two and knew that white lines were cut out onto a mirror and snorted up the nose. I wondered what it would feel like. Nothing weird had ever been in my nostrils before. Water, maybe. Snot bubbles, definitely. But cocaine, no way.

Buzz unzipped his backpack and took out a freezer bag full of white powder. Then, he removed an old-fashioned scale and set it up on the desk. It had two round cradles hanging from a pivoting lever like the scales of justice you might see tattooed on the back of a convict.

"This, my friend, is two ounces of pure Peruvian flake," he said, holding the bag next to his big, square face. "How much of it do you want?"

Not knowing anything about cocaine and its price, I had no idea what to say.

"Uh, I don't know? What do you think? How much do I need? I mean, for this week?" I asked.

I didn't know that asking a drug dealer how much cocaine I needed was like telling a con man I had diamonds under my pillow. A sly, uneven smile stretched across Buzz's teeth.

"How much money you got in your pocket?" he asked. "It is $100 per gram, and I think you should take at least four grams. That should last you the whole week. Believe me—once you start doing this stuff, you won't ever want to stop."

I was planning on spending some of my money on a birthday present for my little sister, but in that moment, she was not a priority. One more stuffed animal would just clutter up her already cluttered room. I reached into my pocket and laid out four $100 bills.

"Yeah, better give me four grams."

"My man, wise choice…wise choice."

He removed four lead weights from a pouch in his knapsack. I had never seen a real cocaine dealer, but he sure looked like one as he scooped the white powder from the bag and dumped it in the cradle. Then, he placed a one-gram weight in the opposite cradle to balance it out. This process took a while, and I felt like I should put on a lab coat and goggles.

The mound of cocaine grew in the saucer until the four lead weights balanced it out. When it was almost overflowing, Buzz dumped it into a plastic bag and handed it to me. In under a second, my cash had vanished. He scooped it up like a blackjack dealer in Vegas and said, "Now for the fun part. Let's sample the product. This is on me."

Using a small spoon, he shoveled a heap of rocky powder into the center square of the chess board. He removed a small razor blade from his pocket and began to chop it. How the hell did he know so much about cocaine?

"You have to chop up all the rocks until it's smooth, like butter," he said.

When he finished chopping, he carved out four perfect lines and stood back to admire them.

"Perfection," he said, then rolled up a hundred-dollar bill and handed it to me. "Do the honors."

I wasn't really sure what to do, but I leaned over anyway and attempted to suck the cocaine into my nostril. I ended up scattering most of it across the board. I felt like such a chump.

"You have to hold the other nostril down tight while you snort," Buzz instructed, "like this."

Buzz grabbed the bill from me and inhaled two lines in a matter of seconds. He leaned on one foot, and his head tilted from side to side like he was limbering up before a fight. I paid close attention so I wouldn't screw up on the second go around. It went much better than the first. The cocaine shot into my nose, causing a nasty chemical taste in the back of my throat. I coughed a few times and felt a numbing in my mouth.

As I stood up and faced Buzz, I could barely focus. A thousand thoughts were stomping on each other and wanted to come out all at once. I felt like I was ten feet tall, and all the worries I'd ever had were gone. I wanted to tell him everything. I wanted to speak the truth. Now. It had to be now. It went something like this.

"Oh, man, I feel *good*. I feel *so much* better, I always really looked up to you and I wanted to be like you and when I thought you were heading up the posse to throw me off the bridge I got really confused because I thought you liked me. I'm worried that I will *never* find friends or be cool even though my mom always tells me I'm a good person and can be *whatever* I want to be in life. I'm not sure what I want to be but I *know* that I just want to have fun and party. I really like to do drugs but not all the time and I'm just *really happy* that you're my friend, thank you for letting me have some of this blow. I feel so *fucking good* I don't know what to do! You know?"

Buzz looked at me with a blank stare.

"Wow, that was a lot. Listen, my man, you should call a girl and get her high. Chicks love to do blow and fool around."

He was the most brilliant person I had ever met. What a suggestion! Yes, a girl. And I loved fooling around, too. When I could, I mean. I hadn't really done it, but I wanted to. *Yeah, I'll call a girl. A girl who wants to do coke with me. Perfect. Yeah, but who?* Who did I know who was fast, or maybe wanted to go fast? I would offer something new, something fresh and dangerous, something she'd only heard about but never done before. I'd be a hero. But most of the girls I knew didn't do cocaine. They went to dance class and studied algebra equations. *Shit.* I was almost ready to admit defeat when her angel face appeared in my mind. Yes, of course—I'll call Natalie.

"I know just the girl," I said.

Natalie was the dream girl who lived up the road from me. She was thirteen, and she was absolutely beautiful. I fantasized about her kissing me when I was in the bathtub. She was in eighth grade but was dating a senior from St. Alban's school who was six foot three and had failed a few grades. I thought he was probably twenty years old, but with the cocaine in my system, he was no match for me.

Although she looked innocent, there was a rebellious side to Natalie. When she walked into a room, everyone stared at her, and she knew it. She had that kind of laugh that said, *I know I'm hot, so what you gonna do about it?* Well, nothing. Nothing until now. Her mom was friends with my mom, and I had met her at a summer barbeque. We talked for a long time while drinking beers and sneaking tequila shots under a picnic table. She had been curious about boarding school and wrote her number down on a napkin for me. I had been way too scared to call her. But now I had no fear, and now I could conquer the universe, and now I would become a man and make her mine. I was absolutely, 100 percent certain of it.

Buzz put away his stuff and gave my hand a shake. I couldn't get him out of there fast enough. I didn't care what he thought of me anymore. As he walked down the long staircase, I looked at him with a new, more relaxed gaze.

"Later, dude," I said with a laugh.

I launched up the stairs to my bedroom and rifled through my desk drawers. There it was on a napkin: the number of all numbers. My ticket to ecstasy. I picked up the phone and dialed. It was her private line, and she picked up immediately.

"Uh, Natalie. Hi, Carder, Carder Stout. We met at—"

"Yes! Oh, my God, Carder! I'm so glad you called. What are you doing?"

"Well, I was wondering if you wanted to come over." I had never done this before—not even close. I felt like I was being shot out of a cannon. "I've got a whole bunch of coke, and I thought it would be fun to do it together."

There was a pause on the other end.

"Yeah, give me about thirty minutes, and I'll be there."

"Okay, cool. See you soon."

The girl of my dreams was about to show up at my door and do a pile of illegal drugs with me. Today was the best day of my life, by far. Was God giving me back pay for all the times I felt like a loser? It sure felt like it.

It was about three o'clock, and I knew that my mother and sisters would be home soon. I was pretty sure my mom would be fine with Natalie coming over, as she had told me like a hundred times to call her. She never made any rules about having guests over, girls or boys. "Just use your good judgment," she would always say. "I trust you." So, when my mom arrived in the kitchen, I let her know my plans. I could hardly contain myself.

"Natalie is coming over, and we're just going to hang in my room for a while," I blurted out.

"Great. That's great. I was hoping you two would hit it off. Have fun and be good," she said, winking at me as if to say *not too good*. I was in the clear—I had my mom's approval, a bushel of South American marching powder, a perfect ten showing up at my door, and a whole lot to say to her. *Life was good.*

Natalie showed up a couple of hours later. After a few exchanges between her and my mom, I whisked her up to my room. I could see that she was nervous, and her hands shook as I locked the bedroom door. She was wearing a pink buttoned-down shirt, and I could see the top of a white, lacy bra sprouting from the open buttons. It was hard to look away.

"I am so glad you invited me over," she said. "I've been thinking about you. I wondered when you'd be home for break."

My heart was about to burst.

"Me too," I said. "I've been thinking about you, too. Have you ever done coke before?"

"No, but I always wanted to. Let's try some now." She smiled. She was flawless.

I removed the chess board from my closet and dumped a huge pile of coke on it. I chopped it up and cut eight long lines.

"Watch how I snort it," I said, as I inhaled the powder. "Now it's your turn."

I handed her a rolled-up $100 bill—my last one—and watched as she breathed it in. We sat on the floor and stared at each other for a while. And then the chatter began.

I wanted her to know everything about me and could not stop the words from coming out of my mouth. I could feel instantly that we were connected, and it felt amazing. I told her about skiing with a guide in the Austrian Alps and staying for a summer in a castle in Normandy. She told me about dancing for the Washington Ballet and that she dreamed of twirling on the stage forever. We talked about our siblings, our parents, the nannies who brought us up—and our deepest fears. Somehow everything important had risen to the surface. We talked of our plans for the future and how we wanted to be together.

Then she brought up something that I had kept a secret from almost everyone. I was surprised she even knew about it and was totally caught off guard.

"So, I heard you have an eating disorder," she said.

I stared at her. "Uh, yeah. I guess so. How did you know that?"

"Well, I have one, too," she replied, "and I guess your mother told my mom about yours. I think they thought maybe we could help each other."

"Not sure I need help," I said.

"I mean, I think we all need help. Don't you?"

The truth was that I did need help. I'd been anorexic for about a year, and every once in a while, I was bulimic, too. It all started when I felt my parents drifting away from each other. I could tell something was different. My dad was spending more time on business trips than at home, and my mom was crying a lot. Sometimes, when she drank too much, she would tell me how much she hated him—but said that she loved him, too. She would cry, and I would put my arm around her. I guess I hated him, too, and wondered if he was going to leave for good. Maybe I didn't hate him, but he really pissed me off. My family breaking into a hundred pieces was too much for me to handle, so I stopped eating.

Not eating felt good at first—it felt like I was in control of something, for once. I blamed myself for everything that went wrong. Over the next few months, I lost about twenty pounds. I stopped eating breakfast and lunch and would only have a small dinner—usually a piece of chicken or something. I chewed endless packs of gum and checked the size of my thighs ten times a day.

It took a while for my parents to notice, and when they did, nothing happened. My father was too embarrassed to say anything. I was his perfect boy, the one who was a star, and I had turned out to be defective. He couldn't deal with it. It made him so mad. One morning at breakfast, he tried to force a piece of toast down my throat. I ran into the downstairs bathroom and locked the heavy wooden door. He pounded and pounded, but I didn't come out.

After a few months, my parents withdrew me from school. I was far too weak to go, and they thought I might hurt myself. My mom took me to see the family doctor, and I lied about the whole situation. The two of them decided to weigh me every Friday for a month or two, and if I had gained a few pounds, they would let me go back to school. So, every Friday morning, I would take an orange juice up to my bathroom and drink as much as I possibly could. I also found that if I taped four D-size batteries between my butt cheeks, I would gain about a pound. I was scared that a battery would drop out of my underwear and ruin everything, but luckily, that never happened.

After my weight went up a few pounds, my parents backed off. I went back to school, but I never stopped starving myself and had no intention of doing so.

"Yeah, I guess I need help, but I don't want any," I said to Natalie.

"What are you doing?" she asked.

"Not eating. How 'bout you?"

"Well, I do eat sometimes, but I throw up after."

"Me too," I said.

"Really? I've never known of any boy to be bulimic. That's cool."

And in that moment, it did feel cool. We were speaking about something that very few people understood.

"What does it feel like when you do it?" I asked.

"It feels good." She sighed. "All my problems go away, and I feel a warm rush of like, happiness, through my body. What does it feel like for you?"

"The same."

Whenever I hunched over the toilet and emptied the contents of my stomach into the bowl, I felt peace in my heart. I would then come out of the bathroom with tons of confidence and a smile on my face. I would forget about all the bad stuff swirling through my brain. In fact, it was kind of like doing a line of coke.

"I never thought I would talk to anyone about this. I mean, like, really talk about it," said Natalie.

"Me neither," I said, "but it feels good to."

I passed the straw to Natalie and held her hair as she snorted two more lines. I did a few more and moved over to my turntable to play some music. I put on The Cars' first album and began to sing the words. We talked and sniffed and laughed through the night. Natalie called her mother and got permission to stay over. There was nothing strange about this, not to us.

When the morning light spilled into my room, there was only one more thing I thought about doing. Her face looked so beautiful. I was in love. I took her hand in mine and leaned in for our first kiss. It was magical. We moved over to my bed and lay down next to each other. She unbuttoned her blouse. I gently touched her nipples and rubbed my body up against her. This was a first for me.

"I can't believe this is happening," I whispered.

"Me neither," she said, staring into my eyes.

And without one more touch or grope or kiss, I came in my pants. She watched as my face contorted. When it was over, I wanted to hide under the bed.

"Don't worry," she reassured me. "I'm glad you did. Now you can last longer the second time."

Second time? I had no idea that there could even be a second time. We took off each other's clothes and lay naked on the bed. I was pretty sure it was going to happen.

My brother would never believe me.

Chapter Seven

2003

I knew little about the drug trade—other than how to buy them—and Flyn was a seasoned veteran holding a lifetime of narcotics wisdom in the palm of his hand. I was to be the benefactor of this knowledge. It was in Flyn's nature to teach, and our classroom was Ghost Town. Every day we spent together was an education, and as days turned into weeks, I began to feel I was earning a gold star for participation.

Flyn's focus wasn't really on the 'hood itself, as that territory was saturated by adolescent Crip initiates lining the streets with their pouches made from paper. He did some deals there—mostly low-risk, cash-ready type deals—but when the sun went down, he focused on delivering his product all over the west side of Los Angeles. His Rolodex was substantial. When he got out of prison, he let all his former clients know he was back in business. Flyn's product was superior—he prided himself on its purity, and this set him apart from the peddlers on the street. He kept a stash of powder cocaine for the Santa Monica crowd and always had an ample amount of crack for the more hardened fiends. I was not invited to attend these nighttime negotiations, but Flyn told me all about them. He delivered to trust fund partiers, trophy wives who were bored with life, has-been actors in rundown mansions, hip-hop producers in makeshift studios, seedy white pimps with their stables of fake blondes, and the gang affiliates that were looking for something special. Flyn was the underground mayor of the drug town, and when he arrived with the dope, there was always a ticker tape parade. I was hoping to get the nod soon.

We spent one night a week at an apartment that Flyn shared with his girlfriend, Alyssa. It was miles from Ghost Town on a rundown block in a crime-ridden neighborhood, but somehow it felt safe. I became the part-time assistant, and Alyssa was the master chef. Much like an old Italian cook who never reveals the precise ingredients of her award-winning Bolognese, her recipe for crack was a well-kept secret. I was allowed to watch her work, but the exact amounts, temperatures, and oven settings were off limits.

Alyssa and Flyn had been together for nearly ten years, and they had each other's names tattooed on their forearms. Like her tattoo, Alyssa was muted, curvy, soft, and small. She was barely five feet tall and avoided direct eye contact due to her painful shyness. Her skin was latte-colored, and her smooth face looked far younger than her twenty-six years.

Flyn and I would play gin rummy and talk while she mixed up the batter. We all looked forward to these nights, away from the danger of the street. One such night, Alyssa asked me to fetch a bottle of tequila. I learned that it was to celebrate: Flyn was going to be a daddy.

"Never thought I'd see the day," Flyn said, grinning.

"And an amazing dad you'll be." I raised my glass. "Here's to all the not-so-amazing dads who did their best but fell short."

"Here's to *not* following in their footsteps," Alyssa said, with a rare burst of sass. I figured that the booze was stripping away her quiet docility. We linked arms and threw back the mescal.

"Here's to Uncle Hollywood," Flyn said, slapping me on the back.

"A white dude in my posse. Lord have mercy," Alyssa said with a laugh. More tequila hit the backs of our throats. As we went around with toasts and shots, the hollowness of my bones began to fill with something unfamiliar. It felt like a radiant heat was healing my limbs. It wasn't the alcohol that instilled this renewed sense of self—it was the company. I had been unwanted for so long.

"Here's to two beautiful people I consider my kin," Flyn said sincerely. My white skin couldn't hide my blush, and Flyn slapped me on the back again. Alyssa got up from the table and moved to the counter to continue mixing. I watched as she poured a large amount of cocaine into a beaker filled with water and stirred it slowly with a wooden spoon. Then she emptied the contents of a box of Arm & Hammer into the same concoction and let it coagulate on the surface.

"You want to know why they will always come back to me, Hollywood?" Flyn asked. He settled back in his chair. "Because my dope is the best merchandise on the market. Everyone stomps and stomps all over their shit. When they finally bake it, only about thirty percent of the cocaine is left. That's what the Crips are working with, and that's fine, but they're going after the low-lifes on the street."

I tried to keep my face neutral—I was one of those low-lifes.

"The stuff I get is a hundred percent pure. Straight from the Mexican jungle. After we mix it, and Alyssa cooks it down, we are still at sixty percent. *Twice* the potency of the rock in the 'hood. One hit, and my number's on speed dial. And when they want the powder, I got that, too. Shit, I had one dude buy 4k of merchandise in one deal. Takes the Crips half a day to make that. *One hour* for me, *by myself.* You'll see. I want you to start coming with me. Now that I'm gonna be a pops, I need someone to watch my back. You cool with that?"

His invite was music to my ears.

"You know it, brother. I was hoping you'd bring me along. I got you." I put my knuckles out, and Flyn gave me a pound.

"And here's the best part. You get a piece of the take. That cool with you?" he said, eyebrows raised.

"More than cool." I put my hand on his shoulder and gave it a shake. "You know me. Don't need much to get by. Just a little something here and there. Product mainly. And a little green on the side."

"I got you covered, Hollywood."

We both watched as Alyssa poured the contents of the beaker into two glass brownie dishes, equally distributing the congealed white paste. She smoothed the top of each compound like a baker applying frosting to a rectangular birthday cake. She slipped the dishes into the hot oven and shut the metal door. It was obvious that she was an expert and took great pride in her work.

"Here's to the best cook in the 'hood," Flyn said lovingly, "the mother of my child! Someone is lookin' out for me, Hollywood. I don't know who it is, but it's somebody."

"To the dude behind the curtain," I said, as we threw back another shot. "May he keep us safe."

The tequila brought out the best in me, and I white-guy danced around the kitchen without a care in the world. They shook their heads and showed me what rhythm looked like. When the crack was fully cooked, Alyssa took it out of the oven to let it cool down.

After a few minutes, she began to cut squares that were about two inches wide and deep. She handed me a sharp kitchen knife.

"Hollywood, take this platter and cut up the dope like it's small brownies." She held her thumb and forefinger out to show me the exact size. I guess I was part of the team now. I had never seen so much crack in my life—the sight of it made my stomach growl.

"Every square you carve out is $350 in our pockets. You should get almost twenty pieces from that tray. You do the math," Flyn said.

Numbers escaped me completely as I focused on my first attempt to divide up a large quantity of illicit drugs. The solidified cocaine had a yellowish color and the consistency of a bar of Dove soap. The knife glided through easily, and each cube retained its own particular shape and character. Some held perfect right angles, and others resembled lumps of crystallized sugar. I realized the booze was affecting my ability to be precise, so I opted to color outside the lines. I pointed to a small Gaza pyramid and smiled.

"What do you think?" I asked Flyn.

"You're a natural. Should have worked in a factory assembling Rubik's Cubes. Or been shaving dice on the Vegas strip," he laughed. "I don't sell anything smaller than this." He picked up one of my nuggets and tossed it toward me. "This is for you."

I had never been in possession of a rock this big and rolled it around in my palm, marveling at it. "Damn."

"I got you, Hollywood. My customers pay three hundred minimum for that. I won't move for less. Isn't worth my time. Most of them want two."

I handed the knife back to Alyssa and took another shot. It was understood that while we were working, no product would be smoked. In the trade, that was an unwritten rule. After the job was done, then it was time to get high. But the booze was taking over now, and I could feel my lids dropping fast. I vaguely remember making plans with Flyn before taking one last shot and passing out on the couch. There I remained until the sound of birds invaded my dreams.

When I approached the alley behind my apartment, the sun had just tapped the horizon on its shoulder. It was the first time I had ever walked through Ghost Town just after dawn, and I had never seen it so peaceful. The houses looked beautiful in the morning light, and I thought about the families that ran through these same streets seventy-five years ago. I imagined their little faces in the downstairs windows as I passed.

In the morning light, it was hard to imagine that anything unpleasant ever happened there, but I knew it had. These streets had watched as Venice grew from a sleepy seaside town into a city wracked by injustice. These were the roadways for freedom riders and sidewalks for picket lines and city blocks for the weary and disenfranchised. These streets were so full of history that it was hard to walk down them without feeling like you were being followed. The suffering on them was palpable, but this morning they were different. They felt like my streets. The ghosts had finally accepted me. This was my place now, and I felt completely at home.

I looked up at the fire escape underneath my second story window. Tisha gazed down at me with a big smile.

"There's my man. Been waitin' all night for you. You best get up here and give me a hug," she said.

When I opened the window, she jumped through, stripped down to her thong, and hopped under my covers in a burst of teenage energy.

"Come snuggle with me," she said.

I was still a little drunk, and her flawless breasts looked more than inviting, but I kept my composure.

"Okay, but no hanky-panky. You're far too good for a guy like me. Understood?" I said.

"Yeah, I got you sweetie, but I don't really get you. But it's cool. You're the first dude I ever met that didn't want to fuck me."

"Exactly."

She looked up at me, perplexed. She didn't understand. I couldn't be like all the rest: the dirty, sweaty, angry men who touched her every day. As I climbed into bed, I saw that her right eye was bruised and swollen.

"Oh, man, what happened to you?"

"I got caught in the eye by this guy's fist last night. He wasn't happy with what I was doing, so he popped me one good. I was knocked out for a minute," she said.

"Don't you have protection against people hitting you? I mean, isn't that what Trech does for you?" I asked, naively.

"Trech the one that did it."

I shot up in bed. "Motherfucker!" I yelled. "What gives him the right to do that to you?"

"I'm his property. He can do what he want. No one ever mess with him. He kills people."

"Listen," I pleaded, "I don't care what you do with yourself and how you make your money. I understand you're doing it for your little girl, but you're nobody's property. No one ever has the right to hurt you."

"No, you listen," she said, her voice suddenly hard. "I'm nineteen. Ain't got no one to look out for me. I'm a ho, and I don't mind. I make my own choices and know what I'm doing. You see me different than I really am."

"No, I see you exactly how you are."

"Oh yeah? How's that?"

"I see a beautiful firecracker of a girl, who is smart and has the best genes of anyone I know."

She softened. "Thank you. That's nice. But I never wear jeans."

I couldn't help but laugh and pull her close.

A few days later, I arrived at Beatrice's door. She invited me in and gave me a hug and a chuckle. "There he is, my handsome friend. Why you been avoiding me? It's bad manners not to stop by and say hello to Ole B."

"I know, I know. I'm sorry. Just got so busy with work and family and things." My nose was growing with every word. I could tell she wanted to believe me.

"Good, good, baby. What kind a work you doin' these days?" she asked.

"Well, I got a little business deal going with Flyn. We're writing a script for a movie and getting a lot of people interested," I lied.

"Well, when you get rich and famous, remember I don't want nothing else from you that I don't have already. Except for maybe a visit from Denzel," she laughed.

"I'll let him know."

Flyn appeared from the back bedroom wearing a nice button-down shirt and V-neck sweater. I looked down at his feet and saw that his white sneakers had been scrubbed clean, and his khaki pants were pressed.

"Dang, where are we going tonight? The prom?"

"Gotta look good when we are doing our thing," said Flyn. "Get your ass over here, and let's work on some hygiene." He grabbed me by the collar and led me into his bathroom.

"The shower is there. Plenty of hot water. I got a fresh razor over here with shaving cream. Make yourself look pretty, and don't flood the place."

Hot water—a luxury I'd done without for months. Personal grooming had gone with it. After a thorough wash, I hopped out of the shower and shaved. Even through the fog on the mirror, I began to recognize myself again. For a moment, the mask was gone, and a young, impressionable boy returned. I waved at him in the mirror and smiled. I missed that boy and wanted him back. I wasn't sure it was possible, but inside this small house surrounded by Beatrice and Flyn, I saw glimpses of him. Being here, with this family, was the medicine I needed. If they had asked me in that moment, I would have packed my bags and moved in.

Flyn called from outside the door, "Meet me in the room across the hall. Leave your clothes in the bathroom and come in a towel."

"But I don't have my lipstick on yet," I joked.

"Just get yo ass in here, please." Flyn wasn't amused. I wrapped the towel tightly around my midsection and waddled into the hallway. Flyn was waiting for me in the doorway of the farthest room down the hall. He motioned me in. He was holding a button-down shirt and pair of jeans in his hands.

"Try these on. They were my brother's. He was about your size when he passed. Nobody's worn these clothes for years. Might as well put 'em to use." He laid them on the bed, glanced around the room, and left.

The full gravity of the situation took a moment to sink in. Beatrice had told me that Flyn's brother had been killed but had not shared any of the details. By the look of the room, he'd been a young teenager when he died. There was a Run DMC poster on the wall next to a Lakers calendar with a purple basketball on the cover. The pillowcase on the bed was made to resemble a football, and there were a few stuffed animals scattered about.

As I inspected the room more closely, I saw a few framed pictures on a bookshelf next to several basketball trophies and blue ribbons. I leaned down and picked one up—a teenage Flyn with his arm around a boy a few years younger. The boy appeared in the other photos as well, sitting next to Beatrice in a more formal studio setting. There was an eight-by-ten pinned to a bulletin board that looked like a school photo, and he was beaming. He looked like the happiest boy who ever lived. I picked up his blue jeans, sat down on the bed, and hesitated. Something about this just didn't feel right. I folded the clothes neatly in a pile and smoothed out the dinosaur bed sheets.

Flyn burst into the room and barked, "Hollywood, what you doing! Why you taking so long?"

"I, uh, man, I don't know. I just feel strange about wearing your brother's clothes. You know, I didn't know him, and—"

"His name was Willy. This was his room. Stayed here weekends, mostly. Lived with his mom during the week, and her neighborhood was even worse. Best point guard his age in California. Could hit three-pointers at will." Flyn motioned like he was shooting a basketball with his hands. "Swoosh. Swoosh. All day long. Smart, too. I had him reading every day. *To Kill a Mockingbird* was his favorite." He pulled a paperback copy off a shelf and handed it to me. "I would take him to school when I could and pick him up, too. There was bad shit goin' down everywhere. I wouldn't let him join the gang, and he was mad at first, but he thanked me for it. B loved him more than she loved anything else in the world."

"What happened?"

"He was with his friends. He played pick-up games all over the city—Compton, South Central, Inglewood, Watts—wherever the court was hot. I told him not to stray too far, but he didn't listen. Some guys rolled up on them, and that was it. Sprayed the whole block with bullets. Willy got hit twice. Didn't see it coming. I never found out who it was. Believe me, I tried. I think it was the Bloods, but I can't be sure. Saddest day of my life. Still hard for me to talk about it."

"Flyn, I'm so sorry man. I can't even imagine."

"It was a long while back. I've done my grieving. You know Kübler-Ross and the stages of grief. I was stuck in anger for years. That's when my mean streak came out. And then the bargaining phase got me. I kept thinking "if only." I was sure that if I had gone with him that day, he'd be alive. I'd been over at my girlfriend's house gettin' some pussy. I thought he'd be okay, but I was wrong. Can't ever take it back. Not ever."

"You know, it's not your fault, man. You can't protect anyone out in the streets. Too many variables. Too much violence," I said.

"Yeah, I know, but I still blame myself. He was my little man. He lives in here now." He pointed to his chest. "Now put on his motherfuckin' threads. He would want you to wear them. That's the way he was," Flyn said.

"You sure?"

"Listen, he worked all summer mowing lawns in Beverly Hills. Saved up $500 and gave it all to the church, anonymously. He never set foot in there, not even once, but he donated every penny—out of respect for B. It's the way he was." Flyn paused. "Much better kid than me."

"That's for damn sure," I joked, but Flyn didn't smile back. I nodded. "Thanks for these."

"Thank *him*. Now get ready. We're going down to the *Hole*."

"The Hole?"

"Don't worry about it. Just get dressed."

The clothes fit perfectly and actually looked pretty damn good. The jeans were well-worn Toughskins that were a little baggy but the right length, and the white oxford looked like it was tailor-made for me. It had been pressed recently and still felt warm to the touch. I wondered if Beatrice was washing his clothes as a way to keep him alive. There was a pair of black suede Adidas at the foot of the bed and I slipped them on without a hitch. I was now officially walking in another man's shoes. Boy's shoes, I mean.

The reception I got from Beatrice was not at all what I expected. She looked me up and down with a stern face and turned away toward the television. I wanted to rip off the clothes and run.

"Grandma B, I shouldn't have put these on. I'm sorry, I'm gonna go change—"

"*I* wanted you to wear them," she said, cutting me off. "I pressed that shirt tonight for you."

"Oh, I thought it was Flyn's idea, for our meeting," I said.

"No, baby. Wasn't Flyn's idea. It was mine. We inviting you into our family now. Seems you ain't got nobody else lookin' after you. We got more than enough to give. Anytime you want, you can stay in Willy's room." She nodded and smiled, but her face was serious.

"Thank you, B, but that's too much."

"Anytime you want," Flyn said, entering the room.

I could feel the tears coming. I put my hands up to my face and let an audible moan escape. I couldn't stop it if I tried. I started crying like a baby. Beatrice stood up and wrapped her arms around me.

"It's okay, baby. It's okay."

"It's just been a long time since anyone was this nice to me." And she rocked me until my shuddering breaths slowed and Flyn put his hand on my shoulder.

"All right, now. If the love fest is over, we got people waiting on us. We got a movie to make, right, Hollywood?" said Flyn.

"Exactly," I replied. "A movie about the 'hood." I assumed that Flyn had confirmed that we were working on a script—a story about the mean streets of Venice. *Not a bad idea*, I thought to myself. Maybe a story about us.

I drove as Flyn guided me down Lincoln Boulevard toward Santa Monica. He hadn't told me anything about my role in the operation. I didn't think of myself as a drug dealer—I was convinced that without possession of the narcotics or money, I was not complicit in the wrongdoing. I thought of myself more as a spectator, like a witness for the justice of the peace or a guy playing tambourine in a '70s folk band. I was just a ride-along who was there to support my friend and father-to-be and, of course, for the excitement of it all. Ready to have my cake and smoke it, too.

We barreled down Lincoln and merged onto the 90 freeway toward no man's land. I had never been to South Central and could feel the nerves tightening up in my neck as we got closer. This was far from my comfort zone, and even with Flyn next to me, I was scared. I had to ignore the urge to pull a U-turn back to Venice. Flyn reached down and unzipped a leather bag. The glint of black steel reflected in the overhead lights as he pulled up a gun.

"You know how to use one of these?" he said, a Glock 9 in his hand.

"What the fuck?" I had no intention of brandishing a pistol. Not for anyone. "No, not really. Why are you holding a gun?"

"I need you to get my back. Just in case. Always gotta strap. These fools don't play around," he said.

Strap? You've got to be fucking kidding me.

"Are you serious, man? I mean…we never talked about me having a gun. Not what I had in mind," I said, suddenly sweating in my borrowed clothes.

"Oh, yeah? Well, what did you have in mind? Having protection is part of the game. Without it, no one takes you seriously. And you wind up *dead*."

"I thought I was the driver. Not the bodyguard."

"You're my partner, right?"

"Yeah, I guess so. But I'd rather be your *gun-free* partner. Besides, last time I shot a pistol, I was eleven years old. Couldn't hit the broad side of a barn. Almost blew my foot off, too."

"It's easy. You just point and squeeze," he said, the pistol in his outstretched arm. His wrist kicked up with each imaginary blast. *Pop. Pop. Pop.* "You probably won't even have to squeeze. But you know how to point, right?"

"Yeah, I know how to point, but I don't want to. If you point a gun, there's a good possibility somebody's gonna point back! I'm *not* cool with that. Not trying to get *killed*." I could hear the panic rising in my voice.

"So you're afraid? If people sense your fear, they'll use it against you. Can't ever let 'em know you're scared. That's a sure-fire way to get killed," he said. "This is serious. These boys don't care. Don't care about me. Don't care about nothing. If you want to come along, then you gotta be prepared."

"Well, I thought I might stay in the car. I mean, if that's okay with you," I said.

"Remember what happened to you last time you stayed in the car? This neighborhood is ten times worse. You can take your chances, but it's probably not a good idea," he said.

He had a point. Waiting in the car, I was easy prey.

"Nah, I'm cool. I'll come with you," I said, nodding to convince myself.

"Besides, how you gonna learn what I do if you're outside?"

I could tell we were getting closer by the look of the streets. We were off the highway and heading south down the boulevard. There were groups of young black men and women huddled on the corners outside liquor stores. I made eye contact with a few of them and was not well-received. Maybe they thought I was the police, or maybe they didn't like me because I was white. Either way, I could tell I wasn't welcome. Once again, I was in a place where I didn't belong. I took a left turn down a residential block and then a right down an alleyway.

"Park here," Flyn said, pointing to the back of a warehouse. "Now, take this gun and put it in your pants." He handed me the Glock. "If anyone tries to fuck with me, pull it out and blast the fool."

No fucking way I am doing this. I took the gun and held it in my hand. I could feel my fingers shaking and my heart beating under my shirt. I looked over at Flyn, and he was smiling like someone had just handed him the keys to a brand-new Cadillac. Then he started to laugh. A real belly-roll, high-pitched, eye-watering kind of laugh. I stared at him, too aware of the gun in my hand to laugh.

"White boy, give me that motherfuckin' gun. You think I was gonna let you walk in there with my gun?" He continued to laugh. "That would be the dumbest thing I could ever do. First off, you don't even know how to use the damn thing. Secondly, if you walk in there strapped, they would pound all over you." He shook his head. "My man, Hollywood, so damn serious sometimes. Gotta lighten up. We havin' fun, right?"

I was stunned. I thought these were the rules of the game! I was so naïve. What did I know about drug dealing? Apparently, very little. I gave the pistol back to him and finally cracked a smile myself.

"Motherfucker. With that poker face, you should be an actor," I said.

"Listen, I was serious about staying in the car, though. Not safe out here. Just follow my lead. Don't say anything. Don't act afraid. Just watch the deal go down from a few steps behind me. This is *real,* so don't do anything stupid."

"Who are these guys, anyway?"

"It's only pimps, low-lifes, wannabe rappers, and thieves that stay in *The Hole,*" he said. "Last I checked, no one's been shot in here for a while. Just be cool and keep your eyes open. You'll be fine." He took the gun and put it in the waistband of his jeans.

"Sounds good. Let's do this." I reminded myself to breathe.

"Stay close," he said as we got out of the car. We walked through a gap in a chain-link fence and down a few steps to a metal door. I could hear music playing from the inside—NWA. Flyn rapped on the door three times, and we waited for a minute with no answer. He pounded again, and it swung open. The sheer enormity of the guy standing in front of us blocked my view of the inside completely. He made Flyn look small. He had to bend down to get through the doorway, and his body barely fit through. His skin was dark black with a few teardrop tattoos falling from his left eye. His eyes were tense but kind as he hugged Flyn, and then he peered over at me.

"Who dis?" he asked immediately.

"Oh, this Hollywood. He my partner. He cool," Flyn responded. His speech went 'hood, and I wondered if I should follow suit. The man stared me down for a few seconds and turned back to Flyn.

"Why you messin' with a white dude?" he said, disapprovingly. "He da police?"

"Nah, nah, nah, Curtis," Flyn said shaking his head. "He my ride. He cool. We do bizness together. Known him for a long time."

"Ain't seen him around before. But if he wit' you—cool. Anything goes down, though, I'm holdin' you personally responsible. You feel me?" Curtis said as he stepped aside and let us in.

"I feel you," Flyn responded. I nodded as I walked past, and just like that, we were down the rabbit hole. The smell of bud was everywhere. On a couch to the right, there was a group of middle-aged men passing a joint back and forth. One of them had a young girl on his lap. They were sort of passing her back and forth, too. It was hard to see through all the smoke, but I could sense that we were in a large industrial space—almost like an old factory. The floors were gray cement, and the walls were exposed cinder blocks. There were couches and tables and chairs all occupied by men, mostly with women flitting around behind them, gyrating slowly to a new song by 50 Cent. A few tables were set up for cards, while the others were crowded with hulking figures sorting through large piles of marijuana with their fingers. There was a makeshift bar at the back of the room with an older woman serving bottled beer and paper plates filled with chicken wings and potato salad. The lights were low, and the smell was bad. The whole place needed a good scrub. I was the only white face for miles, but no one had spotted me just yet. I tucked myself behind Flyn and tried to avoid eye contact. We wove through the sweaty clusters toward a doorway in the far corner. Another herculean figure guarded the door with his arms crossed. Nothing about him looked kind. He slapped hands with Flyn and moved into a sort-of half hug before cracking a smile full of diamonds and rose-colored gold. After exchanging a few pleasantries, he looked over at me and shook his head. "Flyn, man, you know I can't let no cracker into the booth."

Flyn stepped back for a minute and put his arm around me.

"This right here is Hollywood. That's my name for him—can't say his real name 'cuz it's too hot right now." I could see the bouncer taking a second look at me, still unflinching and without any hint of recognition.

"Yo, I don't care if it's Mickey fuckin' Mouse or David Hasselhoff's twin brother—ain't been a cracker in the booth since Iron Mike rolled up in here with a fine Caucasian bitch—but mind you, he was heavyweight champion of the world." He turned toward me and said, "Unless you got some sort of title, a Playboy bunny, a magic wand, or a million dollars—you ain't comin' in. You hear that?"

I nodded my head and shrugged my shoulders as if to say, *I get it, don't worry about it,* but Flyn had a different idea. He leaned over and whispered something into the guy's ear, and in an instant, the man's demeanor changed completely. He looked at me long and hard and began to grin from ear to ear.

"Man, I thought that was you! Sheeet, of course you can come in. I saw that movie, and you was dope, man. Brought my nephew and his boys. That shit was real."

"Thanks, man. Really appreciate you. It was fun. Doing the movie, I mean. Glad you and your nephew liked it," I responded. Flyn had pulled the *Lord of the Rings* card. He gave me a big bear hug and asked for my autograph, which I promptly signed *Viggo*. And that was it—the power of being a celebrity lookalike. We got past the velvet rope and were into the VIP section. I was the first white person since Mike Tyson's lady to have the honor. Lucky me.

We moved up a narrow flight of stairs and down a dark hallway to a large interior window that looked into the mixing booth of an old recording studio. Flyn knocked on the glass, and a well-dressed black guy with a white beard and Jackie O sunglasses waved us in. Next to him was a younger guy in a Chicago Bulls shirt with a thick gold chain around his neck and dark green tattoos covering both of his arms. There was a tall, muscular guy standing next to him who leered at me as I entered—he was obviously the enforcer.

"Must be a special occasion. A cracker in the booth. Somebody call Channel 7 News," said the older gentleman.

"What's up, Flick?" Flyn said giving him a hug. "Always a pleasure. This is my man Hollywood. He's my partner. Thought I'd bring him along."

"Cool, Cool," Flick said with an inviting gesture. "What's up, Hollywood? Come in. Come in."

I remained silent and nodded my head at Flick. The room was small and cramped, and I felt like it was my first day in a new school. I was the variable that brought the unfamiliar into their world, and that wasn't cool in a drug deal. I was smart enough to realize that. I huddled in the corner and kept to myself as Flyn broke out a cellophane bag with several eight balls of crack lining the bottom. Flyn handed the younger man three chunks that we had carved up a few nights before, and I marveled at my own handiwork. I almost wanted to say, *Hey, that's one that I cut up*, but I didn't—of course not. He wouldn't give a fuck, anyway. The young man glanced down at the rocks and then over at me. Our eyes locked. His hair was braided in cornrows, and his pupils were dilated and bloodshot. He had a scar under his left eye. I hadn't seen him smile. He took out his pipe and crumbled a piece onto the waiting screen. His bodyguard leaned over with a lighter and held it under the glass to heat up the crack. He took a long pull and exhaled a cloud of smoke. Instantly, I could smell the burning coke, and it made me want to smoke, too, but that was completely out of the question. I tried to be subtle, but I couldn't stop staring, as if I was passing a burning car on the side of the road.

After a few seconds, he stood up abruptly and, before I could blink, he was right in front of me.

"Why you staring at me, honky? You got somethin' to say?" I was paralyzed and speechless and waited for someone to intervene, but the room was silent and no one moved.

"G-Money, he cool. He wit' me. That Hollywood. Just came along for the ride."

In an instant, G-Money's energy shifted. I knew all about the paranoid episodes that followed a big hit of crack and assumed he was having one. Who could blame him? But I didn't want to get caught in the middle of it. G-Money stepped back and patted me on the shoulder. I could tell by his face that he was beginning to enjoy the ride.

"Hollywood. My man. I seen you before, right? Come wit' me fo' a minute." He reached out his hand and pulled me around the corner into the vocals booth. "Now we gonna bust a track together, white boy." He then turned to Flick and said, "Roll tape."

I watched as Flick began to turn dials and knobs on a massive soundboard and press a button at the top. G-Money put on his headphones and began to rap to a beat that vibrated through the room. He was damn good—I mean, masterful and poetic in his choice of rhymes. I stood next to him, awkwardly bobbing my head up and down—never daring to open my mouth. He closed his eyes, lost in the lyrics. I felt like a plus one on the red carpet and slunk out the side door. After a few more minutes, we exited the club. I could feel my body relax as I slipped into the familiar seat of my car.

"You did good," Flyn said handing me a $100 bill. "This is your take. Don't spend it all in one place."

"Thanks, Flyn. I thought I was gonna have to rap. That would have been bad. I thought—"

"Don't think, man. I got you. Don't worry," he said, cutting me off.

"Okay, good to know. Thanks."

We stayed quiet for the rest of the car ride home. I dropped Flyn off at his grandmother's house and drove a few blocks past my apartment to find a parking spot. The craving to smoke was on me, so I leapt up my stairs, grabbed the narcotics, put a fresh pinch in my stem, and headed toward the walking streets of Venice.

There was something in the atmosphere that had me feeling uneasy before I even took a hit. I had a premonition that something was about to go down, but the compulsion to smoke was too strong to worry about intuition. I darted down a narrow sidewalk that separated several small bungalows. No cars were allowed in the walking streets, and at this hour, nobody was around. I was alone in a quaint, upscale neighborhood and could not wait to fill my brain with the ethers of coca as it evaporated under the flame of my lighter. I stopped, crouched, and began to smoke. When I looked up, there was a middle-aged man standing on his front steps a few feet away. He watched me silently, shaking his head in disapproval, and put a small whistle into his mouth. The sound that ensued was not the police whistle burst that I expected, but the tweeting noise of several birds. He blew the bird call three times, and in an instant, several front lights from bungalows that lined the street turned on. It was obviously some sort of signal. I turned and ran as the ancestors began thundering their alarm bells.

"Run away! They know about you," an old man said.

"Get yo' dumb ass home, or you gonna get caught," Lillie said.

"They want to put you in jail," Maxine said.

And as I ran with all my might, the fear washed over me—the fear of being found out, the fear of losing everything, of being alone, of going to jail, of them coming after me.

It was the same fear that began when I was a teenager on a cold winter's day in a frozen field, surrounded by my friends at Timberock Farm.

Chapter Eight

1986, SEVENTEEN YEARS OLD

Having a car at St. Paul's was strictly *verboten*. Not only were we not allowed to have cars, but we couldn't even ride in them, barring some extraordinary circumstance —which I never witnessed in my three years there as a boarder. Even the handful of day students who lived in nearby Concord had to be dropped off and picked up by parents or older siblings. It was well known that having a car was an easy way to get booted from the school. Therefore, it was rare for anyone to smuggle one even remotely close to the well-manicured campus, but I'd decided that Yellow Cabs and Greyhounds were beneath me, so I took a risk and parked my car in the back of the Concord Hospital two miles away. My plan worked, and it stayed there undetected for the fall term. I hadn't had the courage to take it out. I was waiting for the perfect moment, and soon, in the dead cold of winter, it presented itself.

I was in love, or at least as close to in love as I had ever been. I'd met a girl who thought the world of me. She was unlike any of the girls I'd met before. Her hair was jet black, and her eyes dark brown—a far cry from the country club blondes who usually turned my head. She was witty and awkward and bristling with ideas. In a matter of weeks, we were attached at the hip and spent much of our time scrawling down romantic notes on scraps of paper and slipping them into each other's mailboxes.

Sally was long and lean with a hint of scoliosis in her spine. There was something hidden in her face, as if she held an important secret behind her eyes. She was far more interesting than the predictable trust funders at St. Paul's who wore their Nantucket reds and Izod blues. Her sweaters were hand-knit by her mother, who lived in a sustainable home in the Vermont forest with no running water or electricity. Sally had earned her way into St. Paul's. The school had discovered her untapped potential and offered her a full scholarship. That turned me on as well.

By winter term, we were planning a getaway. We'd decided to spend a weekend in Brookfield at my family's farmhouse in the woods. Not only did we commandeer a bunch of psychedelic mushrooms, but there had been hints that the weekend might include the surrender of Sally's virginity. Both events would be firsts and could possibly happen simultaneously. This both excited and terrified us, but nothing had been set in stone.

Sally had invited her best friend Hannah, and I had included my former roommate, Walter. Hannah and Walter were dating, but their relationship seemed to be unraveling, and they hoped a few nights in the country would patch it back together. The four of us spent a lot of time together at school: smoking cigarettes at the Community Center, hanging out in one another's rooms before check-in, and lazing around on the lawns that connected the dormitories of the school. I loved each of them, and for the first time in a while, I had started to like myself again. I mean, I still had the blues, but I could at least tolerate myself when I was around these three. In fact, Hannah's friendship had much to do with my newfound confidence. She was loyal, stupidly funny, and beautiful. Walter was smarter than me in almost every way. He was celebrated by the faculty as one of the most gifted students in our form. He seemed to effortlessly bang out writing that was worthy of publishing and could retain even the most detailed historical information after one reading. His vast knowledge of the Grateful Dead was merely a side note to the well of information that poured out of him. He wore his blond hair like a hipster with long bangs swept over to the side, and his slender body bounced happily down the path less traveled.

Walter and I had become friends the year before, and he was partly responsible for the transformation of my personal style. He steered me away from rugby shirts and OP shorts into a new realm of bohemian couture. He grew up in New York and had an urban hippy for a mother, who had great taste. This had rubbed off on Walter, and he carried it like a flag—a freak flag, if you will.

As third-formers, we had both tried out for JV hockey, and I made it by the skin of my teeth. Walter quit during tryouts after barfing over the boards, but in most things, Walter was better than me. He was the leader, and I was his follower—at least, this was how I felt. He could smoke several bong hits at night and be fully functional the next morning. It seemed like the weed passed right through him, leaving a residue of genius. I wondered how smoking weed could actually make him smarter while it left me crumpled and speechless.

Earlier that year, on Parents Weekend, Walter's mother and father had waited for us in our room during class. We were met with a less-than-cordial greeting when we got there. Walter's dad was holding a small brass box in his hand, which we used to stash our weed. He held it up to his nose and took a whiff.

"What does that smell like to you?" he said angrily. Walter leaned in and took a sniff.

"Brass?" Walter replied. His father shook his head in disapproval.

"Brass?" he said, raising his voice. "Brass? You mean...Panama brass!"

This may have been the single best thing we'd ever heard, and it was almost impossible to keep a straight face.

"Oh, you think this is funny?" Walter's mother added. "And what is this?" she said, holding up a bottle of Budweiser.

My mother had arrived the night before and brought a case of beer that we hid in our illegal fridge. They found that, too. Bummer. There was nothing we could say to defend ourselves, so I pretended I was mute, excused myself, and let Walter take the heat. From that point on, his parents felt that *I* was the bad influence. The way I saw it, though, we both influenced each other, and most of it was positive.

Walter was as close to a best friend as I'd ever had, but there were still plenty of secrets between us. I hadn't told him about my eating disorders and probably never would. I knew every private bathroom on campus and continued to visit them after mealtime. When I felt stressed, the purging got out of control, and the buzz that followed was brief but soothing. I needed to do this, and no one—not even my best friend—could know. He wouldn't understand, anyway.

But this weekend, I wanted to leave it all behind. Love was in the air, and our farm was one of my favorite places in the world: two hundred acres of rolling pastures, canopied woodlands, and picturesque, kitten-infested barns. My mother's property was only a third of the land, but it was positioned on a hill overlooking an ancient pond that Native Americans had named Quaboag, where bald eagles circled overhead and deer bathed in the morning light. It was pure heaven.

So, on a cold afternoon in February, the four of us hopped in a cab and headed toward the hospital. We had to be sure that no one saw us, so I put up my hood, locked my Ray Bans into place, and tied a blue bandana around my face. I must have looked like a bank robber or something. Each of my friends had a makeshift disguise as well. Sally wrapped a multicolored scarf around her head, Hannah slouched under a heavy woolen peacoat, and Walter covered his face with a pair of leather mittens. We were excited to be heading out of Dodge but had to be careful until we hit the open road.

We jumped into the car and immediately became aware of the cold. It was twenty degrees outside, and it would take time for the heater on the dash to warm us up.

"Fire this baby up, Stout. Let's get the heat cranking," Walter said.

"I'm so fucking psyched for this trip, Stout! This is awesome. Can't wait, can't wait, can't wait to get there!" said Hannah.

We inched our way out to the main road, making sure that our faces were concealed. I nervously watched as each car passed, hoping not to lock eyes with a science teacher or hockey coach returning from the grocery store. When we finally reached the interstate, the whole gang let out a sigh of relief, and Hannah began to cheer from the back seat.

"Wahoo! Next stop, Brookfield!" she exclaimed.

"Hey, pop in the Fox and let's get this party started," Walter said.

One of the most coveted Grateful Dead bootleg tapes we owned was from Fox Theatre in Atlanta. The transition from *Scarlet Begonias* into *Fire on the Mountain* was so legendary that, each year, a fifth-former was given the honor of naming his or her room the Fox's Den. A select group at St. Paul's took their Grateful Dead very seriously and was heavily involved with an underground bartering system of live-recorded tapes. Some of the most seasoned collectors had hundreds of cassettes with illustrated covers coded by date, sound quality, region, and overall ranking. The Fox was considered by many to be the Taj Mahal of Dead shows, and when we listened to certain parts, there was no talking allowed. When I popped the cassette into the tape deck and Jerry Garcia's voice began to bellow from the back speaker, we bobbed our heads in silence.

The drive took us three hours, and by nightfall, we were turning right through the trees into our long, winding driveway. A blanket of fresh snow covered the fence posts and invited us to enter this pure, uncontaminated world. The farm had always been this for me—a place to escape from the pressures of life. I had spent most of my summers here and lost myself in the dense hayfields at dusk, hiding away from anything that bothered me.

One field, in particular, was special. I dreamed about it all the time. In the dream, I was part of a Native American ceremony around a bonfire that burned in the center of the field. I belonged to the tribe that lived there, and we danced and chanted in our paint and feathers. I felt a sense of peace that I never experienced while awake, and a calmness seeped from the ground. I had a strong sense that the field was connected to something sacred as we drove past. I rolled down my window to breathe it in.

"There it is. That's my field of dreams," I said.

"What?" Sally asked.

"That field, I dream about it all the time."

"Wow, that's cool," Sally replied.

"Stout, you are a loony bird," Hannah added from behind.

"We're all loony birds," said Walter, "and about to get a lot crazier from the psilocybin in those 'shrooms."

"When should we take them?" Sally asked.

"Maybe we should wait 'til tomorrow morning, so we can cruise through the woods in the sunshine," Walter said. Everyone nodded in agreement.

We pulled up to the old farmhouse. My mother had purchased it from my grandfather in 1971. He had named it Timberock when he bought the land in 1950. It was not a fancy place, with its gray beadboard siding and black tar roof. Inside, an open living room extended up to the second story, where a narrow, banistered walkway extended around the perimeter. It looked like someone had punched a rectangular hole through the first-floor ceiling and bordered it with railings. This gave the house a festive buzz, as people could walk around the second floor and still be part of the activity below.

The walls were covered with my mother's eclectic art from her days in New York City. A signed Warhol lithograph hung next to an eighteenth-century Swedish landscape. The furniture was a mixture of comfort and style stretching back several generations. Everything fit the rooms just so. The wraparound porch with its view down to the frozen lake was closed off for the winter, and its chairs and tables were piled high in the dining room. The house was built for summer and therefore did not have a working furnace. The water was also shut down so the pipes wouldn't freeze and burst. The only heat we would feel over the weekend would be from the stone fireplace that was the centerpiece of the living room. So, immediately upon entering, Walter and I raced down to the woodshed and loaded our arms with freshly cut pine and red oak. There was no time to waste, as the temperature was dropping rapidly.

A second house on the property was inhabited by our caretaker. His name was Renaldo Portofino Sergio Bontempo, or Renny Good Times, as we called him. We considered him family. He was jovial, chubby, and exceedingly hairy, except for the smoothness of his bald head. He had been working for us for nearly a decade, and when he was not playing the tuba in his tighty whiteys, he loved to tell us the sordid tales of his youth. He had been at Woodstock—the only thing he remembered was taking acid and rolling around in the mud.

Renny kept the woodshed stocked in winter and had gone to the store to provide us with essentials to survive the weekend. This included two cases of beer, a bottle of red wine, a five-gallon jug of water, potato chips, English muffins, butter, a dozen eggs, bacon, ham, spaghetti, tomato sauce, and orange juice, which he had all charged to my mother's running account at the local package store. Walking into a kitchen that was stocked with food had become a luxury that I took for granted over the years. Renny was a reclusive oddity with brown teeth and bloodshot eyes, but he sure took care of us well.

When we got back to the main house, the girls had disappeared upstairs, and Walter and I wrestled with the task of building a fire.

We slapped high fives as the wood began to crackle. Pretty soon, the temperature in the room was bearable, and we gladly shucked a few of our outer layers. With fresh beers in hand, we each lit a cigarette and listened as the girls giggled from my mother's upstairs bedroom.

"Carder, is it okay if we raid your mother's closet?" Sally called from above. Her naked shoulder peeked out of the bedroom seductively.

"Totally. Go for it," I responded.

Moments later, Sally and Hannah emerged wearing two of my mother's embroidered silk gowns—a far cry from the bulky sweaters and wool pants that served as their traditional wardrobe at school. They paraded around the upstairs walkway in an impromptu fashion show, and Walter and I egged them on. We pretended to be photographers.

"More, more, yes, beautiful, now make *love* to the camera," I said.

"*Speen, oui*, twirl. That's right. Perfect, gorgeous, *seemply magnifique*," Walter added in a mock French accent.

In that moment, I was suddenly struck by the sheer absurdity of our situation. We were four horny teenagers with a New England farmhouse at our disposal. We were chock-full of supplies and overactive hormones, and we had no one to answer to but ourselves.

Walter uncorked the red wine and decanted it into four crystal goblets that had belonged to my grandmother. They felt entirely out of place in our fumbling hands, but we held them up in a toast as we ate spaghetti with Ragu sauce.

"Here's to having the best weekend of our lives," I said.

"Here's to your mom for letting us come here. And for letting us borrow her, like, amazing clothes—even if she doesn't know it. And here's to all of those lame motherfuckers that are doing homework right now," Hannah said.

"Here is to exploring uncharted territory with some of the coolest folks I know," Walter said.

"And here's to the new beginnings that this weekend will bring. Here's to the love that I feel for all of you. So much love. And for you, Carder, a special butterflies-in-my-stomach kind of love," Sally said, leaning over and giving me a soft kiss.

"Me too," I whispered back. "Me too."

And it was the truth. I was completely in love with Sally. I loved her as much as I could love anything, which, actually, was not that much. I was making a gallant attempt at letting Sally in, but the well of secrets was too deep. I would never tell Sally about the many things that kept me from falling asleep at night. I wouldn't tell her that underneath the thick blond hair and dimples, my confidence was simply an invention, like the projection of the Great Oz. I would never tell Sally about the sadness that stopped me from eating, or the fact that I had a hard time looking in the mirror. I would never reveal that I was lost and broken and scared of my own shadow. I would never tell her that sometimes I thought about ending it all. I would never tell her these things. Never. Instead, I showed her the best parts of me, and it seemed to work, but I was scared to death she would find out the truth. This was my biggest fear. If she peered behind the curtain, then I was sure to be alone. And I couldn't bear the thought of that.

We sat by the fire and drank beer into the night. My friends smoked weed from a glass-blown pipe, but I refrained. I had become increasingly paranoid when I smoked, as if the THC opened a floodgate that allowed my worries to gush in. I didn't want to visit the dark side, so I watched as they started to laugh at each other, and I did my best to feel included.

I slunk in next to Sally and wrapped my arms around her waist. We looked at each other and both knew that we were only moments away from sleeping together. We had been waiting for the right place and time. We climbed under a big down comforter and started to kiss. Walter and Hannah took the hint and retreated upstairs to my mother's room. We heard the door click behind them, and this was our cue to get naked. Our clothes came off, and we wrapped each other in our smooth, teenage limbs. Sally held both of my hands in hers.

"Is this really about to happen? I mean like full on? Like we're about to do the deed?" she asked, half joking.

"Only if you want to. It's up to you," I said.

"Do you want to?" Sally asked.

"Of course I do. I love you, and this seems like the right thing to do. I mean, I know it's your first time, and that it means something, so...only if you are ready."

"I'm ready," she replied.

"You sure?"

"Yes, I'm sure. Now put that thing in me." She laughed.

So I did. And in a matter of a few hurried and uncomfortable moments, her virginity was wedded to the living room sofa forever. Sally turned to me when it was over (probably in two minutes or less) and told me I was a good lover. How would she know that?

"I'm so glad it's over," she said. That didn't make me feel much better either. "I mean, there was so much build-up, and bang, that was it—no more V card on this broad."

"Glad to help you out with that," I said. "Let me know if I can do anything else to serve you, my good maiden." I reached over to the table and grabbed a cigarette. It was pretty cliché, but I had to do it.

The next morning, we all had smiles on our faces as we gobbled down eggs and bacon. What had happened the night before was so obvious that it didn't need to be discussed. Given the sparkle in Walter's eyes and the appetite with which he devoured his breakfast, I was pretty sure that he had gotten laid, too. We planned to let our food digest for at least an hour before taking the mushrooms so that the plant medicine wouldn't upset our stomachs, as psychedelic mushrooms often induced vomiting.

After we cleaned up, Walter grabbed a large cellophane bag from his knapsack and dumped it onto the kitchen counter. The mushrooms looked strange, with their dried stems and petrified caps. The strong odor of toe cheese emanated from the pile and made me feel queasy, but I held my nose and pulled up a stool.

The pile was divided into four equal quadrants containing two and a half grams each. Walter tried to give each portion with the same number of caps, as they were rumored to pack more of a punch than the stems. They certainly looked more edible, anyway. Hannah was the first to grab a handful of fungus.

"Here goes," she said, wolfing down a cap and a stem. "See you lovely folks on the other side when shit gets weird. Just remember I'm your friend, even if my head turns into a dragon."

After Hannah broke the ice, we all followed suit.

"To all of the wisdom that waits for us on the other side," said Sally.

"If I meet God and stare him in the face, I'll let you guys know what he looks like," Walter said.

"If I don't make it back, tell my mother that I loved her. Let her know that I died with a smile on my face," I said.

The morning light was filtering through the clouds as we twirled around and looked at the sky. The snow was like a sound blanket that removed any echoes from the air, so the only noise we heard was the crunching under our boots. The lake was frozen and looked inviting through the leafless trees as we trudged through a wooded patch toward the ice.

When I was a kid, my grandfather would harness his Belgian horses to an old-fashioned ice shaver and carve out a rink in the middle of the lake. That's where I learned to skate at about five years old. After long mornings on the ice, he would glide us through the forest on a horse-drawn sleigh like we were in Narnia or something. My mother captured these days through the lens of her 35mm Nikon camera and put together a hardbound book of her winter photographs. Those were better times. The thought of them made me smile as we walked along the banks toward our lower corral.

"Whoa, I'm starting to really feel something," Sally said, taking my mittened hand in hers. "I feel like I'm myself, but I'm also someone else."

"Yes!" replied Hannah. "Exactly! I'm, like, seeing all of you around me, and everything looks so fresh and crisp, just like it was put here just for us in this moment."

A surge of energy pulsed through my body, and it felt like all of my cells were alive and filled with color. I took off a mitten and looked at my hand as if I was seeing it for the first time. I got lost in the infinite wrinkles that flowed together like the small rivers of northern Australia. I had never been to Australia, but somehow was eminently aware that the grooves on my palm replicated a pattern of rivers there. It was like someone downloaded a megaton of information into my brain, and I understood every bit of it with clarity and precision.

Everything in the universe is thriving with intelligence and holding a bundle of secret messages. I understand it all. We are here to thrive. All life is connected by the same energy. I can hear the water talking. And the wind. The snowflakes are singing.

I had never experienced such an overwhelming sense of calm and, in that moment, I forgot about fear.

There is no past and no future in this liminal space—only the present. The present is the truth. Nothing else matters. I can hear the heartbeat of the universe.

I got up into a crouch and waved at my friends, who I imagined were going through the exact same thing. I couldn't wait to get moving.

"Let's go into the woods and explore," I said. Without waiting for a response, I was running toward the tree line.

We traversed a shallow riverbed and stopped abruptly to look at the frozen roots of a large pine that had toppled over. The root structure was about six feet in diameter and was solidified by a thick veil of clear icicles. It was one of the most extraordinary examples of life that I had ever witnessed.

The tree is breathing an exhaust of oxygen. I can see it.

I held onto a large, protruding root that was still fastened into the ground, and I could hear the faint heartbeat of the tree.

Yes, I hear you. My name is Carder. What? Okay, I'll tell them.

"This tree was planted in 1896 by a farmer who used to live here," I said. "It is happy to be speaking with us."

The sun glistened off the icicles.

Each of the molecules of water inside is alive. How could I have been so blind to the evolutionary principles of nature for this long?

"The tree ain't talking to me, but it *is* amazing," Walter said. "Look at the network of veins that runs through the roots. Makes you wonder how something like this came to be. I mean, who created it?"

God is the creator of all things.

"It was *God*," I said. "I've never been more sure of anything."

"Jury's still out on that one," said Walter.

"God is all around us *right now*," Sally said. "It's not a man with a white beard, but the feeling we have in our bodies. That's God."

That made sense to all of us, and for the next hour, we really thought we were onto something. We were surrounded by examples in the natural landscape of Timberock. I walked out of the woods with my friends, and we moved into the pasture that had invaded my dreams. We sat down in a circle and inhaled deeply as the mushrooms overtook our senses. Bliss. Rapture. Euphoric insight. Answers. Yes, the answers came. All of the questions I ever had about how the world fit together became clear. There was no more uncertainty about anything. I understood the deeper meaning beneath human existence.

We are here to love one another and, through this quest to find acceptance, we are meant to suffer. The suffering gives us the context from which to appreciate. It's that simple.

I tilted my head back and watched as a thin stream of clouds covered the atmosphere, as if our lives were now enclosed by the curve of a gigantic snow globe. I realized that we were not alone in our field and was not surprised to see the lashes of a prodigious eye blinking over our heads. The eye was compassionate and all-knowing, and I knew that God was looking down. God was present not only in the sky but also in my limbs, flowing through my thoughts and spilling down from my lips.

"Do you feel that? Do you feel God?" I asked my friends.

"I feel something, yeah, something powerful," Sally replied.

"It's as if I know for certain that everything is going to be okay," I said. "I've never felt like this before. God is all around us and wants us to know that we're protected and safe and never have to worry."

"What is God?" Walter asked.

"God is the energy moving through you right now," I said.

Until this point, the afternoon had unfolded in a way that I never thought possible. To be suffused by such gratitude was so distant from my ordinary thought process that I felt completely out of sorts. Perhaps this voice was my soul, and I was just meeting it for the first time. I had always claimed the existence of a soul but had never been quiet enough to listen for it. I suppose I had no idea what it was, really. I had knelt in pews and recited prayers and repeated the word *Amen* so many times growing up that I was completely desensitized. During one service in my childhood, when *Amen* punctuated the end of a prayer, I decided that its real meaning was "Thank God this is over."

We never spoke of God in my house, and it wasn't a subject I'd ever broached with my friends, but religious doctrine was the background music from my childhood. I'm not sure why my parents sent me to schools that held mandatory chapel services four times per week. I never opened a Bible on my own and had no desire to hear the so-called word of the Lord. It was just a story. A parable for a purpose. A Grimm's fairy tale to frighten the weak into submission. I was not buying it. Not at all. Well, not until now, anyway.

There was so much God pumping through my mind that all of my doubt had vanished. I was a believer, a man of faith, a prodigal son, a follower, a disciple, and in the midst of my holy vision, I tried to convert my stoned companions. I may as well have been speaking in tongues.

"How could you not feel Him?" I asked Walter.

"I dunno. Is it, like, warm?"

A bank of dark clouds hovered over the sun and diffused the light into a murky fog. Out of the corner of my eye, I saw something strange.

Is that? Holy fuck. It is! A cop car!

It seemed to be heading right for us, and I wondered how it could be moving so fast through the thick undergrowth of the forest. On second glance, I realized that it was barreling across the ice. My heart skipped a beat.

We have been found out.

"Uh, you guys, I think something bad is about to happen. Something terrible. I have a really bad feeling," I said.

"What are you talking about, man. Everything's cool," Walter replied. "Do you know something I don't?"

"They're coming for us! We have to hurry and get back inside. It's not safe here anymore. Bad guys are coming to get us."

I felt Sally's arm around me. "It's all fine, Carder. Everything's beautiful. You're just thinking something is scary, and it seems real to you. We're all okay."

God is gone! He can't protect us anymore.

I began to hyperventilate wildly, and my body became paralyzed with fear. When I looked up, I could see a swarm of monsters gathering slowly on the horizon. Some of them were human and carried hunting bows like the backwoods inbreds of the film *Deliverance*. Others stood twelve feet tall and had tusks the size of my forearms. A low gargle sprang from behind their yellow fangs, and I could hear the sound of howls coming from every direction.

"We have to go! They'll kill us. We have to move, *now*."

"Stout, calm down. Why are you talking about killing? Wasn't God just all around you?" Hannah asked.

"God left. The monsters are here. We have to get back to the house." I meant this with every fiber of my being. I had looked directly into the eyes of the demons from Hell, and they were coming for us.

"Follow me!" I cried as I stumbled across the open field. My friends trampled through the snow in my wake and were soon ahead of me. I saw them peering into the woods.

The house is our only chance to survive.

For the next several hours, I remained huddled in a ball on the living room couch. Every movement and sound that came from the outside thudded through my eardrums. I heard Sally's soft voice singing me a lullaby, but the sound of claws slashing through the upstairs screen was louder.

Now is our time to die.

"They're out there," I said. I was convinced they'd burst in at any moment. "We're no match for them."

"There's no one here but us," Hannah replied, "and we love you. Nothing bad's about to happen. I'm sure of it. I would never let anything happen to you."

"Don't worry, Stout. You're just having a bad trip. Happens sometimes." Walter's voice sounded distant. "It'll pass. Just hold on tight, and it'll be gone."

"Yeah, but you don't understand. It's real. I can hear them. I can see their faces. I'm not making this up," I said.

We are coming to get you, Carder. You can't hide from us.

"Even if they were real, they can't get inside. They haven't been invited in. And if they did somehow, I would totally fuck them up with this." Walter picked up a wrought iron fire poker and swung it around like a sword.

"And I would give them the old karate chop," Sally said, smiling. She leaned in and smothered me with kisses all over my face and head. "It's gonna be okay, I promise. Look at me. Look into my eyes. I'll never lie to you."

But the fear wouldn't let up. I attempted to close my eyes and lie down, but the gargoyles wouldn't let me rest. I was petrified for the remainder of the afternoon and only began to collect myself after drinking several beers. My friends had offered me a can of Budweiser every twenty minutes, and the alcohol was doing its job. Slowly, I could feel the warmth of the fire. Sally took my hand in hers and rubbed it against her face and chest. She kissed my neck and wrapped her paws around my back, pulling me close. She whispered in my ear, "I thought I'd lost you. Don't leave me like that again, okay? I love you."

"I won't. I promise. I love you, too."

"Now let's get up and walk around a little," she said.

"I'd rather stay here for a bit. With your arms around me. Is that okay? I'm still scared."

"Yes, it's okay. Anything you want."

I poked my head up and smiled at Hannah and Walter.

"Yeah! Stout's back," Walter said, a fist in the air.

"No more of this heinous scary shit, Stout. We are surrounding you in a bubble that nobody can get through. Nobody would even dare," Hannah said.

Part of me knew that she was right. I had slept in this house a thousand times, and the only monster that ever drew blood was a mosquito. But part of me was still paralyzed by an icy dread, and I wondered if it would ever go away. For now, at least, I could tuck it away and carry on, but I was sure that from this day forward, I would forever feel it in my blood.

The next day, no one said a word as we zoomed up the Mass Pike toward Boston. I kept drifting over the yellow line as I searched for the faces of the damned in the rearview mirror.

Chapter Nine

2003

Back in the 'hood, it was business as usual. Flyn and I continued our nightly conquest of addicts from all walks of life. I guarded the door as piles of cocaine were dumped onto gilded mirrors in Brentwood. I watched as our powder was snorted from naked breasts, a signed picture of John Belushi, several leather-bound Bibles, a busted Fender guitar, the cracked dashboard of an old Cadillac El Dorado, and a multitude of toilet seats. I witnessed an eccentric old movie producer and his sycophantic minions rifle through the shag carpet searching for shards of crack and winced as a strung-out couple with pipe burns on their lips begged for another gram. I held my breath as lumps of rock cocaine were passed back and forth by well-armed thugs who refused to make eye contact, and I tried to keep my cool as guns were pointed at me on a regular basis. The more I watched, the less I wanted to smoke, but I wasn't ready to quit just yet. I was too accustomed to the suffering.

One night, we delivered an ounce of powder to the presidential suite of a swanky hotel on Ocean Drive. As we walked in, I marveled at the sight of the twinkling boats making their night voyages across the horizon. We were instantly patted down by a small man with a white moustache and terrible breath. He had a double-holstered rig strapped across his chest holding two matching silver-handled pistols. After a thorough groping, he took Flyn's gun from him and waved his finger back and forth. We got the picture. Flyn surrendered his firearm before entering the well-appointed room. There were two white sofas facing one another, each draped with three beautiful young girls wearing lingerie. It was like a promo for some Playboy special at the mansion, only Hef was nowhere to be found. In his place stood a tall, thin man in a fitted suit who was also smoking from a tobacco pipe.

"Flyn, how are you, my friend? It hus been so lung. Yuri missed you," he said, with a warm smile.

"Good to see you, Yuri. I see you're still surrounding yourself with beautiful things," he said, motioning to the couches.

"Yes, my porsonal stable. All de way from Muscow to your door."

"Yuri, this is my partner, Hollywood. I trust him with my life," Flyn said.

I walked over and shook his hand, and he pulled me toward him. He looked me square in the eyes, up close and personal, then released his grip. He wanted to let me know that he was in charge. But I already knew.

"Good lewking boy. It is time for his initiation after we do business," said Yuri. "Give some pruduct to the girls to keep dem busy for now. Put it on de table."

Flyn dumped a mound of powder in the middle of a large glass coffee table. Yuri placed a gold straw and credit card on either side of the pile—a set of utensils for each couch of women. It became a feeding frenzy. The models began to chop and shove and snort and argue. They squabbled among themselves like baby birds fighting for the same ripe June bug. Yuri sat down in a high-backed leather chair and laughed.

"Who need Pay-Per-View when you have dees?" he said. "Seet back and enjoy de show." He puffed on his own tobacco pipe, and I saw the orange glow of a flame brush against the end of his pointed nose. His black beady eyes, those of a classic villain from the silent era, surveyed the room while he stewed the amber coals with the end of a small blade. He gestured for Flyn to come over, and they began the transaction. I saw Yuri count out several $100 bills and put the product into a wooden box. He looked over at me and motioned toward the girls.

"Which one of dem you vant?" he said.

"Oh no, that's okay. I have a girl, and we're cool. Thanks, though."

His mouth curved downward, and his cheeks hardened.

"We all have good vimen at home, but we are not home now. Enjoy. Dey are de best in de vorld. I insist," he said.

"Thank you so much, but—"

"Now! *Choose!* Are you some sort of faggut?" he yelled at me, as if I had committed some grave offense. Perhaps I had. I'd never been to Russia and had no idea about their customs—especially not the Russian Mafia.

The girls had straightened up at the sound of Yuri's voice and were now giving me sultry bedroom eyes and pursed lips while rubbing their boobs together and licking their teeth. This exact scene may have actually taken place in one of my wet dreams as a teenager, but in reality, their overtures made me feel shy. I reached my arm around a blonde with a pale complexion and soft chin. She barely fit into the teddy she was wearing, and I could see wisps of pubic hair underneath the mesh netting. I was more frightened than aroused. I looked over at Flyn, who nodded his head and attached his eyes to mine with a dead stare. This was not an option.

"Go to de bedroom at de end of de hall," said Yuri, smiling at me with his yellow-stained teeth. And off we went—my personal concubine following close behind like a jeweled tugboat being towed into the harbor. We walked quickly without speaking and entered a large guest room with a king-sized bed.

"Nice place," I said, nervously. I had no intention of sleeping with this girl I didn't know. I was never prone to one-night stands or sex with prostitutes, and I wasn't about to start because some Russian mobster ordered it. Now that we were behind closed doors, I began to relax a little and thought I could persuade this young beauty to simply be my friend. My noble ambitions were thwarted almost immediately.

"You like to fak?" she said, and took off her teddy. Her thin body was perfectly proportioned, and she looked like she was sixteen. I sat down in an upholstered armchair and chose my words carefully.

"Yes, I like to fak, but not right now. I think you are beautiful, but I have a wife, and I want to be faithful," I lied. I could see concern on her teenage face as her cheeks became flushed.

"You need to fak me. I am good. I like strong fakking. I please you," she said.

"I know you would please me. Of course. But I would rather talk to you and get to know you a little."

"Yes, you can. But Yuri is mad if ve cannot fak. He vill punish me. So, you fak me, yes?" she replied.

"How old are you?" I asked.

"Old enough to make good fakking," she said.

"You are. I'm sure. But tell me how old, really."

"I am sixteen years."

I instantly felt sorry for her. I wanted to protect and take care of her—to help her escape. The thought of my younger sisters propelled me into older brother mode.

"You like young? I am fresh and ready. I am tight like wurgin. You see," she said.

"I'm too old for you. More than twice your age. I could be your father," I said.

"Yes, many fadders want to fak me."

"Do you like doing this? Are you happy?" I asked.

"I happy ven you happy. Ven you cam, I happy. Ven you cam, Yuri happy." I felt sad for this girl who was so far away from her parents. I wondered if she had been snatched in the night or sold at auction for a fistful of sweaty rubles. I wanted to help her, but I didn't know how. Not sleeping with her was the obvious choice, but I didn't want her to feel rejected or get into trouble. I went over to the bed, turned down the sheets, and threw the pillows on the floor to feign activity. I rolled around in the bed for a few moments. She stared at me, perplexed.

"Put this back on, please," I said.

"But Yuri—"

"I will tell Yuri that you were the best sex I've ever had in my life. I promise."

She looked a bit hurt but shrugged her shoulders and hopped onto the mattress.

"As you vant," she said.

I sat back down in the chair and watched as the little girl in her appeared. She twirled her hair around and bounced up and down.

"What's your name," I asked.

"Kristina. My name Kristina."

"I'm Carder. Nice to meet you, Kristina. Where are you from? Where did you grow up?" I asked.

"I live in small willage vith two brathers and madder and fadder. I go to school and vurk in de fields. I like dis more better. Yuri give me nice cluthes. Beautiful hotel and French fries. I lub French fries. All day I eat French fries and moostard." She smiled.

"How did you get here? I mean from your village to here."

"Last year, man, he come to willage. He pay much money to Fadder for me. I am like prize. I go to Muscow and then on airplane to Hollyvood. Yuri take good care for me. He like my fadder."

Yes, Yuri was like her father—both of them exploiting her for money. Hearing her story made me never want to have sex again. I couldn't believe how flippant she was about her captivity in the sex trade. She was caught and trafficked and never looked back, and she thought this was a better life for her. I would have picked planting beets and potatoes over getting naked with fat, old, rich men, but what did I know? To her, coming to California was hitting the jackpot, and some carnal activity here and there was her bus ticket to freedom.

We walked down the hall holding hands and reemerged in the palatial living room. I wore a grin on my face like I had just tried heroin for the first time, but I wasn't a very good actor and was hoping he wouldn't sniff me out. Yuri gave me the once-over with his black eyes and drank in my giddy expression.

"She is de best, no?" he said.

"Best sex of my life," I said, as promised. Kristina stood next to me, her fingers ablaze in my hair. I leaned over and gave her a sweet kiss on the cheek. And we said our good-byes.

I pulled up to a stoplight on Main Street and turned to Flyn. "I mean, who the fuck travels around with six teenage girls? Never seen anything like it."

"You fuck her?" Flyn asked.

"Yeah," I lied.

"Good. That's good for business. Don't want to mess with a guy like Yuri. Wind up in a ditch with your throat slit. He's a thug in a thousand-dollar suit."

I simply nodded.

"I got some cash for you," Flyn said, stuffing a few hundreds into my top pocket. "I'll be gone for a few days—heading up north with Lyss. But don't forget about Saturday. It's B's birthday, so come on over at four for a BBQ in the backyard. Get her a gift. She likes that." Flyn hopped out of the car.

Back at my apartment, there was an eviction notice on the door. I tried my key in the lock, but it wouldn't turn. *Motherfucker. Did I just get evicted?* My rat hole was starting to stink, and I hated returning home after our runs, anyway. I guess I wouldn't have to worry about that now. I had a pocket full of dope and a crack pipe in my shoe, so I was good for the next several hours. I knew that the ghosts were waiting on the other side with all of their enthusiastic judgment, and that was the price I had to pay to get high. Sometimes, it felt like it wasn't worth it, and I would hold off for as long as I could, but in the end, my pipe always prevailed. It just sat there begging me to smoke it, and after the third or fourth time of saying no, I caved. I ducked into the back alley and took a big hit.

"Get your ass out the gutter," Lillie said, as I exhaled the chemical smoke from my lungs.

"Watch out for the police, they're out tonight," said Maxine.

I heard the same old song in my head as I strolled down the boulevard. Tonight, for some reason, the voices were getting to me. Maybe the spirits were right. I had to get out of Venice before it was too late. I had to stop smoking. I was killing myself way too fast, and I wasn't ready to die just yet. I still had things to do with my life and didn't want to exit on such a low note. If only I could make some money—I mean real money—then maybe I could fly far away from here. I could find a place where there was no crack and no street dealers and no 'hood. I would find a place where no one had ever heard of me and start over completely. Maybe I could be a farmer or a writer or a teacher. Maybe I could be a father to two beautiful kids who would shout my name and jump into my arms every time I walked through the door. Maybe I could find a woman who loved me and thought I was the cat's meow—or maybe I was just dreaming. These things were for other people—not me. I didn't deserve these happy things. I hadn't earned them. But right there on the street, I got onto my knees and began to pray. I prayed for a way out. I prayed for the strength to put away the pipe and to never do drugs again. The jubilant cheer of my ancestors was deafening.

But for the time being, I needed a place to sleep. Well, not really sleep, as there was no way I could possibly doze off with crack running through my veins. I had never been homeless before—not even close. I had always had a place to return to somewhere in the world. I laughed at myself for a bit. *From a penthouse in SoHo to the streets of Venice. You stupid fuck.* How the hell did this happen to me? Well, I knew exactly how it did—I was definitely not a victim of circumstance. I was suddenly filled with a wave of remorse and disgust like someone had just doused me with a pile of fresh shit. There had to be an end to this, or I wouldn't make it out alive. I walked down to boardwalk and approached a homeless couple sitting on the steps of an abandoned building. It was now or never.

"Hey, how are you guys doing?" I asked.

The guy stood up abruptly, letting me know that he wasn't interested in my pitch.

"Just keep walking, motherfucker. We don't got nothing for you. So move on." He gave me a solid shove, and I reeled backward. I held up my hands and smiled.

"No, man. I'm not asking for anything. I want to give you something. That is, if you want it," I said. He sized me up for a bit.

"Okay, what do you got?"

"I have a brand-new, clean pipe and a fifty piece of pure crack cocaine. The really good shit. I don't want it anymore. It's all yours," I said.

The girl jerked up from her perch and joined her boyfriend.

"Fucking yeah right I want it, bitch," she said, inches from my face. I could smell the stench from her armpits and nearly gagged—rotten cheese in a dumpster. I reached into my pocket and delivered on my promise, handing over two dice-sized nuggets and a pipe. As I gave them away, I felt completely free—like I was standing naked in a downpour of warm rain that cleansed me of my wrongdoings. Maybe this would be the last of it. I walked away without turning back and skipped down the road like I was a little boy.

You see a lot of strange things on the boardwalk at night. Mis-shapen hookers giving hand jobs out in the open air. Old men playing bugles to imaginary flagpoles. Junkies rummaging through trash bins for half-eaten gobs of food. Domestic brawls involving sunburned runaways beating each other down with tent poles. Fits of hysterical laughter and painful crying bouncing back and forth through the hazy night air. Angry hippies playing broken guitars in circles full of confused, underaged dope fiends. I had seen enough and wanted no part of it anymore. I walked as far down the beach as I could, sat down underneath a lifeguard station, and watched the waves until sunup.

I spent the next five nights sleeping in the same spot. I didn't dare return to my apartment, as I imagined my landlord waiting there—demanding that I pay the back rent that was owed. I didn't have it, for one, but I also had no intention of paying it. I didn't want to live there anymore and was ready to pack my things. I just needed somewhere to go. The days of homelessness were a breeze, really. I walked around the streets and alleyways of Venice collecting useful items. I found an old white painting tarp riddled with multicolored stains that would become my blanket for the next week. I found a stack of paperback books behind an apartment building and grabbed a copy of Pablo Neruda's *Extravagaria*, *Crime and Punishment* by Dostoevsky, and *Less than Zero* by Brett Easton Ellis. Over the next few days, I read every word. I sat on the beach moving back and forth to find the shade under palm trees. In the heat of the afternoons, I plunged into the Pacific Ocean in my boxers, washing the grime from my body. The nights were cold and lonely, and I shivered for hours underneath my makeshift blanket, but the sun always came up, and with every new day, I

felt stronger. Saturday rolled around pretty soon, and it was time
to see my friends again. I couldn't wait to get there.

By the time I arrived at B's house, the party was in full swing.
There were friends and family members spilling out onto the street
and crowding her small front lawn like they were waiting for a float
to pass by in the Macy's Thanksgiving Day Parade. And they were
dressed to the nines, too: folks of all ages with their bright eyes
and shiny shoes. There was one commonality that bound them
together in a way that left no room for interpretation, and this was
their brown complexion. I was the odd man out and stared down
at the whiteness of my hands as I walked up the front path. I was
instantly met with turning heads, and eventually, an arm came
down to block the way. It was the long, slender arm of a teenage
boy whose expression said, *Not on my watch.*

"You lost or sumpin', cracker. We ain't ordered no pizza, and
ain't nobody need an encyclopedia or life insurance or no shit like
that. You feel me?" he said, standing up over me. A few other boys
quickly assembled on either side of him.

"Nah, it's cool. B invited me. I'm Hollywood—Flyn's friend."

The three of them looked at me with their brows raised and
mouths open before turning to each other.

"Yo, go check this out. Get my homeboy, Flyn, and let's see 'bout
this," one of them said to the other. At this point, a good portion
of the crowd was now watching me and whispering among themselves. Most times I showed up with Flyn it was like this, so I was
used to it, but it still felt terrible. It reminded me of being picked
last at recess or getting dumped by a girlfriend, only there was a
different kind of hatred involved. I represented all things white
and had therefore earned their distrust in a historic sort of way,

so I accepted their dismissal without taking it personally. Besides, I was getting used to being the minority in the room. I guess Flyn had forgotten to say that a skinny white dude wearing his brother's clothes was invited to the party. For a moment, I felt like hauling ass down the sidewalk, but decided to hold fast.

I stood and waited, feeling clumsy and out of place. From down the interior hallway, I could hear the gleeful bellow of Flyn's voice.

"Hollywood? Hollywood? Get your ass inside," he said, brushing past the teenage watchdogs flanking the front door. He then turned toward everyone on the front lawn and said, "Everybody, this is my brother Hollywood. I know he's white, but he's got a black heart inside his chest." Flyn began to laugh and slap his knee as if he were Richard Pryor or something. Pretty much everyone started laughing—at my expense, of course, but it felt good to get an endorsement, even if it was in jest. Flyn proceeded to take me around the house, introducing me to all sorts of cousins with big hair, friends with kind faces, kids with their butts hanging out of their jeans eating hot dogs on a stick, aunts wearing pointy green shoes, uncles with thick beards smoking thin cigars, neighbors with freckles and shaved heads, and a group that looked like they were flying the blue flag of the Shoreline Crips. This ominous bunch occupied one corner of the backyard. There were about ten of them, all wearing hoodies and bandanas, and I could tell that most of them were strapped. Flyn marched me right up and pushed me in the middle of the circle. Baptism by fire.

"Yo, this is my partner in crime, Hollywood. If you see him around the 'hood, don't shoot him. He's usually with me." The Crips held out their hands one by one and grabbed mine with a firm slap and side shake. They were not a chatty bunch and had no intention of including me, but they weren't giving me attitude, either. I was always safe in Flyn's company. He was like the ambassador of the 'hood, and the guy who appointed him—the president—well, he was standing right next to me.

Treacherous Wallace was a sight to behold. He had a gold chain around his neck that looked like the kind of rope you used to climb in gym class, and at the end of it was a large "T" encrusted with hundreds of diamonds. He was wearing a blue suit and a yellow Edwardian hat with a blue feather protruding from the band. When he walked through the garden, the crowd parted, as if getting too close were a death sentence or something. He tapped his black platform boots to the rhythm of a Run DMC song and tightened his grip around my shoulder.

"I hear you and Flyn is doin' good things around town. You know he my cousin, and we look out for each other," he said, lighting a Benson and Hedges 100 and blowing the smoke at my forehead.

"Yeah, Flyn is taking good care of me."

"Good. As it should be. Flyn is straight up," he said. He paused for a minute and looked at me with a serious expression. "Listen, I gots somethin' I want you to do. Somethin' I gots to get done. Somethin' needs to be picked up. Pays real good. Flyn told me you cool." He paused for a moment, sizing me up. "So, you cool?"

"Yeah, I'm cool," I responded.

Flyn came up from behind us. He pulled me aside. "Listen, Hollywood, I told Trech that you could do something for him. Don't let me down now. Let's go inside and talk for a minute."

And just like that, I was whisked away from any hope of revelry to talk about some business deal that had me spooked. Why would they need me, anyway? Didn't make sense. I managed to blow a kiss to Beatrice as we hurried by and held up my finger to say *I'll be back in a minute.* She smiled at me and waved. It was her day, and she was the center of attention, so I didn't feel like I was being rude.

There was something about Treacherous Wallace that turned my stomach into knots instantly. Maybe it was the fact that he killed people for a living, or maybe it was the way he snatched away Tisha's dignity with his fists, or maybe it was his evangelic confidence that shook me to the core. There was a shiftiness about him that made me feel like I was standing in quicksand; I tried to move, but I was sinking. Rumor had it that he'd committed his first murder at eleven and had added a few dozen since then. He had risen through the ranks of the Shoreline Crips at a meteoric pace and was now overlord of everything that law enforcement tried to stop. He peered down at me as he spoke. I could smell Olde English on his breath.

"So, you gonna do this?"

"I'll do almost anything once," I responded.

"Hollywood is cool, yo. You can trust him. He good peeps," Flyn added.

"My cousin here think you can do the job. You got a car, right?" said Trech.

"Yeah, it's parked down the block."

"And you clean. No arrests, no warrants?"

"No, nothing like that. I've been lucky, I guess," I said.

"Clean and innocent like an Indiana farm girl," Flyn joked.

"Good, good. I need someone got a clean record do a run for me. A *big* run. Some stone-cold criminals holding seven keys for me. At the border. If you go get 'em for me, I'll take care of you. Half now, and half when you deliver. What you think?"

"I'm cool with it. But why me? I know you got plenty of people working."

"True that. True that. But a white dude with a clean record slip in and out just like that, and nobody gonna pay no mind. My people is tracked. You feel me?" he said.

"You're like a ghost. Trech needs him a ghost," Flyn said.

"Yeah, I get it. I'm less conspicuous."

"You's a hot commodity, Hollywood. Ain't no 5-0 looking for you," Trech said.

"When do you need me, and where do I go?" I asked.

"Monday. Eleven AM. Motel 6. At the border. Room 224. You got it?" he said.

"How do you know it's room 224?" I asked.

"Same room as last time. Got it?"

"Yeah, I got it."

He took a small knapsack from under the bed and handed it to me.

"When you get there, give 'em this. Don't open it. Just give it to them. They gonna know you're coming. It's gonna be real. Grab the product and bring it back to me. Here in the 'hood. Ask anybody, an' they'll find me. If anything happens like you get pulled over and arrested—well, that *your* dope. You gonna take the heat. You doin' this alone. And when you get out of jail, 'cuz you lost my money, I'm gonna hurt you real bad. If anything happens to *this* money, anything at all," he said, holding up the knapsack, "like it don't get there or disappears or comes up short even one dollar and you decide to leave town, well, it won't matter, I'll find you and cut off all your fingers before I kill you real slow. Then I'll kill Tisha—I know you sweet on her. Then I'll find your family. I got people all over this world work for me. Ain't nobody gonna hide.

These motherfuckers you dealin' with are mad dangerous. They in the *Car-tel*. They *might* kill you. Always gotta keep that in mind. If they in a bad mood, they probably gonna shoot you. Now you know. Big risk, big reward. Pays ten large. Half now. You wanna back out, that's okay, too. But I needs to know. So, we cool?"

He was right in my face. I felt like I was going to piss my pants. Everything in my body told me to turn down the offer and walk away for good, but I latched onto the bag and stepped back.

"Easy money," Flyn said, "easy money. I'd do it myself, but I promised B I'd look out for her."

"Yeah, we cool," I said, terrified. Trech reached into his pocket and took out a roll of cash as round as a soda can. He moved over to the bed and counted out piles of twenties, fifties, and hundreds. This was the most money I had seen in several years, and I began thinking about how I would spend it. *A new pair of sneakers. A haircut. A necklace for Tish. Turn on the electricity. Go out to eat. Fill my gas tank. Turn on hot water. Get a phone. Buy a carton of Camel Lights.* He stepped away from the bed and wadded up his roll with a thick rubber band before stuffing it into the lining of his velvet jacket.

"When you touch that cash, we in bizness. You feel me?"

I stared at it.

"Go get it," Flyn said.

"Might as well," I said, collecting the bills and putting them in my pocket. It was on. No backing out now. If I backed out, I'd be executed within a week. The Crips were serious about keeping their word and had no tolerance for anyone who broke theirs. It was a code they never strayed from—not for anyone. If they promised you something, they would deliver. If you promised them something and did not deliver, well, that broke the code. When you broke the code, you basically signed your own death warrant, and they would come looking for you. Flyn told me they once tracked down a guy on a sailboat miles off the coast. They came in a Zodiac in the middle of the night and took him out to sea. They chopped him up with an axe and fed him to the sharks before the sun came up. Flyn was full of these stories—many of them he'd witnessed firsthand. He'd told me that his killing days were over, and I believed him, but some days, it seemed like he was itching to pull the trigger just one more time—especially when he hung out with his cousin Trech. Proximity to his cousin brought out the worst in him. I could understand why Beatrice wanted them separated. Just like the Crips, Flyn kept his word, and he had promised to stay away from gang activity. Beatrice made him swear, and that was that.

The door to the bedroom flew open, and there she was in all her glory. The birthday girl at last. She didn't look happy and scanned the room. Flyn looked surprised and guilty.

"What is goin' on in here? Now why you gotta get Codder messed up in some of yo *bull*shit? Franklyn, what's goin' on?"

"We was just telling Trech about our movie idea," I said, quick on the draw.

"Yeah, Trech might want to invest some green in the project. We straight. Nothing bad is going on here. All aboveboard," Flyn said.

"Yeah, we straight," Trech confirmed.

Beatrice turned to Trech with a suspicious eye.

"Now, you is my nephew, and I do love you, but I know what you doin'. I ain't no fool. Do what you want, but don't drag my children with you. You hear me? Franklyn's not been out of prison but for a bit. He ain't goin' back," Beatrice said.

Trech nodded his head.

"We hear you, loud and clear," I responded. "Don't worry, B, I wouldn't get involved in anything bad. We're talking about the movie idea. That's it."

"Word," said Trech.

"BeeMa, come on now. It's your birthday. Don't get all riled up about nothing. Let's get back to the party. You got people waiting on you," Flyn said.

Trech walked past us and slithered his way through the door without looking back. Flyn attempted to grab B's arm, but she brushed him off and put her hand on my shoulder.

"Franklyn, I'll be out in a minute. Let me and Codder talk for a bit. I'll see you out back, and you better not be lyin' to me. If you is—gonna be hell to pay," she said.

"All right, BeeMa, I'll be right outside," he said, exiting the room and closing the door behind him.

I felt a little sheepish, like I had been caught watching an X-rated movie by my mother or something. Here we were, back in Willy's room with all of the trophies and photos that I had seen before. Here I was, wearing his creased shirt, jeans, and Adidas—didn't seem right that such a nefarious conversation had just taken place in here. I was ashamed, really, and took a deep breath to clear my mind of the self-loathing that was pooling below the surface. I tried to crack a smile.

"I come in here every day. Makes me feel like I'm still his grandma. Wash his clothes, change the sheets like he's gonna come home with his basketball. He used to bounce it all over my floors. Drove me crazy," she said.

I had no idea how to respond, so I just stood there and listened.

"So senseless. These streets is poison, baby. If you walk on them for too long, that poison gonna rise up through your feet and land in your heart. You ain't got no business bein' in the game, Codder. Gonna end up getting hurt."

"I can take care of myself, B. Thank you. I'm careful and won't do anything dangerous," I lied.

"Willy was just walking to the bus stop. He was careful, too. Look what happened. I don't want you to get hurt, baby," she said.

I reached into my back pocket and produced a small box that I had wrapped in silver paper with a gold string and bow. I thought now would be an appropriate time to change the subject. I handed it to B and watched as her eyes lit up.

"For me? You didn't need to get nothing for Ole B, but thank you. I likes me a gift," she said.

"I heard that," I said.

I watched as she unwrapped the paper carefully and folded it neatly on the chair. She put the small cardboard box next to her ear, shook it a few times, and her smile got bigger.

"The keys to the kingdom?" she asked.

"Well, kind of, go ahead and open it."

Beatrice took off the lid and pulled out a shiny silver chain with a small cross at the end. I had found it at a junk shop on Abbot Kinney and was told by the owner that it was an antique. Anything to make a sale, I guess. But I thought it was perfect and would fit the occasion nicely, as I knew of B's dedication to the Lord. She instantly put it around her neck and stood up to glance in the mirror.

"This is my favorite gift of all of them. Thank you. Means so much to me. I love you, baby."

"I love you, too, B."

It had been quite some time since I'd used that phrase, and even longer since I'd actually meant it, but it rolled off my tongue with the full sincerity of everything I believed in—which wasn't that much, really. But it still was a powerful statement of how I felt about her. She was part Lillie B., part mother, and part friend. I desperately needed her in my life to remind me of the goodness I still had. In a strange way, I felt her suffering dissipate when I allowed her to care for me. She was ready to assume the role of my guardian, and I was happy to have her. I didn't want to let her down. I didn't want to lie anymore. I had no idea how to stop. Beatrice gave me a hug and headed toward the door. She opened it and turned toward me.

"Listen baby, what you doin' tomorrow morning?" she asked.

"Nothing. No plans."

"Be here at 9:30 in the morning. I got something I want you to do," she said.

"I'll do anything for you, B. I hope you know that," I said.

"I do, baby. I do."

My desire to smoke had left me. Perhaps it was because I felt connected to someone that was considerate and kind. I lay down in the back seat of my car and tried to forget about the deal I had made with the devil. I closed my eyes and waited for sleep to come—and it did. The birds woke me up at dawn and, for once, I didn't hate them so much.

I rang the doorbell, and Beatrice pulled me inside with a laugh. She was wearing a polyester floral dress, mid-calf in length, and the cross I had given her shone from the cradle of her neck. I saw that she had makeup on and wondered why she was so dressed up. We stood in the front hallway for a moment as she gathered her things.

"Do you need me to give you a ride somewhere? My car's outside."

"No baby, we don't need the car. We walkin' this morning. We walkin' to church," she said.

I was dumbfounded. *Church. Church. Fucking church.* Served me right. I regretted giving her the necklace immediately—wished I had brought flowers instead. The last time I had been in any kind of formal church setting was back at St. Paul's. I hated it back then and swore off organized religion moving forward. But maybe a bit of the gospel would push me forward toward salvation—whatever that was.

"Go back into Willy's room. I pressed a shirt for you. It's laying on the bed," she said, patting my chest.

The shirt was bright blue, and it fit perfectly. I surveyed the room and winced when I thought of the dirty bag of gang money I had strapped to my back. I hadn't taken it off since last night. I turned to a glossy shot of Willy smiling at the camera and addressed the photo.

"I'm sorry, Willy. You deserve better."

Out on the street, the 'hood was quiet. It seemed like no one was awake yet, or at least not the people I associated with. Beatrice linked her arm in mine, and we walked slowly down the sidewalk. I felt proud to be on her arm—much more satisfied than walking down the red carpet with the flavor of the month back in New York. I realized that this was the first time I was in the 'hood for noble purposes, unrelated to the solicitation, selling, or manufacturing of narcotics. There was life on the other side. This was a new beginning. At least, that's how it felt as we walked down Seventh Street.

"You know, baby, Willy used to walk me to church sometimes. He'd drop me down the block, though. Never went inside, not even once. And Flyn, well, you couldn't drag him this way if you tried.

Somethin' 'bout the Lord disagreed with those boys. Don't matter. We all got our beliefs. Don't make me love 'em any less. I know what I believe, though. Part of who I am. Don't go every Sunday, though—just once in a while. God lives in my heart. Don't need a church to prove that. What do you believe, Codder?" she said.

I thought for a few seconds.

"That's a good question, B. I'm not sure how to answer. Not sure what I believe."

"Give it a try," she said, squeezing my hand.

"Okay, well, I know there is an afterlife. Of that, I'm sure. I talk to my ancestors all the time. They speak to me. Sounds crazy, I know, but it happens. I don't know where they are, but I imagine it's some sort of heaven. I mean, not like the Christian heaven up in the clouds, but more like some other dimension or something," I said.

"Good, baby. That's good. We all gotta believe. The good Lord knows you and will do right by you if you let Him," she said.

As we walked down the block, I could see other families moving toward the church a few streets down. Grandsons in brown and black suits walked arm in arm with their radiant grandmothers. Children of all ages in their Sunday best scampered down the street, girls with their tights pulled high and red ribbons bouncing on their braids. People stopped to greet one another and gathered in small circles up and down the block. As we got closer, the stares began. At first, they were racial in nature, but then there was more of a look of amazement on their faces, like someone had just jumped out of a cake or parachuted from the sky. We approached a large cluster of family clogging the divine pathway, so we stopped for a minute to wait our turn.

The mother of the bunch turned to B and spoke. "Beatrice, how are you, dear. Haven't seen you for a bit. You look nice."

"Thank you. You do, too. This is my friend, Codder. He's walkin' me to church today," Beatrice said.

"Oh, isn't that nice," she responded. "Beautiful morning for church."

I hadn't realized that I'd been invited to the most prestigious social event of the week. It was like the Met Ball of the 'hood, and tickets were hard to come by. If I had come with anyone else, I would have been stopped at the gate. As we came closer to the church, I recognized a few of the younger folk sitting outside on a brick wall. They were the dealers that I had scored from so many times. They seemed embarrassed to be all gussied up in their starched collars and buckled shoes, but they cocked their necks back to acknowledge me anyway. I smiled back as if to say, *How funny to see you here.* They were each flanked by family members—younger brothers and sisters, mothers and grandmothers. Today, there would be no selling crack to strangers. Today, everyone got a free pass, and no one would get shot. Not on Sunday. Sunday in the 'hood.

Beatrice continued to introduce me around, and I actually started enjoying myself. I said things like "What a beautiful dress" and "Your son looks just like you" and "So happy to meet you," and for once, I felt like a human being in the 'hood. I had walked these sidewalks so many times desperate to score, with my head pounding and tongue hanging out. Beatrice was showing me a side that I had never known. There was a tight community here of families who had grown up together while drugs ravaged the sidewalks outside their bedroom windows. It was a different face, and I immediately wanted to kiss it on the cheek, but I held back and tried my best to be cordial.

When we got to the front door of the church, we were greeted by the minister. He held out his hand to me and said, "We are all welcome in God's house. I am so happy you could join us this morning."

"Thank you, sir. It's a beautiful church, and what a perfect morning for a service, but I'm just walking Miss Beatrice to her seat," I said.

"Great to see you, B," he said, giving her a hug. "Well, please come join us some other time, then."

This was my invite.

"I will. Yes, I will."

I walked Beatrice to the second row and helped her sit down. The church was almost full now, and I was the only white man for miles. I knew that this wasn't my place, but a big part of me wished it was. I felt better than I had in years.

"Thank you, Codder. The Lord loves you," B said.

"My pleasure, B. I know he does."

I took one last look at the rows of smiling faces before heading out the door.

Chapter Ten

1997, TWENTY-EIGHT YEARS OLD

The whole place was a front, and it was obvious if you were looking. The shelves were barely stocked with anything worthwhile—just a row of Cup O' Noodles and endless cans of refried beans and crushed tomatoes. I had never seen anyone make a food purchase or even buy cigarettes. People didn't come here for those things—they went to the deli for their groceries and smokes. No, this was a distribution center for good cocaine. The coke hadn't been stepped on too badly and delivered a great high. I couldn't wait to get my hands on some. I walked past the understocked shelves and knocked four times on a metal door in the back. That was the secret code.

I placed my money on a metal card table and watched as two Hispanic men counted it. They had dealt to me a few times before, so they seemed at ease as they slid five plastic bags my way—each holding a gram. I saluted, smiled, and hurried back to the cab that was double-parked outside. I would be the hero of the night. I decided to sample the product before I got there, so I used my apartment key to scoop from a baggie as we headed down Houston Street. I shoveled a blast into each of my nostrils, and within seconds, the ringing in my ears was so loud that I could barely hear the driver when he turned around.

"Hey, I'd put that away. We're getting pulled over."

"What?" I said frantically, as a million thoughts rushed through my brain. Man, this is good shit. I was blasting off to another planet.

"The cops. They're walking up now. Be cool," he said.

How could I possibly be cool right now? I'm way too high. Fuck, I'm done for.

The knocking of a flashlight on both back windows of a cab is not a pleasant sound when you have dope in your pocket. The right back door flew open, and a middle-aged officer with a moustache leaned in.

"Sir, I'm gonna need you to step out of the car," he said.

No way I can pull this off. Slap the cuffs on me right now. Save yourself some time. Jail. Shit. I don't want to go to fucking jail.

"Is there an issue, officer? Can I help you with something?" I asked, desperate.

"Please get out of the car, now. Don't make me ask you again."

He knows I'm high. It's so obvious. What the fuck is going on?

I got out of the cab and stood in front of two of New York's finest. They didn't look pleased. They sized me up before speaking.

"What's your name," a short stump of a cop asked, looking up at me with a frown.

"Carder," I stammered.

I'm gonna have a heart attack right here. They won't need to take me to jail. I'll never make it.

"Let me see your license, Carder," he replied. I handed it to him, and he read it aloud.

"Carder Stout, 29 King Street, Penthouse B," he replied and turned to his partner. "This kid lives in a penthouse. Must be nice. What's it like living in a penthouse?"

Are you serious? Is this a test? What the fuck?

"It's nice," I said.

"There are no penthouses where you're going tonight. More like the opposite of a penthouse, really," a cop said.

"Yeah, more like a basement studio with no windows," his partner said, laughing.

Why are they laughing at me? Who are these guys? I could run away right now. Down Houston. Bad idea, bad idea. Shit.

"I'm not sure what's going on, sir. I was just in a cab going to meet some friends. Not sure why you pulled me over," I said.

I know why. They saw me buy coke. They saw me snort coke. They know what I have in my pocket. I'm so high right now.

The taller cop scratched his blond moustache and put his arm around me.

"Right now is one of the most important moments of your life. If you lie to us, we're gonna take you to jail. It's probably not where you want to go tonight. But, if you tell the truth, well, we may be a bit more lenient. So I'm gonna ask you this once and only once. Were you in that bodega on Tenth Street buying cocaine?"

Motherfucker. If I say yes, they'll bust me and I'll go to jail. If I say no, then they'll know I'm lying and bust me and put me in jail.

There's no way out of this. Fuck. I wish my mother were here. She'd know what to say. I miss you Mom.

"Sir, I was just getting some—"

"Remember what happens if you lie," the fire hydrant of a cop said, cutting me off. *Oh, what the fuck.* As I said the words, I couldn't believe they were coming out of my mouth. I was doomed.

"Yes, I was buying cocaine," I said.

"Let me see it," the blond cop said.

Really? You're about to give drugs to a cop. This is a Class A felony. If you hand it over, you'll regret it for the rest of your life. You'll lose everything. Everyone will find out you're a drug addict.

I reached into my pocket and took out one of the blue plastic baggies. I handed it over and stared at the ground. I could feel my whole body shaking and my heart pounding. This was it. The officer opened the baggie and tasted it. He passed it to his partner.

"Yup, it's the blue baggies. It's the same stuff. It's what we're looking for."

His partner held the baggie for a minute and handed it back. Then all eyes were on me.

"Tell us everything," he said. "In great detail. If you leave anything out, we're gonna book you," the officer said.

They're gonna book me anyway, so what the fuck.

"I went to the bodega. A friend told me about it. I went to the back room and gave him money and bought the drugs," I lied.

"What was the guy's name? What did he look like?" the cop asked.

"I don't know his name. It's the first time I've ever done anything like this. He was like forty and Hispanic."

The tall cop looked at his partner.

"What do you think?"

"I think he's being straight with us," the other replied.

"Me too." He turned back to me and added, "Don't ever go there again. If you do, we'll bust you. We know who you are and where you live." With that, he grabbed my hand, turned it over, and put the baggie back in my palm. "Thanks for your cooperation. Have a nice night and enjoy yourself." The two of them walked to their car, got in, and sped down the road.

That did not just happen. Is this some kind of strange joke? Are they gonna follow me? I'm the luckiest guy in the world. This is the last time I'm ever doing cocaine. Never again. No way.

Back in my apartment, I emptied a baggie onto my glass coffee table and cut out two monster lines. I couldn't inhale them fast enough. I sat back on my couch and waited for my friends to arrive. And when they did, the six of us didn't leave my living room until late the next afternoon. There was way too much powder and too many things to say.

I had arrived in the city years earlier with a bachelor's degree in nothingness from an expensive liberal arts college in New England. It took me four years to realize that I had learned very little. I had mastered a few new skills, though, like the art of long-term procrastination, the satisfaction of responsibility avoidance, and the subtle gradations of embracing laziness. Wearing my cap and gown, I was certainly much less equipped to face society than when I had arrived as a freshman. But the city called, and I got my first job as an executive assistant at an age-old Madison Avenue ad agency. My parents were ecstatic that I had a job and bragged to their friends that I was on the rise. My dad bought me a few suits from Brooks Brothers—all of them wool, so I dripped with sweat on summer mornings walking down Fortieth Street. The days I was hungover outnumbered the days I was well-rested. After two years of a rigorously underwhelming performance, I limped away from midtown and got hired at a theatrical casting office in the Warner Brothers' suites. This is when my life got interesting. This is when I moved onto the cobblestones of Greenwich Village. This is when I met Shane for the first time.

I didn't like him at first—not at all. He hogged the conversation, for one, and had too many alluring things to say. Things I knew nothing about, like who was dating Charlie Chaplin back in the twenties and what color the writing was on the jacket cover of a first-edition copy of *Catcher in the Rye*. He sat next to me in a booth at a dive bar on Christopher Street but never included me in his conversation. He was far too preoccupied with the two actresses sitting across the table, both blonde, both hanging on his every word. I had never been ignored so conspicuously. What was I doing there, anyway? Perhaps I didn't belong. But as the booze flowed, I began to relax a bit and wedged a few words in here and there. I spoke about the casting office, mainly, which piqued the interest of the wispy girls across the way. But Shane, well, he didn't seem to be impressed or even remotely curious about anyone I had auditioned or how they performed in front of the camera. He was driving fast in his own lane, and there was no room to pass. By the end of the night, we had made each other laugh a few times, and he hugged me goodbye, his bristly whiskers tickling the side of my face.

A few weeks later, he invited me to the opening night of a play he'd written at a small theater on Forty Second Street. I learned that he was an accomplished playwright who had won numerous awards and was well known for someone in his mid-twenties. He wrote most of the material for a fledgling off-Broadway theater company founded by a celebrated young movie star. I was both surprised and honored to be included in such an exclusive event, but it was evident that I was out of my league. I mean, what did I know about plays or movie stars? Almost nothing, really.

But I invited my college girlfriend into the city with the distinct purpose of showing her that I had assimilated well and had a host of new artistic friends. I thought it would impress her and keep her invested in a relationship that was slowly fading out. We arrived together, arm in arm, with expectations of an exciting evening that we could talk about over coffee and pie at a late-night diner somewhere. When we arrived at the box office, I asked for our tickets, but sadly there were none to be found. I asked if someone could go find Shane, as I was sure there must have been a clerical mistake. I was correct in my assumption—my name had never been heard by the clerk. Shane came out wearing a wrinkled white button-down and oversized khaki pants, looking much like the disheveled writers I had created in my imagination. He paced around sheepishly with a red pen in hand and scrawled madly on white note cards as he spoke. His apology was profuse as he revealed that the show had been sold out for several weeks, and there was nothing he could do. I was heartbroken and embarrassed that I had dragged my girlfriend in from Hartford to get aced at the door. Through the bristle and shag of Shane's bangs, I could see the melancholy in his eyes—he was actually sorry. I forgave him then and there and hailed a cab toward home.

Weeks later, I saw him again at a downtown bar called Mondo Cane, and we huddled in a corner as we watched the comedic antics of a band called the Niagras. That was the night when everything changed for me. I had been looking for a friend—a colorful friend who could teach me the ways of lower Manhattan—and there he was. Shane was different than anyone I had known, and although I found him repellent at first, it was this uniqueness that drew me in. First of all, he had something to say about everything. No topic was off limits, and his inventory of facts was an education. He was an artist who painted with words, and his canvas was the New York night. In fact, I'm not sure if Shane ever saw daylight. In the first few months of our deepening friendship, I saw him only after the sun had set. We usually met up at about 10 PM and carried on until the bars closed at four.

It seemed like the nights never ended. We hopped from place to place, hitting the corner payphones for updates from his home answering machine. He may have been the most popular guy in New York and had at least five new messages every time he checked, mostly from girls. As he listened, he would take out his red pen and scrawl detailed notes on a pad while incessantly popping the SweeTARTS he stowed in his pants pocket. He introduced me to every young New Yorker who was worth a salt, and we hooted and hollered together like moonshiners bubbling a fresh batch of firewater in the Appalachian woods. I bought a leather jacket and black jeans and grew my hair long. I was a pig in shit. When the morning light hit, it was like razor blades in my eyes, and I would stumble into the casting office reeking of vodka. Good thing I had my own little cubicle to hide in.

For the first time in my adult life, I felt like I was a part of something important—a movement, perhaps. That's what we convinced ourselves of, anyway. We perfected the game of Truth or Dare—it went something like this:

"Truth or dare?" said a girl in a light blue dress.

"Dare," I replied.

"I dare you to kiss me."

So I did.

We were oversexed, libido-driven twenty-somethings without regular jobs to go to in the morning. We drank and laughed and carried on like we were invincible. Everyone kissed everyone, and no one got herpes—at least, not that I could see in the dimly lit living rooms of lower Manhattan.

When I moved into 29 King, the party got louder. I had exhausted my trust fund buying an eleven-hundred-square-foot penthouse with a massive outdoor terrace. The place was epic. It was like Warhol's factory without the soup cans, and in place of Andy's 8mm camera, there was a Polaroid Captiva. I documented every musician, actor, writer, director, film executive, and bon vivant who streamed in. I had a shoebox filled with photos of the Who's Who of young New York—many of them in compromising positions. Just like the Factory, everyone stopped by at least once. We partied 'til dawn. I provided the space, and everyone else brought the party favors. I was in heaven.

I quit my job in casting and became an independent movie producer, whatever that was. I made a few mediocre films that paid the bills for a while and affirmed to the masses that I was a creative talent with something to offer. I played the part well and began to attract a contingent of A-listers into my orbit. They may have liked my penthouse more than they liked me, but they all showed up and stayed for a while. Gwyneth began to introduce me as her good friend. Leo said that one day he wanted to have muscles like me so he could get the girls (I assured him he would). Liev jumped into my Sharper Image blow-up pool with his wallet in his pocket. I put it in the microwave to dry it out and melted his credit cards. Ray Donovan has killed people for less. Brad put his arm around me and suggested I put a putting green on my terrace so we could play golf at night. Tobey, Billy, Alessandro, Shane, Adrien, and I dressed up as cave girls one Halloween and took the subway to a party in Chelsea with our plastic clubs in tow. It was long before *Spiderman, Almost Famous,* or *Jurassic Park III,* so no one asked for autographs as we thundered uptown. One morning on my terrace, Peter got his hair cut by a former Miss West Virginia. He wasn't under contract to keep it long, as *Game of Thrones* hadn't been conceived yet. I went to private dinners hosted by Anna Wintour, movie premieres, and invite-only after-parties in swanky clubs. I was part of the entourage, and the velvet rope always parted when I arrived.

As the nights continued, I felt more and more out of place. I knew that I wasn't one of them, but merely a hanger-on with a winning smile and pronounced jawbone. My prosaic accomplishments could be counted on one hand, and they paled in comparison. The more I spent time with this crowd of fantastic notables, the worse I began to feel. I was an imposter, an opportunist, a charlatan. I had nothing to offer them, really, and as their career trajectories shot into the atmosphere, mine ground to a halt. I was a great host—that was about it, and my appeal was wearing thin. One by one, the glamorous jet-setters began to peel away, and there was nothing I could do to stop it. They were friends one day and acquaintances the next. But Shane never left or turned his back on me. We drank away our sorrows (he had different ones), and when the alcohol wasn't working anymore, I turned to cocaine.

Cocaine was the perfect drug for the New York night. It provided the fuel, the courage, and the confidence that was needed to keep up the façade. I was far more charming when I did the stuff. My fear and self-doubt went away. When it hit my brain, I felt alive and virile and brilliantly funny. I was quick with a joke, especially when I was getting attention from a cute girl who knew little about me. I pretended that I was a number of things—none of them needy or dark. And when the lights turned on at the bar, a few of us would head back to 29 King, dump the contents of our baggies on the coffee table, and snort 'til dawn. We all tried to have the last word, cutting one another off during a conversation full of impassioned nonsequiturs and hyperbole. This, of course, was before I realized it was more fun to do it alone.

I went through a phase of becoming a serious writer. I would do a line, scratch down a few disjointed memories from my childhood in a notebook, do another, claw out a nonsensical poem about unrequited love, snort some more, and get lost in meaningless anecdotes that I would scribble onto the page. At night, with a brain full of powder, the words arrived.

So, who is the protagonist? Carlton. No, Caleb. Ooh, Caleb, that works.

And maybe he should have a chipped tooth. Chipped tooth. Chipped tooth. No, that's too much like me. A chipped bone.

Yes, of course. A chipped elbow bone.

He chipped his elbow throwing the javelin. No, that wouldn't chip the bone—that might strain it or pull it out of the socket.

Ooh, he got hit by a javelin while he was walking his dog by the river.

A stray javelin hit him in the elbow.

Maybe it wasn't a stray.

Maybe the dog was a stray but the javelin was deliberate.

He was an Olympic athlete who turned on his country and was being hunted down by the other athletes.

And the discus. It's an evil weapon, that discus. It could cut a man's head clean off.

The bad guy uses a discus to make it look like an accident. Like a track-and-field accident. Like someone was just practicing for a tournament and threw it too far.

And there's a girl. Tinga. No, Tinka. No, Tara.

And her father is a bishop in the Catholic Church.

Yes, good, good.

But behind the scenes, he's in the mob. His holy ways are just a front, and he's really into high-stakes poker. That's his thing.

He tries to get the athletes to gamble and then turns them into assassins. He was once a champion shot putter.

Nice. Nice, I like it. This is really coming together.

"Carder, we're in here," a voice whispered.

Wait. What? Is someone here? I better hide the coke. Shit. What are they doing?

"Hello? Hello? Who is that? What are you doing here?"

No response. Silence.

Maybe it was just a drip in the sink. Who would be hiding in my bathroom, anyway? The cops? Fuck, is it the cops? They know where I live.

"Carder, it's us. We're here," a faint voice said.

Who the fuck is that? How did they get in?

I got up from the living room couch and thrust open the bathroom door. I pulled the shower curtain open and checked the cabinets under the sink. The coast was clear.

That's weird. I know I heard something. Maybe I'm losing my mind.
If they try to get in, I'll stash the coke under the table.

I went to the front door and checked the bolt. Locked tight.

Let 'em try. Good luck, little piggies.

Now, where was I?

For a while, my coke-fueled ramblings—Pulitzer-worthy, in my mind—distracted me from the voices and my sorry state. Shane introduced me to a painter named Ariel, an even better distraction. I was instantly struck by her beauty. She had straight, blonde hair that fell to her shoulders and baby-white skin that glowed in the dark. Her intense blue eyes had bits of green in the iris, and they rarely blinked. She told me that she lived inside her paintings and that her artistic expression was drawn from experiences she had as a teenager. She asked if I would like to see her work. There was nothing in the world I wanted more.

In a matter of months, we were deeply in love. I was in love with her, at least. For a brief spell, it felt like my life had meaning again. We would make love on lazy afternoons and walk the streets of SoHo hand in hand. She took me to art galleries and openings and showed me the paintings that inspired her work. She listened when I spoke about my family and the mixed-up childhood that took half my front tooth. I believed in myself when we were together, and I thought that she might be the one. I never told her about the cocaine, which I was still doing with regularity. She never told me about the ex-boyfriend who she still loved and visited in secret. We were even, I guess.

On a certain Friday in the summer, I had plans to visit my mother in DC but, at the last minute, procured two tickets to *La Bohéme* at the Met. I was excited to share the news with Ariel and left a message on her machine. When I hadn't heard back from her by lunchtime I started to get worried. She was supposed to be in the city. She told me that she would be here all weekend and would be available to talk if I called, but my phone didn't ring. I sat in my apartment, staring at it. I was concerned—maybe something had happened to her. I opened a handle of vodka and smoked a pack of cigarettes. But the football phone in my kitchen never rang, and my mood began to slip away into the dark abyss. She had been dating her professor from Harvard before we met but had assured me it was over.

She must be with him. Fucking tramp. Fucking strumpet. Fucking liar.

The thought of her betrayal was like a branding iron on my neck. Six PM and no call. Seven. Eight. The tickets were useless now. I had to get outside. Where the hell was Shane when I needed him most?

I found him at a bar called Rose's Turn on West Fourth Street. It was a cabaret joint where members of the audience could get up and perform songs when piano veterans were in between sets. I once sang *Space Oddity* to a large crowd of old women who were less than cordial with their response. But tonight, I had no intention of singing or even listening to anyone else tickle the ivories—I just needed my friend. When I saw him seated at a crowded table, I burst into tears. There was nothing I could do to hold them back. Ariel had confirmed my deepest fears—that I was disposable and unworthy.

"Buddy, come here. Sit down. Tell me what's going on," he said.

"It's Ariel. I think she's off with her old boyfriend. I'm sure she is." And the tears came even harder. "I had tickets to the Met, and I've been calling her all day. She won't call back. I know something is up. I can feel it."

"Maybe she went out of town for the weekend. I know she digs you. Can't see her doing something like this," he said.

"It's that teacher. The one she used to date. I know it's him! I'm done. Fuck her. It's over," I sniffled. But that's the last thing I wanted. I couldn't get her out of my head—not for a second. I mean, who was I kidding? I had cheated on most of my girlfriends over the years, and it didn't mean I loved them any less. But when it was done to me, it felt so much worse. I was the Grand Poobah of double standards.

"Have you tried to go over there?"

That was fucking brilliant. What a great idea. I would go catch her in the act with her hack of an ex-boyfriend. I needed a few drinks first, and they came one after the other, each kamikaze shot thrusting a knife into my heart. I borrowed Shane's red pen and began to write a poem on a cocktail napkin. It was titled "A Day without Ariel," and it flowed out of me like water.

A day without Ariel
Is Piglet and no Pooh
Cinderella in Converse
Nurseries without their rhymes

As I wrote each verse, I passed it to Shane, and he would nod his head in concern.

"I hate to see you this way, buddy. This is one of the most deplorable heartsick drivels that has ever come out of you. She shouldn't make you feel this way. I mean, the ladies are supposed to enhance our lives, right? And we're supposed to enhance theirs. If that ain't working, then it doesn't seem like a good fit. Makes me sad, though. I thought you guys were good for each other," he said.

I nodded in agreement. "But I guess not. I can't forgive her for this. It's way too fucked up. I mean, I'm so in love with her. It's not good for me."

"Be yourself, buddy. Ain't nothing wrong with the C. Never forget that," he said.

"Thanks, buddy."

"So, go find your lady. And if he's there, see if they're into a threesome. You can be 'Lucky Pierre.'"

I laughed for the first time all day.

I had half a gram of blow hidden in a ceramic Buddha on my mantelpiece. I snorted every bit of it before launching my full-frontal assault on Ariel.

I stood in front of her apartment building on Second and Avenue B with the veins popping from my arms. I was fuming—arguably the most pissed I'd ever been in my life. *How fucking dare she?* I was ready to break the door down if she didn't answer and had a jumbled speech in my head that I was ready to vomit all over her cheating face. All those things she said to me. *Lies.* All those promises. *Broken.* All those whispers. *Bullshit.* Our future together. *Done.*

I was ready to brawl, and there would be considerable collateral damage if he was with her. I would pound his fucking face. I'd never been in a fistfight before, but I would still smash him in the teeth. She was in for the surprise of her life. *Here I come!*

I leaned on the buzzer with everything I had and waited for a reply. Nothing. I pressed it again and again and again. I knew she was in there. I buzzed everyone in the building, lighting up the switchboard with pure hate. A voice came over the intercom system.

"Hello? Who is this? Do you know it's twelve o'clock at night?" someone said.

"So sorry, I lost my key. Could you buzz me in?"

"Who is this? I know everyone in the building. What is your name?"

I didn't respond, and the entryway went silent. I buzzed a few others but got nothing. Time for plan B. I walked down the front steps and looked up at the black iron fire escape that crawled up the front of the building. The metal ladder was stowed on the second-floor landing to prevent people like me from climbing up. The bottom rung was about eight feet above the sidewalk. Like a maniacal cat burglar, I stood up on a plastic trash can and jumped. I pulled myself up with sheer cocaine-induced adrenaline and clambered up the iron steps to the fourth floor. The living room windows were locked, and no matter how hard I pulled, they wouldn't budge. I pounded and pounded and screamed her name.

They're hiding in the bedroom. Naked fuckers. I'll break these goddamn windows.

But before I hammered through the glass, I saw that there was a small bathroom window cracked open about six feet to the right of the fire escape. I was now fifty feet above the pavement, but there was no stopping me. I climbed over the railing and held on with my left arm as I prepared to launch. If I fell, I would probably die. But I didn't give a fuck. I would go down in a blaze of glory. She'd know how much she hurt me.

In spite of the coke pulsing through my heart, when I released from the guardrail, everything slowed to a halt. I could feel myself suspended in midair, four stories above the street. I hung there for seconds, what seemed like minutes, before my body crunched against the brick exterior of the building. The side of my head hit the sill with a thud. Blood poured onto my shirt. I frantically waved my arm inside the window and clutched a towel rack. My feet scurried upward and propelled me halfway inside the bathroom, and I crashed onto the tile floor, leaving smears of blood next to the bathtub. I had done it. I was in. *Now, where the fuck are they?*

I burst into the bedroom and jumped onto the comforter without saying a word. I rolled around punching the pillows before realizing that no one was there. I checked the closets, opened the cupboards, reached under the sofa, and looked into the fridge. Nothing. And then I saw a simple little square pack of Dunhill cigarettes sitting on the coffee table: Exhibit A. Evidence. *You are now found guilty of cheating on me.* Ariel never smoked, so they must have been his. I scrunched the small box in my hand and threw it across the room. I would wait them out. When they got home from their pathetic romantic stroll, I would be waiting in the shadows. *I'm ready for you, motherfuckers.*

But after an hour, the cocaine began to wear off. I had to get out of there. I picked up a pen and wrote a note on a pad of yellow lined paper I found in the kitchen.

It read, "I hope TC gets VD from me." I placed it on her now bloodstained pillow and read it out loud. I wanted to hurt her, taunt her, scare her, and make her suffer. I had never contracted any kind of VD in my life, but she didn't know that. Her ex-boyfriend shithead fucking asshole was named Tom Callahan. TC gets VD— had a nice ring to it. It rhymed, even. It was quite possibly the best thing I'd ever written.

I ran down the stairs and grabbed a taxi toward home, feeling a deluded sense of accomplishment. The city looked bleak and dirty as we approached Sixth Avenue. I needed to get the fuck out of here. I needed to clean up my act. I needed a lobotomy.

No, I needed more coke.

Chapter Eleven

2003

Tisha looked like an angel standing on the street corner—a fallen angel. I couldn't take my eyes off her. She was not a churchgoer and had no interest in joining the exalted crowd that had gathered down the block. She was in business mode, and I watched as she tried to flag down a passing car. I didn't think that Sunday morning would be the most optimal time to turn tricks, but what did I know? The dirt of the sidewalks had ravaged her white stockings, and I wondered if it had found its way underneath. Still, in her tatters and rags, she looked better than most. My heart felt heavy as I approached her, and I realized that I was falling hard.

"Hey there, good lookin', save some of that for me," I said as I gave her a hug.

"Ain't nothin' here you ain't seen before," she said with a twirl.

"What you got going on today?" I asked.

"You know, girl's gotta work. Bills to pay."

"How 'bout tonight I pay all your bills, and you come away with me for a bit? Like on a trip?" I said.

Her eyes widened with a mixture of skepticism and disbelief.

"Yeah, right. You my prince charmin' all of a sudden? What kinda trip you talkin' about, anyway? I can't go too far. Got a few dates set up. People wantin' to see me."

"That's cool," I said, "but I'm offering to take you away for a few nights. All expenses paid: Hotel. Dinner. Beach. Pool. All of it. I gotta drive down the coast, and I want you to come with me. A romantic getaway for the two of us. What do you think?"

"Is you shittin' me?"

"I'm dead serious. Everybody needs a vacation once in a while."

"That's for damn sure. I know I do. Shit, yeah, I'll come with you, baby," she said, "but I gotta do it on the sly. Can't let Trech find out. He'd kill me. Gets jealous, you know."

"It'll be our little secret," I grinned. She jumped up in my arms.

"You surprise me like a mofo! Takin' a vacation with my man. Sheeet. I'm a lucky lady. Gotta get a few things from my storage locker, baby. You know, a girl's gotta look right for a fancy hotel."

I put my hand in hers, and we strode down the street. Maybe she was my girlfriend after all. Everything in my body told me so as we jumped into my car and drove toward Rose Avenue. Her locker was on the first floor of a huge public storage facility. It was more like a small room that was sparsely kept, with a few blankets on the floor. There were two light blue Samsonite suitcases lying open with clothes strewn inside, and that was about it. This was obviously the place she slept—her little hideaway cubby when the asphalt got too cold. She scrambled about, putting items from one suitcase into the other with a shuffle and a spin. I realized this may have been the first vacation she ever took.

"I got an idea. Just bring it all. Just in case you need something. We may be gone for a few days—who knows, maybe even a week. I wouldn't want you to forget something important."

"Really, baby? You got room for all this stuff?" she asked.

"I do. In the trunk. No problem. Let's bring it all just to be safe."

"Okay. Tish is gonna show you such a good time. We's gonna have so much fun. Where we goin'? What hotel we stayin' at?" she said. She leaned in and gave me a long, sloppy kiss on the lips. She bubbled like a girl who had just been asked to the prom. It felt amazing to see her so happy and carefree—the way she should be, at her age.

"Down the coast. Just north of San Diego. There's a town called La Jolla. Right by the ocean. All we need is a double bed and a view, right?"

"Ooh, La Jolla. I like the sound of that, baby. Sounds expensive. I like that."

"It's one of the most beautiful towns I've ever been to. You're gonna love it. Now let's get going," I said.

I snapped together the clasps on her plastic luggage and dragged it out the door. She wouldn't sleep in a locker tonight, or eat leftovers from a dumpster in back of a barbeque joint. I was going to do everything in my power to give her the five-star treatment.

She jabbered away in the car like nothing was bothering her. Maybe it wasn't. But it bothered *me* that she made her living on her back in junked-up cars and burned-out tenements, whispering into the ears of married men with their zippers down. Maybe she didn't care as much as I did. I was feeling possessive. Maybe I could talk her out of it. Maybe we could get on a cruise ship to Mexico and never look back. A hundred grand could go a long way if you lived on the cheap. We could get married and move to Bali and change our names. Trech would never find us there. I could get away from this life. Maybe I was full of shit.

"Why you in such a good mood, baby? Never seen you like this," she said as we sped down the 405.

"I don't know. I guess it's because I got my girl riding shotgun on a beautiful day in sunny California," I said.

"Yeah, but there's somethin' else. You got a secret. What's the secret, baby?"

She was right, I did have a secret, but there was no way she'd get it out of me—not yet. I would tell her at the last possible moment, when the decks were stacked in my favor. But there was something else I wanted to share—something that had eluded me for the better part of a year. Something that I had been chasing my whole adult life. Something I had prayed for on many nights when I stared at the ceiling, feeling sorry for myself.

I was sober. I hadn't smoked crack in six days and had no desire to do it ever again. She must have noticed a difference. I sure did.

"I'm not smoking anymore. No more rock. I'll sell the shit to make money, but that's it. I quit," I said. I couldn't stop smiling.

Tisha looked over at me, and I could see the tears in her eyes.

"You serious, baby? I mean you tellin' the truth?"

"The complete and utter truth. No more of that shit for me. I don't want to be a paranoid freak anymore." I glanced at her. "Must have been hard to watch."

"It was. I don't know why you was doin' it in the first place. You was always scared and talkin' to people and goin' crazy. It made me feel sad for you."

I nodded. "There were a lot of reasons I smoked—no good ones. But not anymore. I left my pipe at home. Got nothing on me. Never again." I paused for a few seconds and reached into my pocket. "But I *will* smoke one of these. Will you light one for me? We can share it." I passed her a box of Camel Lights and a lighter.

"That sounds good, baby. I loves me my man. And you him. So, I guess that means I love you!" She giggled.

I almost said it back but refrained. I didn't want to lead her on or make promises I couldn't keep. We must have smoked ten cigarettes before pulling into a seaside hotel in La Jolla. It was stunning. I had seen pictures of the coastline in a magazine left at the laundromat on Rose and Fifth. I had always wanted to stay there—the beaches seemed so pristine. It felt like nothing bad could happen there. No one could get shot or killed or sell their ass for a dime bag. I would bet my life's savings that no one had ever smoked crack in the rooms.

Up at the front desk, the concierge was less than cordial. He took one look at Tish and started to brim with attitude.

"I'm not sure we have any rooms available tonight," he said. I knew he was lying because the parking lot outside was nearly empty. Ignorant fuck. If he only knew what she'd been through.

"I don't want a room. I must not have made myself clear. I want a suite with an ocean view. The best view available. Like right over the ocean, if you know what I'm saying," I said with a polite smile.

He looked down his nose at me and chuckled. I felt like sounding the racist alarm but kept my composure.

"Yes, sir. We do have a suite available, but it is $500 per night. I imagine that will be too much for you—"

"I'll take it," I said, cutting him off at the knees.

Tisha stood there and grinned at him with her best *fuck you* face. I laid out $800 in cash on the desk. He stammered a bit before printing out some paperwork and asking me to sign on the dotted line. It felt amazing. There was more money coming when I got back to Venice, so I wasn't worried. You know, when in Rome.

"This should take care of any room service we order. Thank you for being so kind," I said. He handed over the key and pointed us in the right direction. When we got in the elevator, we both started to laugh.

"That's the kind of motherfucker that picks me up off the street. Just like that. All slick and hoity-toity. But underneath it all, he's just a scared little bitch," she said. It was so perfectly stated that I almost had nothing to add.

"When we're eating room service and taking bubble baths, he's gonna be picking his ass at the front desk," I said. Tisha leaned in and gave me a passionate kiss as we rose up to the fourth floor.

The room was impeccable. A small living area with an over-stuffed yellow sofa adjoined an elegant master bedroom. The wooden venetian blinds were raised to a sprawling view of the Pacific Ocean. The water was dark blue and calm, and the misty afternoon sun refracted through the waves into our private haven, leaving a golden hue on the green wallpaper. It was quiet—not the usual horns and engines I had grown accustomed to in Venice, but a tranquil nothingness that caused a sense of withdrawal in my ear drums. The setting was the antithesis of anything we had experienced together, and for a moment, I felt like a foreigner in a strange land. I laid on the bed, and Tisha curled up next to me. We were safe for now.

"Let's get in the tub and stay there all afternoon. There's a bottle of champagne in the fridge, and we can lounge around sipping bubbly like we're the king and queen of Spain."

"What's Spain?" she asked innocently.

I guess she had never heard of it. She probably had never opened a history book in her life, but she was street smart, and that's what mattered. That's what had kept her alive for so long against odds that were anything but favorable.

"It's a place. A place across the sea where people love to dance and paint and enjoy themselves," I said.

"Sounds nice. Can we go there sometime—me and you? I mean, if it's not too much of a bother," she said. No one had been nice to her for a long time.

"I would love to take you to Spain sometime. Nothing would make me happier."

I propped myself up on my elbow and looked into her dark eyes. "You know, I'd give you the world if I could."

She looked at me with the innocence of a child.

"Why are you so good to me? I'm just a teenage girl from a bad neighborhood with nothing. Why you like me, baby?"

That was a hard question and not something I could answer right away. I needed to think about it for a while. I smiled and winked.

"You make me feel good, for one. And you make me want to stop smoking, for two. And for three, well, I'll tell you when we're underneath some bubbles."

I jumped up, grabbed her feet, and pulled her from the king bed. The bathroom was like a kingdom unto itself. It sparkled with brass, gold, and marble, like the inside of an Arabian palace. We undressed politely together. The gigantic porcelain soaker tub stared at us with an inviting grin, and I turned the chrome knob toward warm before stepping in. Tisha took her eyes off me for a moment to navigate her entry, and I got a long look at her in the light. There were scars, cuts, and bruises all the way down her back. How had I not noticed them before? It seemed the culmination of years of abuse. Instantly, one name sliced through my head like a razor blade. Fucking Trech. Was he capable of something so utterly disgusting? Yes, he was. Fucking coward. Fucking loser.

And when our eyes met, she knew that I had seen. She sat down in the tub, looking scared.

"Who did that to you?" I demanded.

No response. Only tears.

"Who the fuck did that to you?" I yelled.

The sound of bathwater was my only answer.

"Was it him? That *fucking* asshole. That *low-life* pimp. That *scumbag*."

She nodded her head and began to sob.

I knew it was him. Treacherous Wallace. The lowest of the low. A cockroach dipped in shit. A puss-filled maggot. A psychopathic masochist, a pedophilic child abuser, the stone-cold killer who was also my employer. I guess my soul was only worth about ten grand. Pathetic. Maybe we *should* hop the ferry and head down to Argentina. The idea seemed even better now.

"I'm so sorry. No one should ever do this to you. If I had a pistol, I'd shoot him in the heart," I said.

"No," she wailed. "He'll kill you. Like he does everyone. Please don't do nothin'."

I tried to steady my breathing. "Okay, love, I won't. Don't worry. Come here. Give me a hug," I said.

As she shifted her weight in the tub and fell onto my chest, I could feel her body quivering. Her sobs became loud, like those of a small child who had skinned her knee. I did my best to comfort her.

"It's gonna be okay. I'm here. No need to worry. I'm not gonna leave you. You're safe," I whispered.

"He's gonna kill me. I know it. One of these days, his lead pipe's gonna take the life from me. Sometimes he hits me so hard. I don't want my baby girl to be alone," she said, gasping for breath.

"I'll take care of this. Don't you worry. It's all going to be okay. I promise."

I rubbed the side of her cheek with my thumb and kissed her on the forehead. It was the only thing I could do.

"I understand if you don't want to be with me no more, baby. On account that I'm so ugly. I used to be pretty, but I ain't no more. I'm ugly now." She sobbed.

This was hard to hear and so untrue.

"You're not ugly, Tish. You're beautiful. You're one of the most beautiful girls I've ever seen. I'm being serious."

"You think I'm ugly. I know it. I'm sorry, baby. I wanted to be pretty for you. You never gonna want me now."

It was now or never.

"I love you," I said to her face. She looked up from her crying and hugged me even tighter.

"Say it again," she said, "so I can see it in your eyes if you telling the truth."

"I love you," I said, again. And this time I knew she believed me. Now if I could just believe it myself. I was pretty sure that I did—love her, I mean. In fact, in that moment, I was dead certain. I kissed her on the cheek and turned her around so that her back was facing me.

"Is it okay if I wash your back? I really want to wash you."

"If you love me, it's okay, baby. Only if you love me."

I took a fresh washcloth from the rack and dipped it in the clear water. With the palm of my hand, I rubbed a bar of soap in a circular motion, coating the cloth with a thin film. I began on her neck and ever so gently swept the grime from the grooves that lay under her hair. I moved to her shoulders and upper back, delicately swabbing in between the new cuts and irritated scabs. She winced several times but never said a word. I descended slowly down her spine, brushing her bruises with a gentle hand. These were her battle scars, and she hid them well. I was ashamed that I had done nothing to stop this from happening. Never again. I would not let this happen again. There was no way I could stand up to a man like Trech and live to speak about it. A direct confrontation was out of the question—it would be a suicide mission, and I wasn't ready to die just yet.

"We could run away together. Me and you. Go somewhere warm like Guatemala or Tahiti. Spend our days lying in the sun and drinking Pina Coladas. What do you think?" I said, playfully.

"I can't go nowhere without my daughter," she said.

"Of course not," I said. We sat in the tub for another thirty minutes and remained quiet. The terrycloth robes felt like they were made of feathers when we put them on and jumped back on the king bed. I picked up the phone to order room service for the both of us.

"Uh, yeah, this is room 416. I'd like to order room service. Yes. We would like two filet mignons, medium rare, and two glasses of red wine, and some chocolate-covered strawberries. Yup. Put it on my tab," I said. I hadn't put anything on a tab since I lived in New York. Felt good to say those words again.

"What's a fillit minnon? I ain't wantin' nothing like that. Call him back, I wants a steak."

"Think of the softest, leanest steak you ever had, and then cook it in butter. That's a filet mignon," I said.

"That's what I want, baby. Exactly."

We ate dinner on the bed, watched a Sandra Bullock movie, and fell asleep on top of the covers.

I popped the trunk of the car and found that the backpack with the money was gone. Several Crips were chasing me with machine guns, and I was cornered on the edge of the cliffs of Dover.

I woke up in a panic. I scanned the room in search of the bag. Jesus Christ, had I left it inside the fucking car? How could I be so goddamn stupid? My entire life was tied to that bag. I leapt out of bed and turned the corner into the living room, but it wasn't there. I was ready to burst out the door naked when I saw it sitting on a wooden chair in the hallway. Motherfucker, that was close. I checked inside the bag and saw that the rolls of bills were still there. I might just pull this off. Just maybe, if I have some luck, and the gods are smiling on me, I might not die today.

I dropped Tish off at a Starbucks in San Diego and told her I'd be back in an hour or so. I gave her a twenty and told her to get some breakfast and to have a latte waiting for me.

"What the fuck's a latte?" she said.

It was game time, and somehow, I was not terrified. It was like some superhero had inhabited my body, and I had turned bullet-proof or something. The thrill of buying seven kilos of pure cocaine from the Mexican cartel wasn't something that happened every day. I had to be invincible, or I'd be dead before sundown.

I pulled into the parking lot of the Motel 6, and my dashboard clock read 10:45. I rolled the windows up in my Taurus and clutched the backpack to my chest. It was now or never. I figured it would be okay to be a few minutes early, but what did I know about the cartel? Only a few things, really, like the fact that a seedy motel near the border was the perfect place to execute a white boy. I hardly ever prayed, but now seemed like a good time to start.

"God, if you're up there, and you're not too pissed at me for all the bad shit I've done, please let me live through this so I can do better things," I said, out loud. And a few moments later, I was standing outside room 224 with the delivery. I knocked on the door three times and heard a commotion from inside followed by several words in Spanish. I watched as a young mother and her daughter exited the next room, and I waved at them. If they only knew who was staying next door. I waited patiently and no one answered, so I knocked again. One of the first rules of a drug deal was that you shouldn't stand outside for too long. People would take notice and sometimes feel the need to call it in—especially if you were in a bad part of town. If they didn't answer in another few seconds, I would call it off and head out of Dodge. Fuck it, my freedom was more important to me than another five thousand. Besides, I had a bag full of loot, and Tish and I could go anywhere in the world with this kind of money. Part of me was hoping the door wouldn't open—a big part.

But it did, and a small Mexican man grabbed my shoulder and pulled me into the dark room.

Another man frisked me and took the bag from my hands.

A third man flipped me around, zip-tied my wrists behind my back, and pushed me to the ground. I turned my head to look up, and it was met with the butt end of a machine gun. Jesus, that hurt.

Two of them scooped me up off the floor and threw me onto a wooden chair in the corner.

For the first time, I could see who I was dealing with, and they were obviously not in a good mood. All three were in their late twenties, and each one of them brandished a machine gun.

Their faces were exposed to me, which was not a good sign. I could identify them now, and this put me in grave danger. It was easier to kill someone than take the risk that they could finger you later. One of them dumped the contents of the bag on the bed and began to count. The others parted the curtains with the muzzles of their guns and began speaking to each other in low, hushed tones.

"Es una coche de la policia," one said.

"La policia?" the other replied.

"Si, claro que si."

One of them came over to the corner and stood in front of me. He had a tattoo of a knife dripping blood on his arm and deep pits on his face like someone had mashed it with a cheese grater.

"Why is you police car?" he said in broken English. He brought the barrel of the machine gun close to my face and pretended to pull the trigger.

"No, that's not a police car. It's a Ford Taurus. Police drive around in Crown Victorias," I said.

"You police? Yes? Undercover police? You like to die, yes?"

"No, no. I'm Hollywood. Treacherous sent me to do the deal. I'm not the police. I swear. I work for Trech," I pleaded.

"You work Treacherous? Why you have police car? You police?" he said, pretending to pull the trigger, again. Each time he did this, I closed my eyes and waited for the bullets. The guy counting money on the bed—obviously, the leader—motioned for him to step aside. He spoke perfect English.

"Trech told me he was sending someone new. A white guy. Are you him?"

"I'm him. I'm Hollywood. Listen, I'm supposed to get the dope, and that's all. I'm cool. You don't have to worry."

"You don't look too cool, and I'm not worried about anything," he said, laughing. His two cronies laughed with him and pointed their guns at me. "Maybe I'll take this money and send you back without the kilos. But you'll be alive. How does that sound?"

"If I don't come back with the dope, I'm already dead. You know that," I said.

"So who do you want to kill you? Me or Trech? It's your choice." He laughed again, and his minions followed suit.

"Neither. I just came to do a deal and drive home. Trech told me you were cool. I don't want any trouble. I have a son," I lied. Maybe I could appeal to his softer side—if he had one.

"Yeah, I got a son, too. So what? You play in this game, and you probably get killed. That's it. Don't know where. Don't know when," he said.

"Listen, it's my son's birthday tomorrow. Got a big party planned and everything. A pinata. Homemade tortillas. All his friends. Please let me go," I said.

He gave me a long stare and took a deep breath. With a swift hand gesture, he motioned for his subordinates to untie my wrists. They stood me up and brought me over to the bed.

"This is seven kilos of the finest cocaine in the world. A present for you and your son on his birthday," he said, handing over a small duffle bag. "Take care, and tell Treacherous we will contact him soon."

"Thank you. I will. See you later," I said. I hurried out the door, and as I walked down the steps, I saw the same mother and daughter coming toward me. If I hadn't seen them before, I never would have thought up my fictional son. They had inadvertently saved my life. Maybe God had heard me after all.

When I picked up Tish at the Starbucks, she had a latte waiting for me. She was so proud as she handed it over.

"I think it's still hot, and I told them to make extra foam on top. Lattes are damn good," she said, smiling.

"Thank you, darling. You have no idea how much I need this right now."

"Now take me to Spain," she said, beaming.

The cars moved slowly going up the 405, but I didn't mind. There were far worse places I could be than in the middle of a traffic jam. I had done something this morning that I never thought I would do—officially become a drug dealer—but I considered it a one-time thing. It was a means to an end, and as the road signs passed by the window, I could sense that an end was near. Tish lay her head on my shoulder and began to hum a tune that sounded familiar. It was a happy tune, full of promise, and it sweetened the already confection-like ambiance in my car. When the humming stopped, I knew she had fallen asleep.

Instead of taking the freeway up to Venice, I veered off course toward downtown. In an hour or so, I exited toward the city center with a specific destination in mind. I had the element of surprise on my side—she would never expect this. I hoped that she would see it my way. As we clunked into the parking lot, she began to stir. She opened her eyes blankly and reached her arms up in a stretch.

"Are we home, baby?" she said.

"Not yet, sweet girl. But that's where you're going. You're going home."

"Wait. What? Where are we?" she asked. She sat up in the seat and looked in front of us at a big sign that read GREYHOUND.

"Wait. Baby, why we at the bus station? Where we goin? We going to Spain?"

"I'm sending you home, Tish. Back to Detroit. Back to your little girl and your momma," I said.

She looked at me with a combination of confusion and dismay.

"What? Back to *Detroit*? I can't go back just yet. I got people who see me regular. And Trech, he never gonna let me leave. Nah, nah, I can't go," she said, backing away from me in the seat.

"Yes you can, Tish. Your little girl needs you. No one will ever know where you went. Treacherous Wallace doesn't own you. He can't keep you here. There's nothing here for you anymore," I said.

"But what about you?" she said, starting to cry. "You told me that you loved me."

"I do love you, Tish. That's why I'm doing this. The streets are no place for you. You told me yourself that one of these days, Trech is gonna kill you with that lead pipe. You need to be with your daughter, not dead."

"But what you gonna do?"

"I'll be okay. Don't worry about me. You have to start over, Tish. I do, too. I'm gonna quit the game soon. I'll come visit you," I said, but I knew I never would.

"Are you for real?" she said. She turned to look out the window. "I do miss my baby. But I got nothing to give her. How's I gonna live? What I gonna do, baby?"

"You're gonna live with your momma and get a job. Something clean. Something safe," I said.

"But Trech, he'll come looking for me. I know it. I'm his favorite girl. He'll find me and bring me back," she said.

"What's your middle name," I asked.

"Ivory."

"Okay, from now on, your name is Ivy. He won't come looking for anyone named Ivy. Don't walk the streets anymore, and he'll never find you."

She nodded.

"You promise?" I said.

"I promise," she said, hugging me tight. I reached down into my pocket and pulled out a roll of bills. I handed them to her.

"This is $4,000. It's all the money I have in the world. This is for you and your daughter to start a new life."

She began to cry even harder and shook her head from side to side.

"I can't, baby. I can't take it from you. That wouldn't be right," she sobbed.

I forced her hand open and placed the money in it.

"I saved this up for you. This is for you and nobody else. I don't want it. It's for your new life."

She looked at me with her sad eyes and nodded her head, acknowledging that what I said was right. She took the money and put it in her purse, closing the clasp tightly. Our lips came together for one last time.

"No one has ever given me a chance, baby. No one has ever treated me like you. I love you. I love you so much," she cried.

"I love you, too," I said.

We waited on a bench in silence for the bus to come. Her hand was in mine—our fingers interlocked, our sadness palpable. I was sending away one of the people I cared most about in the world, and my heart felt like it had been gut-punched, but underneath the pain was a feeling of satisfaction that trumped any crack high I'd ever had. As the bus door opened and we embraced, I knew that I would never see her again—this lovely girl with bruises on her skin. Although I would miss her, pride surged though my body. I was doing the right thing. For once in my fucking life, I was doing the right thing.

Maybe I was a good person after all.

Chapter Twelve

2002, THIRTY-TWO YEARS OLD

"Hits you like a motherfucker, huh?" Dave said, taking the crack pipe from my sweaty fingers. I looked up and saw a crown of thorns on his head. *What the fuck?*

I felt different. Better than I ever had, maybe.

"Look at you, man. You're really high. I've never seen you so high," he said. And with that, he loaded the pipe with more crack and took a long hit. He sat back on the couch and began to drool.

"What *is* this stuff?" I said.

"It's crack, motherfucker. Once you go crack, you never go back."

I got up and began to dance. Embarrassment at my insufficient rhythm was gone. I felt like someone had branded me on my chest with a big S, and I actually tried to fly. I got up on the coffee table, jumped off, and crashed to the floor.

Dave laughed hard. He was having a hard time speaking, so he just sat on the couch and giggled at me. I didn't mind at all.

I don't care about anything. Life is beautiful. This is the way I'm supposed to feel. I never want it to end.

"Give me another hit of that shit. It tastes like gold," I said.

I watched as Dave loaded the pipe. He stuffed the end with a pebble of yellow cocaine and heated the glass underneath. A crackling sound emanated from the tube, and he looked up at me and smiled.

"Snap, crackle, pop, motherfucker." He handed it over and giggled like a lunatic. I tugged on the end with my lips and felt a chemical burn in the back of my lungs. My ears rang loudly. I forgot where I was. My ability to speak disintegrated. I felt like a burning piece of newspaper, blackened to ash, floating up the chimney and over the red clay rooftops of Hollywood Hills. When I came back down, I wanted more. It wasn't enough. Not nearly enough. Another, please. And another. And another.

We barely spoke. My mind was numb. The doorbell rang. It was Massimo, the dealer. He looked like he was about to die, with black leather bags under his crimson eyes. He hobbled through the room and plopped into a chair.

"What's up, you crack fiends?" he said in a thick Italian accent. We looked up at him in silence, trying to find words—any words. "Isn't it dee best? I have more for you, and sometheeng else. Sometheeng special."

He unwrapped a marble-sized ball of black tar heroin.

"Dis will take away da jeetters and make you cum in your mind," he said. Disgusting image. Disgusting human being. I wanted more of the yellow stuff, not anything black.

"We'll take it," Dave said, handing him a $100 bill.

"That'll be two beels," he said. I had never done heroin before. It had been an imaginary line that I proclaimed I would never cross.

"Not for me," I said, a few of my words coming back. "If you get hooked on that shit, you're done."

I watched as Dave dropped a small crumb of heroin in the center of a piece of tin foil, lit the bottom with a flame, and sucked up the smoke with a rolled-up twenty. Once heated up, the heroin would glide down the foil, leaving a brown, tear-like streak. As it began to liquefy, a plume of smoke streamed upward.

He slid it across the table toward me.

"Don't be such a bitch," he said.

"Nah. I'm good."

"You won't get hooked. Take the ride. Come on the magic carpet with me."

His eyes glazed over. He looked calm.

"It's better dan de white. Try it. You will fall een love," Massimo chimed in.

That was the problem. I knew myself too well. I didn't want to fall in love with heroin. But maybe I could try it just once, just to get it off my bucket list. Rules were meant to be broken, and I broke them often. Tonight was the night, I guess.

"What the fuck. Give me the lighter," I said.

"Bravo! You tank me later when you sheeting yourself in de corner," Massimo grinned. Disgusting man.

I heated up the foil and sucked up a sizeable amount of mud-colored smoke. Nothing was happening, nothing at all. I wasn't hallucinating or seeing shapes and colors, or even feeling calm. What a gyp.

"Hey, you guys, this stuff is lame. I don't get it. It's not doing a thing," I said.

"Your pupils are leetle pins. Look in de mirror." Massimo laughed.

"Fuck you." I slowly raised my body to stand. I felt like a newborn calf that hadn't found its footing yet. I wavered over to the hall mirror and looked into my eyes. He was right: My lids were almost closed. No wonder I couldn't see anything. My whole body was wonky, and my mind was sort of breezy and warm, like the leather interior of an old Citroën parked near the beach on a lazy afternoon in the south of France. I suddenly had an uncontrollable urge to lie down on the floor, and as I did, the room became a shadow. It wasn't a scary one that jumps out at you from behind a door—more like a friendly shadow. My body became a weightless bag of feathers.

This was the best I had ever felt. It brought down the crazy frenetic surge of the crack high and left me in a puddle of golden honey on the floor. My thoughts were of warm, natural hot springs, angels calling my name, and golden retriever puppies licking my face. I could get used to this. I wanted more—a lot more—and in the months that followed, my wish would come true.

I lived in a Spanish-style Hollywood bungalow in Beachwood Canyon that was built in the 1920s. I had arrived in LA a few years before with aspirations of becoming a seasoned TV producer and even had a few projects that were close to being sold. I networked with the young film executive crowd, and interviewed for jobs at the big movie studios and talent agencies. To my dismay, no one seemed to want me. I became increasingly disillusioned with the business—or maybe it was the rejection I didn't like. I had sold my New York apartment and made a sizeable profit of $200,000, but after buying a steel blue vintage Porsche, a bunch of Armani, and hosting a continuous stream of bloodsucking party friends for the better part of two years, most of the money was gone. My place was decorated to the nines with the overflow of my mother's antique furniture from Georgetown. She had even loaned me a signed Warhol that was prominently placed above my mantelpiece. The exterior of the bungalow was coated with a thick skin of ivy and bougainvillea that blossomed with red flowers in the spring and covered the windows. It felt like a regal cave when you walked in. I even painted the dining room a deep burgundy to enhance the mood.

At first, the people who came by were the friends who had jobs and careers and ambition—you know, the educated transplants from back east who came out to LA to be discovered. There was a legendary party house up the road on Temple Hill Drive that was inhabited by old buddies from St. Paul's and a Harvard grad. We called ourselves the varsity squad because we could take more chemicals than anyone and still remain functional, so to speak. We snorted and chewed and guzzled our way through the better part of two years alongside heiresses, actors, agents, and other generally well-bred—and always beautiful—people. I spent a lot of time up there planning my next moves in the industry, gaining contacts, flirting with women, and taking recreational drugs. That all stopped completely when I started smoking crack and heroin.

Within six months of my new daily habit, my pedigreed, fair-weather friends could sense that I was on the decline and had no interest in rolling around in the gutter with me. Who could blame them? So, a group of new friends began to arrive each week on the scooter of my Italian drug dealer, Massimo. He would pull up on his Vespa and drop off the goods, often leaving one or two of his depraved customers on my doorstep. I didn't mind. I was happy to have the company of other drug fiends; we could smoke together and pass the time talking about nonsensical bullshit. People would crash out on my couches, sometimes for days at a time. As long as the drugs were flowing, they loved me. Somehow, it didn't bother me that these were true bottom-feeders looking for a handout and willing to do whatever it took to get high. The drugs took away my libido, so I never really deviated to the realm of sexual darkness, but many of them did. Besides, I was happy to give my drugs away for free. It made me feel popular and adored. But this didn't last long—the good times never do.

The money began to dwindle, but my thirst for crack and heroin intensified. I no longer wanted to share. I grew suspicious of everyone. I kicked people out so I could be alone in my dungeon of narcotic haze, with the shackles of addiction clamped around my heart. *Fuck them. All of them.*

But after the fanatics headed out the door, the room got silent, and the silence was a reminder that I had failed to live up to even the most modest of expectations. I had no career, no girlfriend, hardly any money, no connection to my family, and no hope for the future. I wallowed in this misery for a few weeks until a new group of people began to speak to me—and they were angry. One morning, they showed up in the sky like invisible storm clouds. They had me surrounded.

"He's in there. The first bungalow on the left. Right inside," a woman's voice said.

Wait, who is that? I'm not expecting a delivery. I hope it's not one of those lame-asses I asked to leave. Fucking drug addicts.

I walked over to the front door and opened it wide. No one was there. Funny. I walked back to the couch and continued scraping my crack pipe for resin hits—something I did often when the rocks had run dry.

"He's in there. Up to the same old stuff. When will he learn? Such a stupid shame," a man said.

I heard that. I definitely heard that. Who are they calling stupid and shameful?

I walked back to the door and went outside. I scanned the parking lot for the perpetrators. There was no one in sight. I scaled up my neighbor's stone fence and looked down onto his patio. Empty. Where were they?

"I want you to know I can hear you. I can hear you loud and clear. Why don't you go judge someone else? Like yourself, maybe," I said to the air.

Silence. I waited outside for a few minutes, hoping to catch a glimpse of them. Nothing. I returned to my living room and continued pushing the screen through the pipe with a straightened coat hanger. I took a hit.

"I told you he's getting high. That foolish boy is smoking again," a woman said.

I jumped up from the couch and raced out the door.

"Leave me alone, you assholes! Fuck you and the high horse you rode in on!" I yelled at no one. I couldn't let them get away with it. Who were they?

"Carder, we can see you. We know what you're doing," a woman said.

Who were these ghosts? Why couldn't they leave me be? I pulled back the curtains to confront them. I put my ear to the floorboards.

Maybe they were hiding down there. I hid in my closet for an hour. I locked myself in the bathroom, watching for shadows underneath the door. I heard them on the roof, whispering from up above, so I climbed onto the shingles and sat for the rest of the afternoon. They heckled me like monkeys throwing their poop.

"We see you. Don't forget about us. We're coming for you," they said.

Who the fuck is this? Am I being followed? Are there people after me? Is it the drugs? Am I being watched?

I surveyed the rooftops and hillsides around me, and I began to see flashes of cameras and the red lights of video recorders. I was under surveillance. I was a target. It was the police and the FBI and the CIA. They were onto me. They knew about the drugs. They had my place bugged. I was fucked. Completely fucked. They would put me in jail, and I would be killed by murdering rapists.

Man, I have to calm down. I need heroin. Lots of heroin.

I managed to come down and get into bed after a large hit of heroin, but when I woke up the next morning, they were back. After my first hit of crack, they came at me even harder.

"Look at what you're doing. It's despicable. You're killing yourself. You're in a lot of trouble. We'll be there soon," they said.

"Leave me the fuck alone," I yelled. But they wouldn't stop.

Heroin: yes please, another hit of the brown.

I inhaled the thick smoke and was better for a moment. I took a colossal hit of crack.

"We're right outside your door," they said.

"Leave me alone, you bastards! Can't you see I'm trying to get high? Don't think you're fooling me for a second. I know what you want. You stupid pig fuckers. You want to drag me through the town square. I'm not gonna let you do it. I'm smarter than you, so watch out, assholes. Here I come!" I screamed at the wall.

My one-sided conversation lasted for the next several weeks—months, actually. Whenever I smoked crack, the voices came. I guess it was fair. I deserved to be criticized and laughed at like some rodeo clown. Look at what my life had become.

When I wanted them to stop, I filled my lungs with black tar. *Heroin. Yes, heroin.* I laid on the bed for several hours in a pool of sweat, watching myself slide down a rainbow into a pool of psychedelic bliss. I never wanted to get out—I was safe, for now.

But the pipe kept calling my name. I tried to cover my ears, but it was no use. There was nothing I could do—nothing at all. It always won.

I put a small yellow nugget on the screen and sucked until my face turned blue.

"What? Go away. Stop talking to me. I know I'm in trouble. Come arrest me, then. Let's get this whole thing over with."

"We're outside your door. We're coming for you now. You need to learn a lesson," they taunted.

I ran outside and circled my bungalow three times, but I still couldn't find them. I could hear their police radios squawking back and forth in the distance.

"Yup, he's over there. He's outside now. I'm looking at him right now. I feel bad for him. He has no idea what's in store," a man said.

I crawled underneath the foundation of my bungalow, slithering like a garden snake. Maybe they would lose track of me if I stayed really quiet. I could smell the damp scent of decaying earth and mold as I lay face down on the ground.

"He's under there. Yes, under the damn house. He's gone crazy. We have to get him out," a woman said.

Let them try. Let them fucking try. I'm not going down lightly. I'll scratch and kick and claw my way out if I have to, and I don't care if they get hurt in the process. No one is going to take me in alive—no fucking way. I'm not going to jail. Not today, not ever.

Footsteps were everywhere. I could hear them inside my bungalow, walking across the wooden floorboards—creaking their way around my rooms. It was my neighbors, too; they were all in on it. They must have ratted me out and called it in. I'd been noticing that they were looking at me strangely and keeping their distance out in the parking lot. Now I knew for sure. It was a big fucking conspiracy, and I was the fall guy. I didn't deserve this. *Help me, please. Somebody help me.*

I was stuck. I had wedged my way in between a wall of cinder blocks and a mound of dirt. I reached my hand out into the open air and tapped the ivy as loud as I could.

"Help! Please help me. I'm stuck. Help!" I yelled from my hole.

I could hear more circling around me like coyotes surrounding a stray. I was no match for them.

"Who is that? Let me pull you out. Grab my hand," a voice said.

I reached as far as I could and clasped fingers with one of them. I could hear the handcuffs opening and the prison keys clacking and the vehicles arriving for backup. I felt myself jostling loose, and the hand pulled harder, discharging me from the tomb underneath my house. My next-door neighbor gazed down at me with the look of a concerned parent whose child had just swallowed poison.

"What the hell were you doing down there?"

"I was looking for something. I dropped something, and I was looking for it," I said. I couldn't stop twitching in my left eye. My nostrils flared like a thoroughbred.

"What did you drop?" he asked.

"Are you helping them? Are you in on it?"

He looked at me with a strange expression. Guilt, no doubt. I backed away, shaking my head.

"Helping who?"

"*You* know *who*," I said. I could hear them chattering away in the background. "Them." I gestured to the bushes, the house, and the hills above.

"Who is them?" he said with a sly smile. And in that instant, I *knew* he was in on it. They're all out to get me. *He's just a decoy to distract me from what's really going on.*

"You're not fooling me," I said. "I know what you're doing."

"Are you okay?"

"I'm fine. Never better. Now leave me the fuck alone and stop pretending you're a good guy. I *know* you called them."

He put his hands on his hips. He was getting angry—just what I thought.

"Listen, I don't know what you're talking about, and I don't appreciate you accusing me of doing something. I have no idea what you mean. Take care. And you're welcome," he said, walking back into his bungalow.

"Thanks *a lot*," I said sarcastically. "Thanks for being so *reliable* and *trustworthy*. Fucking Judas!" A car pulled up to the curb, and I could hear them get out. It wouldn't be long now. I rushed back into my bungalow and slammed the door. I was out of heroin, but a mound of crack glared at me from the dining room table. I had to smoke some more before it was too late. When they caught me, I would never be able to smoke again.

I stripped out of my dirty pants down to my boxers. I had been wearing the same clothes for four days, and I hadn't slept during that time. Shadowy figures lurched from behind the furniture and swirled around the corners of my ceiling. Iridescent bubbles with eyes floated by the living room mirror. Rats traversed the rug and watched me as I prepared my pipe. I crammed the stem with as much crack as it could hold and began to melt it on the screen. If this was going to be my last hit, it was going to be the biggest one I'd ever taken.

I heated the glass with a green lighter until the crack was bubbling from the end. I pulled and toked and sucked on the glass until I thought I would suffocate. I held it in for a few more seconds. When the first puff of smoke streamed from my lips, I heard the sirens. This was for real. I sprinted to my bathroom and flushed the pipe down the toilet. I had to run—it was the only way. I picked up a shirt off the floor and slung it over my back. My shoes. Shit, where were they? The sirens grew louder. The megaphones blared.

"Come out with your hands up. We know you're in there," a voice bellowed. My shoes. Fucking shoes. I slipped my feet into a pair of bunny ear slippers—the only ones I could find. My mother had sent them in a care package for Easter. Something on my feet. Anything. I grabbed the large chunk of crack and put it inside my mouth. If they caught me, I would swallow hard. I opened the bathroom window and lowered myself onto a narrow dirt path behind my bungalow. I vaulted myself over a rusty chain-link fence and into an alleyway. As soon as I hit the ground, I started to run faster than I'd ever run before.

"It's no use. We're going to catch you," the voices echoed. "Run all you want, but remember, we're right behind you."

I leapt over trash cans and through backyards, hoping to find my way out of the neighborhood. I had to get as far away as possible. I shimmied down the side of a stucco house and saw that the coast was clear. It was now or never. I barreled down the street for as long as my lungs would let me, and when they felt like they would explode, I crouched behind a tree and doubled over, dry heaving. I double-checked, and the crack was still safely under my lip.

There it is—that car. That black car is following me with the man wearing a hat in the front seat. I've seen him before, I know it.

He looked over at me while talking into his cell phone, and the wheels of his car came slowly to a halt. Shit, I'd been spotted.

A helicopter. I hear a helicopter, maybe two.

Blades whirling and engines blasting away. It was nearby and loud and full of hate. I booked across the street into an open garage. I crawled behind an old Chevy station wagon with wood panel siding and crouched. I waited until the street was clear.

I walked down a side street and took a left down Beachwood Drive—the main thoroughfare in the canyon. A man in a hat was walking his dog across the street, and he talked incessantly into his phone as he looked up. He was one of them. They were everywhere. He was giving my coordinates to his agent friends up the road. I bolted down the center of the avenue in my fuzzy, bunny-eared slippers and purple silk underwear. A car passed, and two girls hung out the window whistling at me. The whistle was obviously another signal.

"There he is," a voice roared, "in the middle of the street wearing slippers. You can't miss him." The fuzz of a radio answered back.

"Copy that."

I arced left onto Franklin Avenue, nearly bowling over a group of old ladies wearing flowered hats. It was clear that hats were an integral part of the spy uniform—it's how they identified one another. They looked at me from underneath their brims. I had to get inside before it was too late. There was a record store just around the corner. I had been there before. It was small and well-lit and had a back door. I slunk inside.

A young guy with long hair and mutton-chop sideburns looked up from the register and tilted his head back in greeting. I hunched down on my heels and ducked behind a stack of records, peering out the plate glass window every few seconds.

"Hey, man, you okay? You don't look so good. Can I help you with something?" he said. I could tell that he was on my side.

"Can you see them out there? All those people in their hats? They're all after me. Is it okay if I stay in here a while?" I asked.

"You can stay here as long as you want, man. There's a back room, too, if you need to stash yourself away. Who is it that's looking for you?"

I straightened up. "CIA and FBI, mainly. Local law enforcement, sheriffs, DEA. Special task force."

"Damn. That's a lot of pigs after one dude. What'd you do? Rob a bank or something?"

If I could make it out of there alive, I had a friend named Lars who lived down Franklin Avenue. He usually had heroin. I needed a hit of the black really bad.

"No, I got caught up in some dope deals and stuff. They've had me under surveillance. They came for me today, and I barely got away," I said.

"Damn, dude. Let me know how I can help you. I got friends been busted before, and it's no cakewalk. You need a ride somewhere? I could close the store and take you somewhere safe," he said.

"No, it's cool. But if I could leave out the back, I can get to Lars's place. He's got a watchdog that won't let anyone inside. I'll be safe there. If they come asking about me, please throw them off the scent," I said.

"Of course, amigo. I never saw you. The back door is through here," he motioned toward the rear of the store.

In the crowded parking lot, I inched from one fender to the next, using the side view mirrors like periscopes to survey the adjacent street. When there were no hats in sight, I made a break for it. I had done the impossible and eluded the police for the better part of an hour. Drenched in sweat and dirt, with one hell of a story to tell, I arrived at Lars's door with a mouthful of crack.

"Carder," he said, as he opened the door. "Dude, what the fuck."

"Lock the door behind me. Quickly. They're looking for me," I said, panting.

"Yo, look at your getup. Sweet bunny slippers. Are you wearing boxers? Wait, how did you get here?" he said.

"I ran all the way from my house," I said. I paced around the room and peeked out the window.

"What about your Porsche?"

I crouched below the window sill and pulled down the blind. I watched the street through the slats. Lars stood and watched.

"It's bugged. Can't drive it anymore."

I got up quickly and moved quietly into the hallway—out of sight.

"Dude, you're kinda freaking me out. What's going on? Who is after you?"

"CIA, FBI, DEA. They were staking out my place. They were coming in for the bust, and I made it out by the skin of my teeth," I said.

"No shit? Man. That sounds terrible. Well, it's safe here. You don't need to worry. Barley won't let anyone in here. Will you, girl?" he said, bending down to pat his small, bear-like companion.

"You sure it's safe? Maybe they saw me come in."

"Listen, if anyone even comes up the stairs, Barley will bark. Don't be so paranoid. Everything is cool. But if you have any of the white, you should give it to me. I'll put it in a safe place. Give me the drugs. I'll keep them for you," he said.

I took the soggy wad of crack from my mouth and handed it to him.

"I'm gonna stow this away soon, in a safe place, but first I want to take a few hits. Just one or two to tide me over." Lars sat down at his desk and took a glass pipe from his drawer. He began to pull apart the blackened screen with his fingers to clear out the resin.

"Yeah, good idea. Hide it for me. They're not after you. If you had a hit of black, it would really help me out," I said.

"As a matter of fact, I do. Just a pinch. I'm saving it for later, but I'll give you a little dollop," he said. He pulled a jelly bean–sized nugget of heroin from his drawer and smudged it onto a square piece of tinfoil. I grabbed a rolled-up dollar bill and took two hits in rapid succession. If the feds were going to catch me, at least I wouldn't be filled with so much fear.

"Man, I feel better. So much better. If they find us and break down the door, do you have enough time to stash the dope?" I asked.

"Are you sure it wasn't just the fashion police that were after you?" Lars said, grinning. He nodded toward my feet.

"No, it was the Feds," I said. "I not only heard them coming, but I saw them everywhere."

"Really? Shit, what did they look like?" Lars said, exhaling a huge cloud of crack smoke into the air.

"Serious. And mean. All plain clothes. Most of them wearing hats. Undercover. Some of them were driving black Suburbans."

"Damn, dude. That's hairy. Are you sure some of them weren't just normal people out on the street walking their dogs and shit?"

"Listen, bro. I know the difference between an old lady and an undercover agent, okay? I'm not crazy," I said, annoyed.

He put his hands up. "Okay, okay, I hear you. Just glad you got away. Hey, can you pass that black over my way? You want a little hit of the white?"

I considered his question for a moment. If I smoked, there was a distinct possibility that the cops would zero in on me again. It happened that way every time, but I had never once refused a loaded crack pipe from a friend.

"Don't mind if I do. Just a small one," I said.

As I pulled the smoke into my mouth, the alarm bells started ringing immediately. Sirens everywhere. Megaphones blaring.

They're here. Right outside the goddamn building. The fuckers were waiting for me to smoke so they could catch me in the act. They've been videotaping from across the street. They saw me take a hit. They have proof. I'm a goner.

"Put the dope away! They're outside!"

Lars looked at me, bewildered.

"Who's outside? What do you mean?" he asked, putting the pipe and crack in his drawer.

"Can't you hear them? Those sirens? The megaphone calling my name?"

I heard it plain as day.

"We've got the place surrounded. You need to come out now. You're in a lot of trouble," a voice said.

"I don't hear anything," Lars said. "I think it's all in your head. Calm down. Everything's cool. We're not doing anything wrong. If someone came in, they would just see us here having a conversation. Two handsome dudes, chilling."

I got up from my chair and rushed into the bathroom. I locked the door quickly behind me and lay down in the bathtub, pulling the shower curtain shut.

If they come in, I'll pretend I'm taking a bath. Just me in the tub. But why would I be in my clothes? That would look strange. Maybe I should be naked in the tub, and then I won't look like I'm high. I'll seem normal. Just a normal guy taking a bath. But they already know. Shit.

I raised my eyes to the level of the window and peered at the street below. A black SUV sat parked across the street, and I could see a man's arm leaning from the window, holding a cigarette. It was a stakeout for sure. I took off my clothes and drew a shallow bath, attempting to scrub the scent of crack from my skin. I shivered in the warm water and listened to every sound my ears could detect. And then the footsteps came. They were outside the bathroom door. I stared at the doorknob turning slowly to the right. I was petrified. *Goodbye, freedom.*

"Carder, are you in there? What are you doing, bro? The coast is clear. I promise, it's cool." Lars's voice sounded shaky. Maybe they were behind the door, coercing him to talk so he could coax me into a trap. But I couldn't stay in there forever.

When I emerged from the bathroom, the room was calm. Lars sat at the desk, pushing the screen through the crack pipe. Barley lay at his feet in a cozy afternoon slumber. Her paws twitched like she was running through a field full of rabbits.

"Sit down. Take a load off. I saved a hit of black for you. Looks like you need it," he said.

Where were they? All my enemies huddling together outside the door? Had Lars sent them away?

"Thanks, man. I need it. Really bad."

Thank God for heroin.

Back at my bungalow, things were quiet. I waited for my dealer to arrive and was hoping he could provide me with enough of the black to ease me into sleep. I had been awake for way too long—four days—and my body throbbed. But the salty Italian hustler arrived with only a pouch full of white, and I wanted no part of it. Instead, he offered me a two-milligram tablet of Rohypnol and said it would take away the pain. I had heard it called the "date rape drug," so I escorted him to the gate before swallowing it. You can never be too careful. I sat on the floor and waited for the yellow pill to take effect. I drifted in and out until there was a loud knock at the door. It was well after midnight, and I had not invited anyone else, but for some reason, I knew they had to come in.

"The door's unlocked," I called from the floor.

As it swung open with a groan, I sat transfixed on the wool carpet. Lillie B. walked in, and behind her was my grandmother,

Maxine. Lillie wore a pair of white polyester pants and a small yellow halter top that stretched tightly across her ample chest. Her brown face was vibrant and kind, with the eyes of understanding that had consoled me so many times when I was a boy. My grandmother was in a blue dress with a beautiful gold brooch pinned to her lapel. Her thinning red hair fell about the wrinkles on her face. They sat down on the floor facing me, and our bodies formed an impromptu circle, as if there was a low-burning campfire that separated us.

"But you're both dead," I said, confused.

"No one ever dies," Maxine said. "We just go to a different place. A place on the other side. We've been watching you."

"I want to go there with you," I said.

"It's not your time yet, Coda. But you're close now. Closer than you've ever been," Lillie said.

I started to cry. "I don't want to be here anymore. There's nothing here for me."

"You need to stop hurting yourself. You have many good things to come. You're going to help a lot of people," Maxine said.

"I don't believe you. I can't help anyone. I'm lost!"

"You gonna find love, Coda. You gonna raise children. But not if you keep doin' this. You got one foot on the other side. We come to put it back," Lillie said.

"I miss you, Lillie," I said, frowning at her through tears.

"We're always here for you, dear. We've been talking to you. It's our voices that you hear in your head. The spirits of your ancestors," Maxine said.

"Wait, that was you? I thought I was going crazy. I was scared," I said.

"We watch over you. All of us. We will help you," Maxine said.

"I love you, Grammy." I held out my hand, but for some reason, she wouldn't take it. Maybe it was forbidden to touch someone from the other side.

"You have a gift, Coda. Listen when we talk to you. Everything's gonna be fine, my chil'. Take care of youself. We love you," Lillie said.

The two of them rose and walked toward the door. Their footsteps made no sound at all. They wanted me to give life another try. I wasn't sure I could.

Thirty-two hours later, I woke up heaving on the bathroom floor. It was only a matter of days before my family arrived unannounced and brought me to Promises Treatment Center in West Los Angeles—a mere stone's throw from the middle of Ghost Town.

Chapter Thirteen

2003

The sights and sounds of the 'hood blazed through my open window as I rolled onto Brooks Avenue. A group of teenagers clustered together on a stone wall outside the community center. I wasn't there for them. An older couple walked arm in arm down the street, carrying a tattered lawn chair. A homeless man rummaged through a trash heap. Police tape cordoned off a long stretch of sidewalk where there had been a fight the night before. A small boy played tag with his sister in the forbidden area, running directly over the blood stains. Cars pulled over and stopped at the corners to dance with the dealers that occupied them. It was just another day in Ghost Town.

Trech told me to find him when I got back, so I drove up and down the streets until I noticed his Escalade double-parked on Broadway. It wasn't hard to spot with its tinted windows and gold rims. He was sitting in the driver's seat listening to rap and watching the block. No surprises there. My hate for him had grown exponentially in the past few days, but I had to keep my cool until the transaction was over. I imagined putting a bullet in his head as I pulled alongside him.

"Hey, Trech. I'm back from doing that thing. Everything's cool. Should I meet you somewhere?" I said.

He seemed relieved to see me and smiled like I had just brought him a new underage girl. I should have turned him in—called the cops right then and there—but I was too involved and didn't want to implicate myself. Maybe I would make an anonymous tip after our business was settled—drop a dime on him, so to speak. I knew how he operated, and that would be valuable info to the police. I didn't care that he was a scumbag drug dealer who recruited young kids to do his bidding. It was what he did to Tisha. He had carved her back with the uncut carats of his diamond rings. I wanted to punish him—but maybe I already had. She was gone, and he would never touch her again. This would probably hurt him more than a bullet.

"Pull over. Park over there and get in. We'll go for a ride," he said.

I grabbed the duffel from the front seat and walked toward the SUV. I had become a drug dealer overnight. I wasn't proud of myself. There wasn't a person that I hated more than Treacherous Wallace, and he was about to pat me on the back and tell me I'd done good. I had to pretend I was grateful for the opportunity. It was not going to be easy. I took a deep breath and put my poker face on.

I jumped into the passenger seat and he accelerated off the curb. He dipped into a back alley and, moments later, pulled into an open garage.

"Now let's see what you got for me," he said.

He unzipped the black duffle and dumped the contents onto

his lap. Fifteen pounds of pure cocaine is not something you see every day. He cut into one of the kilos with a pen knife and tasted the thin film of powder on the blade. He nodded his head.

"Yeah, this is the shit. This is the *primo dope*. The finest of the finest. White boy, you done good. My cousin was right about you. You cool," he said.

"Thanks. So everything's cool?" I said, fighting off the urge to smack him in the mouth.

"Yeah, we cool. We good. Listen, I got another load needing a pickup in a few weeks. What you think?" he said.

I had to be careful about how I answered this. I didn't want to offend him but there was absolutely no way I could say yes.

"I'll think about it." I gave him a lame smile. "Thank you for the offer, but that was some crazy shit. Those Mexicans don't fuck around. Had me zip-tied in a chair with machine guns in my face. Not sure it's worth it."

"I don't *fuck around* neither," he said, staring me down. "I ain't askin'. There's another load needs to be picked up. I'll tell you when. Now that you in. *You in*. You can't walk away. Don't work like that. You feel me?" he said. His voice filled the SUV.

I was not going to argue with the head of the Shoreline Crips in a back alley in Ghost Town. I had to agree, and do it with conviction.

"Yeah, I'm cool with that," I lied.

"All right. See you 'round the 'hood," he said, hinting that our time was done.

"But what about the other five grand you owe me?" I said, holding my eyes on his. I wasn't going to flinch.

"What five large you talking about?" he asked, staring back at me.

"You said five now and five on delivery. Flyn told me you was straight and wouldn't fuck me over. You feel me?" I said, standing my ground.

He kept the staring contest going for a minute, then cracked a smile.

"Shit, if you wasn't my cousin's friend, I'd kill you right now. But seeing that you is, I guess I should pay up." He laughed. "But don't *ever* fuck with me, white boy, 'cuz if you do, I'll hurt you. Bizness is bizness. You in the *game* now."

Trech took a stack of bills out of the center console and counted out $5,000. I folded up the cash and stuffed it deep into my front pocket. I reached for the door handle, but he grabbed my arm and yanked it toward him. He was no longer smiling.

"One more thing. You seen Tisha around? I ain't seen her for a *minute*," he said. He stared hard at my face.

"I haven't seen her since Saturday. I'll keep an eye out, though."

"So you didn't bring her with you? To San Diego?"

This may have been the most important moment of my life. If I answered wrong or showed deception of any kind, I would be another statistic. I inhaled a shallow breath.

"No. No way. I went by myself," I said.

"Okay, 'cuz if you did, that would be a bad thing. You feel me?" he said.

"I feel you. Don't worry, I'm sure she'll turn up," I said, exiting the car. I tried to slam the door just the right way—not too hard, not too soft. I was at least twenty feet away before I exhaled. I was in the game now. Shit. This was a game that I'd rather watch safely from the bench. Cruising around with Flyn to serve his fancy clientele was one thing, but becoming a drug runner for the Crips?

I felt safe with Flyn—for the most part. He would see a way out of this—I was sure of it.

Beatrice's house smelled like fresh-baked muffins when I walked through the door. It reminded me of the kitchen in Georgetown when I was a boy. I would help Lillie B. mix the batter for her world-famous banana bread and watch through the oven door as it rose in the pan. The smell made me feel like I was coming home. Now, this modest house on Vernon Avenue was more of a home to me than anywhere else. I had searched for this feeling my whole life, and it had finally arrived in the most unlikely of places. This family could never know what it was to live in my privileged skin, and I would never comprehend the struggles they had endured in the 'hood, but none of this seemed to matter. They had adopted a stray by choice.

Beatrice stood in front of the stove wearing a red apron that said, "Kiss the Cook," so I walked up and planted one on her cheek. She beamed back at me.

"Codder! So happy you came fo' a visit. You can help me in the kitchen. Ole B is gonna bake all afternoon."

"Nothing would make me happier," I said.

Over at the kitchen table, Flyn and Alyssa sipped iced tea from tall, frosted glasses. The bump on Alyssa's stomach was protruding over her waistband, and she had a flush about her cheeks that looked like a benevolent sunburn. I joined them with a slap on Flyn's back.

"Hollywood, what's up, my man?" Flyn said. "We been talkin' about you. Your ears must have been burning."

"Talking about how handsome I am again?" I grinned.

"How did you know?" Beatrice laughed. "You hear us talking through the walls?"

"Something like that," Flyn said. "Sometimes, he hears his grandma talking."

"Flyn!" I said, eyes wide. Would he tell Beatrice my secret?

"I'm only foolin'. Don't get so riled up. It's Flyn here—your brother from another mother."

"And father," Alyssa added, with a wink.

"So, my educated, adopted white brother, we been talking about Willy's room and how empty it looks. We think you should move in and stay with us. Together as a family. We like having you around. Nobody will think we're racist anymore." He laughed.

I was a deer in the headlights.

"Seriously? Wow. I don't know what to say. That's a lot to think about, but I really appreciate the offer," I said. They were putting me on the spot, and although I wanted to say yes, I knew I should mull it over.

"You could help me out with the groceries and keep me company. I would love to have the company, baby," Beatrice added.

"Lord knows I'm not gonna help with the cooking. Last time I tried, I nearly set the house on fire," Flyn said.

"Mmm-hmm," Alyssa said.

"How far are you along?" I asked Alyssa.

"Five months. We're going to the doctor tomorrow to find out if it's a boy or a girl. I think it's a girl," she said with pride.

I looked over at Flyn, and he was shaking his head back and forth.

"Nah, that's a boy. That's my son in there. Flyn Jr. He's gonna be our first black president," he said.

"President of what?" B said, sarcastically.

"You know what," Flyn replied, "president of everything. He's gonna take the world by storm. There is nothing can stop that little nappy-headed boy in there." He rubbed Alyssa's belly.

"I didn't know you could have an afro inside the tummy. Must be a black thing," I said. I hoped this wasn't too off-color for the room, but they erupted in laughter.

"Sheeet, that boy ain't got no nappy-headed afro inside the womb. Flyn, you's crazy," Beatrice said, slapping him playfully with her oven mitt.

"You think about moving in. Uncle Hollywood should be here, too," Alyssa said to me in a low voice. Her words landed directly on my heart.

"Uncle Hollywood. I like the sound of it," I said back.

I turned to Flyn and pointed toward the backyard. He nodded his head, and we got up together.

"Where you boys going? I ain't through with you just yet," Beatrice said.

"Just got a few things to discuss with my brother. Man talk, you know. We'll be back shortly," he said.

We sat facing each other in two weather-beaten lawn chairs. The sun was setting over the slanted rooftops. There was so much to say, but we sat quietly for a few minutes, watching the sky. Flyn broke the silence first.

"How was the trip down to San Diego? Didn't expect you back so soon," he said.

"I'm glad it's over," I said. "It was pretty hairy. I'm not really cut out for it."

"I'm sorry, man. I never should have put you in the game like that. I just thought that you could use the money. Save it up. Get your ass out of the 'hood back to where you belong," he said.

"I belong here just as much as anyone," I said.

"No, you don't."

Who was I trying to fool? I was a white boy from the right side of the tracks. I didn't want to hear the truth, but maybe it was time to go.

I blinked. "You're right."

"Listen, I was trying to look out for you, but it was the wrong move. I'm sorry. I'm glad you got back safe," he said.

"Don't worry. It was my decision. It's all good."

"I've been thinking a lot about what we've been doing." He paused. "I don't want my son to grow up with a drug dealer as a father. Been thinking about cooling it for a while. Maybe for good."

This was music to my ears. I smiled.

"I think that's a good idea. I've been thinking the same thing. I quit smoking dope. I've been sober for a week now," I said.

"My man, Hollywood. No more talking with your ancestors. Good move. Solid."

"But when I made the delivery to Trech, he told me I couldn't walk away now. He wants me to do another pickup. Can you talk to him for me?" I said.

"Consider it done. Don't worry about a thing. I got you covered," he said. The tightness in my chest eased. I'd be okay. Flyn would make sure of it.

It was getting dark now, and the expression on Flyn's face grew somber. "I've done a lot of bad shit in my life, and I don't want to be that guy anymore," he said. "These streets are full of ghosts. I want to be around when my boy grows up. I don't want him to hurt like I did, looking at old photographs of a daddy he never knew. I want to hold him in my hands and swing him from my shoulders and tuck him in at night. That's all I want."

"And that's what you're gonna get," I said.

I reached down and took off my right shoe. I could feel the cash bundled up next to my toes. It was time to repay Flyn for the education he had given me. I peeled off $1000 and reached it toward him.

"This is for all you've done for me," I said.

He looked back at me and smiled.

"You keep it. It's yours. I've saved up a bundle. I'm straight. Take that money and buy yourself a ticket home. Somebody out there misses you," he said.

He was right. My whole family was out there, and they missed the person I used to be: the golden child with the chipped smile and all the answers. But I was no longer him.

"I can't leave now. Who would do the grocery shopping for B?" I said.

He leaned forward. "Listen, if anything ever happens to me, do your best to take care of things, okay? Whatever you can do. I've lived a lot longer than I thought I would. If my number comes up, take care of things for me, okay?"

"Nothing's going to happen to you. But it's a deal. You have my word."

We got up from the chairs and slapped our palms together, going in for a half hug. Flyn seemed melancholy, and his request sat heavily on my mind. We spent the rest of the evening around the kitchen table eating cold chicken and ribs. Beatrice rifled through a stack of old Motown records and kept the music flowing from the old Victrola in the living room. I talked about Craig and running away under the bridge. Flyn spoke about his dreams of becoming the first black lifeguard in Venice. He said he had a crush on

Pamela Anderson and used to look for her jogging down the beach. Beatrice reminisced about Los Angeles in the seventies and how she used to let her hair down with the Black Panthers. It was one of the best nights I could remember. I agreed to pick up Flyn and Alyssa the next afternoon to take them to the doctor's office. I was excited to know if it was a boy or a girl.

It was time to return to my apartment, so I walked up the fire escape and pulled myself through an open window. It was piled with layers of neglect. I stepped over my dirty clothes like I was a stranger in someone else's bedroom. It sure felt like it after a week sober. There were drippings of white wax adhered to the furniture and burn holes in the stained mattress. How had I ever lived this way? It was such a stark contrast to the warm, lamp-lit kitchen at Beatrice's house, and I wanted to go back. There was nothing here for me anymore. Even my mother's paintings looked foreign, like I was visiting some run-down gallery in a bad part of town. I didn't care about any of this stuff. I lay back on the fetid pillows and thought about the months to come. I imagined Flyn bouncing his baby boy in the garden as I readied an iron skillet for a mountain of scrambled eggs. I saw a birthday party with Uncle Hollywood dressed up in a clown suit, tripping over his oversized shoes. I saw Beatrice planting tulips in the garden and twirling around the kitchen to Otis Redding in her bare feet. I saw Alyssa walking down the block pushing a baby with a huge afro in an old-fashioned bassinet. I saw the future, and I couldn't wait to get there. I closed my eyes, and sleep took me away.

The next morning, it was time to clean up my mess. I walked down to the corner store and bought trash bags, sponges, and a bottle of Fantastik All-Purpose Disinfectant spray. If I was going to move out today, I wanted the place to be respectable. I took a butter knife and attempted to dislodge the solidified wax that had pooled on the oriental carpet and red ultra-suede chair. I wiped down the counters and scrubbed the bathroom floor with an old Chore Boy steel wool pad I found underneath the kitchen sink. I would no longer need its shavings for my crack pipe. I balled up piles of clothes, threw them into two yellow laundry bags, and headed toward the fluff and fold on Rose Avenue. I did not want to bring my matted shirts and soiled undergarments to my new home. It just didn't seem right. When I returned to the apartment, I was surprised at its sparkle—somehow, a six-month crack binge hadn't stripped the dignity off the crown molding. I packed a suitcase full of fresh-smelling garments and said my goodbyes. I would return later to put the rest in storage.

The activity on the block was at a lull as I walked up the front steps to Flyn's house. I felt like a kid on the first day of camp, about to walk into a cabin full of friends. I pushed open the door, hardly able to contain my joy.

"Hey guys, I'm here! I made a decision," I yelled down the hall-way. But I got no response. I could hear sobbing coming from the back, so I picked up the pace. As I rounded the corner, I saw Beatrice sitting on her bed, all dressed up in her finest things. Tears rolled down her cheeks, and she clutched a black-and-white photo to her chest. Alyssa sat in a chair in the corner of the room. She was also crying.

"What's wrong?" My thoughts went quickly to the baby. Had they lost the baby? But Alyssa's bump was as visible as ever, and she rubbed it gently back and forth.

"They got my boy! They got him," Beatrice wailed.

My heart sank into my stomach.

"What do you mean, they got him? I don't understand," I said.

"His old friend called last night. He went to meet him, and the police were there. He got caught up in some bullshit," Alyssa said quietly.

Beatrice kept looking at a photo, pressing it against her face as if this would somehow bring him back.

"I asked you to take care of him, Codder. You promised me you was gonna look after my boy so he wouldn't get into trouble. You *promised* me," she cried. An atom bomb of shame detonated in my bones. I could find nothing to say.

"Another one of my boys. They takin' *everything* away from me! I can't go on like this. It's too much." Beatrice's shoulders hunched as she sobbed.

"Well, let's go bail him out," I said. "Where's he at? I'll go get him out right now, and we can figure this out."

"Ain't no bail, Hollywood, and they ain't letting him go. Not now. Not ever," Alyssa said.

I stared at her. "What do you mean, 'Not ever'? I'll get him a good lawyer. I know one who's really good. He'll be able to get him out," I said.

"*You don't get it.* This his *third* strike. He ain't got no more chances. They putting him away for life. He goin' in for life," she said, the tears dripping down her cheeks.

Then it hit me—the full gravity of the situation. Flyn told me that he'd been convicted twice for selling dope and done time for both offenses. There was a three strikes law in California that put hardened criminals behind bars for twenty-five years to life. This was his third strike, and the law was clear. It would be a long time before he saw the outside again. He would never hold his baby in his arms or walk his child to school. He would only see him behind a thick window of bulletproof glass. My friend was gone, and there was nothing I could do to bring him back. I fell to my knees and looked up at Beatrice.

"Is there anything I can do? Anything at all to help?"

"No, baby, what's done is done," she replied.

I got up from the floor and moved over to her, but she blocked my attempt and pushed me away with Flyn's photo.

"I'll be back in a minute," I said, leaving the room and shutting the door behind me. I needed a minute to think my way out of this. I had never been in jail before, and it seemed futile to forge any sort of plan. I walked past Willy's room and paused for a moment. Maybe there was one thing I could do. I went into the room and sat down on the single bed. I took off my shoe and extricated the roll of blood money from underneath my toes. Five hundred dollars was all I would need to survive—the rest would be for Beatrice. Flyn had asked me to look after them as best I could, and right now, this was the most viable way.

I wondered if he had felt the danger lurking nearby. I figured his request the night before had been a cautionary measure. He must have had a premonition, felt the cold breath of captivity on the back of his neck, or realized that his number was up. I had never believed in coincidences, but his somber appeal had been out of character. Maybe he even knew something and had kept it a secret. It didn't matter now. I placed $4,500 on the bookshelf underneath a photo of Flyn and Willy. It was the best I could do.

Alyssa stopped me as I walked down the hallway toward the front door.

"You don't have to worry. Flyn's no snitch. He's not gonna tell them about you," she whispered, so Beatrice couldn't hear.

This thought had never even crossed my mind, but it made perfect sense.

"But I'd lay low for a while. I don't know if they been watching us or what."

"We were going to stop, anyway. Flyn wanted to start over for the baby. We were quitting. We talked about it last night," I said, sadly.

"I know. He was doin' it for me. I asked him to quit," she said. She took a deep breath.

"Can I go visit him? I mean, go see him in jail?" I asked.

Alyssa looked stone-faced and shook her head.

"Flyn don't want nobody to see him. Not even me. Makes it harder to do this kinda time when you got things on the outside. Forget about him," she said.

This was not the response I was expecting at all. It was inconceivable that I would never see him again. I shook my head.

"I can't. He's my friend. I can't forget about him," I said.

She looked out the living room window. "Thinking about moving to Atlanta. Better place to raise my son. Better place for B. I got family there who can look after us. Nothin' keeping us here no more," she said. Her face hardened, and her tears were gone. She had experienced loss before. There was no more emotion left.

"Your son? It's a boy?"

"Yeah. I already knew." She smiled weakly. "Gonna name him Willy," she said.

I gave her a hug and squeezed her as tight as she would let me. I walked down the hall. Beatrice was inconsolable. It took everything I had not to run away. I sat next to her on the bed in silence, holding her hand as she cried.

"I left something in Willy's room for you. Everything's going to be okay. Lyssa will take good care of you, and you have a new baby to look after. I love you, B," I said.

She looked at me through her big brown eyes full of water and nodded her head.

"I love you, too, Codder."

That was the last time I ever saw her.

In the span of an hour, my life had unraveled.

There was no point in being sober now. I had no future anymore. Everything I loved was gone.

I had never felt this sorry for myself in all my life.

Give me a fucking hit. I looked at the suitcase mocking me from the passenger's seat. *Load up the fucking pipe and give me the lighter.* All those neatly packed clothes and bundles of fresh socks. *Put the rock in the cylinder, and heat up the glass.* All of the jokes and laughter and fresh-baked muffins. *Step aside while I slowly kill myself with hunks of pure cocaine.* My black brother, Uncle Hollywood, and the perfect little makeshift family. *Fuck all of it. It was never real.* Who was I trying to fool with all of this Hallmark Hall of Fame after-school special bullshit? Life doesn't work that way. *Give me the fucking pipe.*

I knew it was safer to make a buy at night, so I waited patiently in my car until the sun fell to the ocean. There was a distinct possibility that the police had eyes on me, and it would be harder to detect my nefarious activity in the dark. I drove around the 'hood for a while and spotted a dealer on San Juan who had served me before. He was in his late teens, always had good dope, and usually engaged me with a kind word. Most of the street dealers were all business, but Dash liked to interact with his customers as if he were a local barber cutting hair for a living. He always had a yarn to spin and wanted to extract as much information as he could about the car you were driving, where you were headed, and what thoughts you might have about the climate on the block. He walked across the street quickly and sidled up to my front window.

"Hey, Dash, what's up?" I asked.

He was unusually tight-lipped. He looked a bit nervous, even.

"What's up, Hollywood. These streets is getting dangerous. Might be time for you to find someplace else. You feel me?" he said.

"Let me get a quick twenty," I said, handing him a fresh bill.

He unfolded a piece of wax paper and gave me a healthy rock.

"Listen. I can't sell to you no more. This is the last time. It ain't safe no more. Not for you," he said.

"I know," I replied. "The cops are out hard right now. Did you hear they got Flyn? Motherfuckers got Flyn."

"I heard that. This place is hot right now. You need to watch your back, shorty. This is a warning. Don't come back here," he said.

As he stepped aside, I could see a cluster of young dealers with their blue hoodies up gathering across the street. One of them walked slowly toward my car, and I barely caught a glimpse of the black reflection in his right hand before it happened.

In one swift motion, he raised his arm up and pointed my way. *Blam!* A bomb shattered my eardrum.

In slow motion, I could see a gold projectile pass inches from my forehead. I turned my head toward him and thrust my foot onto the gas petal.

Blam. Blam. He fired two more shots as I sped away.

What the fuck just happened? I had done hundreds of deals in the 'hood before and never had a gun pulled on me. Everyone knew I was with Flyn, so I was protected from harm. The way he came for me was unlike anything I'd witnessed before. He was like an assassin. The adrenaline rush in my body was so strong that I forgot about the brakes. I ran every stop sign in the 'hood doing seventy miles an hour until I hit the stoplight on Main Street.

I had literally just dodged a bullet—something I thought I would never do. The addict took hold; I had a healthy rock of crack in my pocket, and that was all that mattered. My car began to sputter and groan as I turned up the alley toward home. It coughed and wheezed and came to a complete halt behind my building. I sprinted up the stairs and into my apartment. In eleven seconds flat, I had loaded up the pipe, heated up the glass, and taken a colossal hit.

This time, it was only Lillie B. and Maxine who walked through the portal in my mind, but their voices sounded like hurricane winds.

"Coda, Goddamn stupid chil'. Don't you know they's coming? You need to get outta there!" Lillie said.

"Who is coming?"

"Bad people. Bad people who want to hurt you," Maxine said.

"Are you guys trying to scare me tonight? 'Cause if you are, it's working. What bad people? Did you know I just got shot at?" I could feel the blood pumping in my veins.

"We know," they answered in unison.

"Get out the house. Take a walk. Stay away," Lillie said.

Nobody ever had to ask me twice to leave my hovel, especially when I was high and paranoid. Were the cops headed my way? I wasn't going to wait to find out. I grabbed my pipe and the remainder of the drugs, put on my blue Boston Red Sox cap, and headed toward the canals. I zigzagged through the walking street for about a mile with the faint echo of birdcalls trailing me in the distance. I

moved briskly, keeping my head down like I was absolutely certain
where I was going and hell-bent on getting there.

A few lights flickered on in my wake, and I heard the slam
of a screen door or two as I passed. There were light footsteps
approaching from everywhere, and I hunted for their origins, but
I could discern only a few shadowy figures moving in the distance.
I turned around to see if I was being followed. Was I imagining all
this in my mind?

The canals were peaceful as usual. At this time of night, they
were deserted except for the random lovesick couple playing kissy
face on a sloping bank or a resident scooping up designer dog
shit with a perfumed green baggie. I watched the moon dangle
its arms through the rippling pools and wondered if anyone had
ever jumped off one of the bridges, falling to a pathetically shallow
death. Maybe I would be the first. I would stand up on the ledge and
plummet the excruciating ten feet down into several feet of muck.
Knowing me, I would probably sprain an ankle and have to hobble
home with only my spirit broken. But it was already smashed and
shattered like a tea set dropped from the Empire State Building. I
tried to imagine how I could pick up the pieces, but came up blank.

After two hours of tromping the entirety of Abbot Kinney's
waterway matrix, I plunged onward to find a quiet walking street
where I could cop a squat behind a hedge and smoke my horn on
the fly. Sobriety had been wishful thinking. The peril of the streets
was far too grave for a spoiled kid from DC. What would I do now?

I found the perfect spot for my next hit. The tranquility of the
setting was inviting to a drug fiend like me. There were twenty small
structures lining either side of a narrow cement sidewalk, most of
them authentic bungalows from the twenties, freezing time in their

little Venice enclave. I walked silently to the center of the block and crouched down behind a white picket fence. My stem was already prepared, and my whole body was salivating.

Flick.

The flame rose from the lighter and rested on the yellow, crumbling chemical stones. I filled my lungs and blew a long stream of smoke over the bushes.

Flick.

The flame rose again, and as it touched the glass, I could sense a presence behind me. I twirled quickly and saw a middle-aged woman standing on her front stoop with a bird whistle in her mouth.

"*Tweet. Tweet. Tweet.*"

Within a few moments, every bungalow on the street had turned on its outdoor lights like a runway preparing for an oncoming jet. It was a setup. Screen doors opened in unison, and men and women popped out in their pajamas, wielding baseball bats and golf clubs. Each of them had a whistle in their mouths, blowing the insidious chirps that would haunt me forever. I slowly backed down the walk, and the residents began to follow me. As I passed by their stoops, each of them peeled off into the growing surge of humanity. It was an angry mob.

"*Get off our streets! We have children who live here.*"

"*Fucking crackhead son-of-a-bitch loser!*"

"*Never come back!*"

"*You're ruining our neighborhood.*"

"*The police will be here soon.*"

I began to run, and the unruly horde chased me. I picked up the pace, and at least five or six of them stayed on my heels. They had blood on their minds. I was in a full sprint now. I could see the ocean up ahead and hightailed it toward the beach, where it was pitch black. They were chasing me out of town. If they had horses, I would have been dragged through the town square before being tarred and feathered. I looked over my shoulder, and the last of them had slowed down as I ramped over the boardwalk to the sand. I continued for another quarter mile until I was safely out of reach. I had worn out my welcome on both sides of the poverty line.

I sat down, hyperventilated, and then wept like a baby. I was terrorized, like I'd eaten a bunch of bad mushrooms, only this time, my friends were not there to console me. I sat alone and cried to an audience of stars that barely twinkled back. My life was a waste. Maybe I had earned a one-way ticket to the bottom of the ocean.

I took off my shoes and walked toward the water. *Will anyone miss me if I do it? Will I miss myself?* I rolled up my pants and invited the foam to meet my toes. *Is this the night?* I stood and watched as the waves came one after another, and I realized that I was a wave that had already crashed. I was drifting now back out to sea. It wasn't so bad, this drifting. I would find land again, someday.

Chapter Fourteen

2003

For the time being, the voices had stopped. I didn't want them to return anytime soon—perhaps ever again. The blue light of a passing tanker drifted along the horizon. The waves pounded the shore like the slow heartbeat of a whale, and I stood there until my own heart slowed. The angry mob had nearly pushed me to cardiac arrest.

The cold waves beckoned, but I wasn't ready to disappear into them yet—a part of me was still living. I turned toward the Santa Monica pier. I had all the time in the world.

As I approached the wooden pylons, I remembered playing make-believe under the thick-hewn beams of the docks on Long Island. Craig and I were pirates digging for Spanish gold lost at sea when their galleons went down in a blaze of glory. It had been six months since I'd spoken to my brother. I missed the way he stood next to me. We hid under those docks together, evading the wrath of our father. I had broken a window, and he was coming like a storm.

When he slapped my cheek, Craig stayed by my side. I needed him now more than ever—my beautiful brother with the cape on his back.

I sat down and rested against an old retaining wall that had been constructed with vertical slabs of battered driftwood. I didn't flinch when a jagged nail protruded into my shoulder. I wondered if I was still welcome at Beatrice's house, but I knew that I had no place there without my friend. I would be a constant reminder of the life that put him behind bars. Atlanta would be good for Beatrice, Alyssa, and the baby. There was no room for a secondhand white boy in the car. I thought of the coffee-colored girl who threw herself to the wolves so her daughter could have heat in winter. I pictured them sitting together on a rusty tire swing in some broken-down playground in Detroit. Any place would be better than here. Sending her home was the only thing that turned out right. When dawn broke, it was time to get moving.

Fishermen cast their long lines into the shallows as I walked by. A lifeguard drove his red truck past me and raised his hand in a wave. I kept walking until I found a patch of shore that was free of human activity and stood facing the ocean. The pipe felt warm in my hand as I removed it from my pocket. The morning sun had heated up the glass through my jeans pocket, and the warm glass gave me a momentary erotic charge. It was time to break up with my mistress. I had taken her back in desperation, but this time, it would be for good. With all of the strength I could muster—which wasn't much—I hurled the pipe out to sea.

"Goodbye, old friend. May we never meet again," I said. And I meant it. Everything else would become clear if the crack pipe stayed away from my lips. I was sure of it.

It was mid-morning by the time I reached the front steps of my building. I tromped up the stairs, heading toward the fire escape, but as I approached, I realized it wasn't necessary. The door was wide open. The lock looked intact. Maybe I had left it open in my crack-induced frenzy the night before. I scanned the room and saw nothing amiss. I lowered the venetian blinds and fell fast asleep sitting up in my mother's upholstered chair.

I dreamed of the farm in Massachusetts and the sacred Native American field that bordered the lake on our property. Once again, there was a big bonfire, and a village of large teepees surrounded an ongoing ceremony. Flyn sat before the fire in a feathered head-dress, and next to him were Alyssa and their newborn son. I walked toward them, but with each step, they moved farther and farther away. Tisha and Beatrice stepped out of a teepee and sat down next to them. I yelled their names, but they couldn't hear me over the crackling of the flames. I ran faster and faster toward them but gained no ground. I could hear the loud thump of a fist landing on the skin of a drum. The beat got louder and louder and faster and faster—*Bang. Bang. Bang.* I bolted up and for a second was still in my dream. The farm. I could go live at the farm.

"*Yo Hollywood, it's Jamal. You in there? I needs to talk to you.*"

I opened the door and he burst in, looking disheveled and serious.

"Hey man, good to see you. What's up?" I said.

"What, you sleeping? It's like five o'clock," he said.

"Shit, I must have needed to sleep. Some dude shot at me last night. And then a bunch of people from Venice chased me down the street. Craziest night of my life."

But Jamal didn't come to hear about my night. I could tell by the look on his face. He looked scared.

"Forget about all that. I got something to say. It ain't safe for you no more," he said. "Trech knows what you did."

"What do you mean?" I said.

"Tisha, man."

This was not good.

"What about her? I haven't seen her around lately," I said, casually.

"Listen, man, it's me. Jamal. I'm your boy. You can be straight wit' me. You know I don't give a fuck what you do."

"What about Tish? Is she okay?" I asked.

"She called Trech from a payphone. Said she was on a bus to Detroit. Said you took her to the bus station after goin' to San Diego. Said *you* paid for her ticket home."

I couldn't believe it. After all I had done for her. "Shit."

"Listen, the whole 'hood talking about it. They comin' for you, man."

"Coming for me? What does that mean?" I said.

"They's a contract out on you. Trech took a contract out on yo *life*. You gots to leave now."

The weight of the situation was setting in. I had to go. Now. I went to the sink to splash some water on my face and saw something that I'd missed earlier in the day. A forty of Olde English sat upright next to the drain. They had already been here.

I whipped around. "How much time do I have?"

"They coming for you at dark. Might be watching from outside now. I's crazy to be here. But I didn't want you to get killed. You looked out for me before." He was twitchy and skittish, but he'd put his life on the line for me.

"Thanks, Jamal. I got to pack a few things and go. I appreciate you, man. Thank you. You saved my life."

"Yo life ain't saved yet. Not 'til you a thousand miles away. Now *get*," he said.

He gave me a quick hug and was gone. What did I need to bring? My passport. The Gottlieb. A photo album. A change of clothes. I hurried around the room and stuffed a few things into a small backpack. I ripped the painting off the wall and shut the door behind me as I left. They might be watching the front door, so I opened a window in the hall and climbed out onto a fire escape that led to a back alley. I jumped down and grabbed the car keys from my pocket. My hands were shaking so badly that it took a minute to get inside, and when I did, I felt no sense of relief. Last night, a bullet had passed through my open window. Another could arrive at any moment.

I inserted the key into the ignition and stomped on the gas pedal. Nothing. Complete silence. I took the key out, wedged it back in, and thrust my wrist to the right. *Dead.* It was completely dead. How could this be happening? I remembered that it had lurched to a stop the night before. I could not have cared less at the time. Now it would mean my life. I had no way to get out of town, and night was coming soon. They would have me surrounded before the sun went down. I turned the key one last time, praying for a miracle. No response at all.

There was a basement in my building, and sometimes, the outside door was left ajar. It was dark down there. I grabbed my backpack, opened the car door, and crawled on my hands and knees toward the cellar. They knew the car I drove and would probably assume I was hiding somewhere. I had to find a place to camp out for the night. A place where no one could see me. If they caught even a glimpse, I would be six feet under.

There was a stack of wooden crates in the basement that had a small space behind it, and I wedged my body tightly inside the crevice. The lights were out, and I watched the last of the sun's shadow drifting up the wall. I crouched in the same position for several hours. My bones ached and my head was splitting, but I didn't make a sound. Suddenly, a flurry of activity overhead. Several people marched up and down the stairs of the building, and whispers came through the floor. Was that my name? I heard a faint calling.

"Holly-wood. Holly-wood. Where you at, Hollywood?"

I recognized the voice. It was Trech.

"We see yo car, Hollywood. We know you here. Come talk to me, Hollywood. Don't be afraid," I heard through the wall. He was getting closer and closer. He had found me. I was a goner.

The cellar door opened, and he walked slowly down the stairs.

I wish you were here to protect me, Craig. I need you now. I love you, bro.

His body moved through the darkness. It wouldn't be long now.

"Come out, come out, wherever you are!"

He kicked a few boxes and ducked into the next room. The footsteps thundered overhead. I was surrounded.

Will I feel the bullet cut though my skin? Will it hurt?

"Hollywood, you down here? It's Trech. Treacherous Wallace. I just want to talk to you. You don't need to hide no more. It's all good. Just want to hear your side of the story. Come out."

The conversation would be short. It would begin and end with a bullet.

"Hollywood? You back there?"

I was convinced he could see me.

He clanked the gun against the wall, and I shifted a bit.

I wish I had been a better person. I wish I hadn't let everyone down. If I could only have one more chance, things would be different.

"I got a surprise for you. Don't worry. It's not gonna hurt."

I could see the gun in his hand. It had killed so many. Now it was my turn.

I want to have kids and fall in love and move far from here.

I could see his face.

"Time to pay for what you did, Hollywood."

Please, God, receive me with open arms. I know I've been bad, and I'm sorry.

He was two feet away.

"You can't hide forever."

I bit my lip, waiting for the bullet. I closed my eyes and said goodbye.

"I'm coming for you, Hollywood."

But instead of pulling the trigger, he turned around and shuffled through the blackness.

"We gonna find you one way or another, Hollywood. I can promise you that. You got no place to go."

He was a monster in a bad dream. I heard the sound of his footsteps retreating up the stairs and the door slamming. How had he not seen me? Had God intervened?

"Nah, he ain't down there," he said from the other side of the door. I listened as the mass of bodies scurried away, but soon they came back and continued the search. I sat in the corner until the morning came. It was the longest night of my life.

I could hear the roar of a bus engine a few blocks away on Pacific. They started to run at 6 AM, and there was a stop on the corner adjacent to my building. It was now or never. I bounded up the stairs and thrust the steel door open with my palms, fully expecting to enter a hail of bullets, but none came. I ran across the street and flagged down the bus just as it was pulling away. The glass doors swung open, and I hopped inside. I slapped a crumpled twenty into the driver's hand.

"Does this bus go to the airport?" I said.

"Last stop LAX," he replied.

As we glided south toward Jefferson, I saw a familiar shape in the distance. I could tell immediately that it was Trech. He was standing in the middle of the street, looking down an alleyway. As the bus passed by, he turned around, and his eyes locked onto mine. He nodded twice, letting me know he'd seen me, and in a flash, I was gone.

I looked down at the beautiful California coastline. At an altitude of ten thousand feet, I almost felt safe, but I continued to check the rows behind me for a blue hooded sweatshirt. For many years, I would hear footsteps throughout the night and dream that he was following me. Blue had once been my favorite color. Now it made my ears ring.

Through the airplane window, I could see the cars rolling down Abbot Kinney, turning right onto Brooks Avenue—stopping at the corners for rock cocaine.

I wouldn't miss it. Not at all. The view from the clouds was better.

EPILOGUE

I heard from Flyn a few years later. He had been released from jail (apparently, the charges didn't stick) and had moved down South with his family. He called to tell me that Beatrice had passed and we wept together for a long while—talking about her smile, her sense of humor, and the way she touched our lives. We laughed, too—about our time in the hood barreling down alleyways with the radio blazing. He asked me to rap for old times, sake, and I thought about it for a minute but politely declined. I could hear his muffled giggles through the phone receiver. Sadly, he died soon after. My beautiful friends from Ghost Town were gone and had no idea they had saved my life. Tisha never came back to California. Last I heard she was off the streets, working a steady job and taking care of her daughter.

As for me, well, after leaving Venice I bounced around the East Coast for awhile until I finally got sober. Really Sober. It was a treatment center in Santa Fe, New Mexico, that finished the job. I had a therapist there that helped me heal the last bits of trauma lingering in my psyche. I was so moved by the work he did that I decided to go back to school to study psychology. I had no money in those days—I mean, none. My family had cut me off financially and I had to borrow a few bucks from a friend just to get a modest roof over my head. My rent per month was $300 and that was hard to come by. But I worked hard and studied every night. Four years later I had earned my master's degree.

In 2008, I moved back to Los Angeles and entered a doctoral program in psychology. I worked at several rehabs up in Malibu until finally starting my private practice. There were many nights I doubted myself. I mean, who was I kidding? From homelessness to earning a PhD—not possible. But it was. After ten years of graduate school, I became a doctor. It was one of my proudest moments. I was rebuilding my life one piece at a time. I now have a practice filled with regular folks, celebrities, billionaires, and people who can't afford to pay. I work with a few pro bono clients each year as a way to give back. Every day I hear stories of sadness and triumph and feel so blessed to be included in this ritual of healing. My clients are so wise, so brave, so colorful.

My brother Craig and I stayed best friends throughout our adulthood. I was there when his second son was born. We talked on most days, mostly about nothing important, and often laughed about the adventures of our childhood. He continued to look after me until he succumbed to cancer. That was the hardest day of my life. He lives in my heart now and shows up in my dreams from time to time.

I found love again and married my beautiful wife Jennie in 2012. We live on a hillside in the Santa Monica mountains six minutes from the Pacific Ocean. We have two remarkable children, Maxine and Sebastian, who teach me to be curious and kind. These are the good times. My life has grown full and continues to expand with every passing minute.

My story is not meant to be a cautionary tale, but a reminder that love transcends pain, that wounds are healed through friendship, and that hope resides just around the corner. Sometimes, it's hard to believe these things really happened to me, but they did.

I leave you with one last thought. No matter how far you have fallen, you can always rise up again. There is always a way out if you believe it's possible. And it is possible, I promise you that. I am living proof.

ACKNOWLEDGMENTS

Special Thanks To: Gwyneth Paltrow for believing in me and giving me the courage to write again, Jonathan Marc Sherman for being such a beautiful man, Richard Dupont for your mind-blowing artwork, Cristina Cuomo for standing in my corner time and time again, Nick Paumgarten for your unabashed truth, Alessandro Nivola for your unwavering friendship, Craig Borten for being my partner in crime, Seth Herzog for Wonder Woman and Sweet Bong, Mr. Blue for the light that shines from your heart, Lillie Beatrice Johnson for giving me hope, Lane Heymont for being a superagent, Billy Crudup, Jason Blum, Alexandra Shiva, Will Arnett, Fernanda Niven, Thomas Lennon, Elise Loehnen, Katherine Butler, Syd Butler, Kay Kendall, Jack Davies, Sam Trammell, Jennifer Todd, Jessica Queller, Jeffrey Clifford, Helen Stubbs, Sara Daley, Ingrid Mach, Julie Miesionczek, Allison Janse, Meryl Moss, Kiki Koroshetz, Nancy Reynolds Bagley, Kevin Chaffee, Jonathan Mahler, John Dickerson, Mike Nasatir, Lyn Stout, Becky Wright, Michael McDonald, Bree Jeppson, John Jeppson III, Wendy Benchley, Skye Raiser, all the folks at HCI and Simon & Schuster, Mom and Dad for lending me your color,